The
Claim
Game

The
Claim
Game

A Homeowner's Guide to Avoiding an Insurance

Catastrophe

Andrew Wallingford

Quarter Sawn
Books

North Liberty, Iowa

The Claim Game: A Homeowner's Guide to Avoiding an Insurance Catastrophe

By Andrew Wallingford

Copyright ©2009 Quarter Sawn Books

Quarter Sawn Books
P.O. Box 635
North Liberty, IA 52317
www.QuarterSawnBooks.com

First Edition
Printed in the United States of America

Publisher's Cataloging-in-Publication

Wallingford, Andrew
      The claim game: a homeowner's guide to avoiding an
      insurance catastrophe/Andrew Wallingford, 1st ed.
      p.cm
      Includes bibliographical references and index.
      ISBN: 978-0-615-28278-7
      Library of Congress Catalog Number: 2009925831

      1. Homeowners insurance—handbooks, manuals, etc.
      2. Insurance—adjustment of claims, handbooks, manuals,
      etc. 3. Property insurance—handbooks, manuals, etc. 4. Insurance claims—handbooks, manual, etc.
      I. Title
      HOM010000   REF028000

Cover design and typesetting by Cicatrix Media, LLC. www.TheCicatrix.com

For free downloadable forms go to www.ClaimGameBook.com.

Wood that is cut in a quarter sawn fashion presents a finer grain that is considered more desirable than plain sawn wood. Quarter Sawn Books endeavors to publish works of an equally superior quality and desirability.

Contents

Part 4: Common Losses and Issues 171

Introduction

So there I was, eight o'clock in the morning, clinging precariously to the peak of a very steep Cape Cod-style roof, writhing, desperate—though not actually awake enough to be frightened, exhausted from two straight months of 16-hour days—making sudden irrational vows to take up bullfighting or dismantling landmines, anything safer and slightly less ridiculous than inspecting houses for storm damage. I was hundreds of miles from home and was beginning to wonder if coming here, Indiana, was a huge mistake—and wondering, too, if my entire career path was some monumental lapse in judgment. I looked left, then right: an archipelago of roofs, sun-splashed gabled ends, glistening patches of lawn—not a person in sight, not a single rescuer to be had. Woozy with exhaustion, I daydreamed of a Chihuahua, a speedy little wiry thing with a cask of espresso looped around his proud neck—a sort of Juan Valdez version of the St. Bernard—determined to climb my ladder and bring me a hearty gulp of sweet wakefulness. But then I realized something. "Oh, no thank you, Mr. Chihuahua," I would've had to say. "I don't drink coffee: it's bad for your health." As opposed to, say, falling off a roof. I called for help, practically raising my voice to a whisper. Luckily, no one answered. While it was a fine morning—fair and dry with only the faintest trace of the July humidity that would soon envelope the limbs and furrows of every animate object—I realized I could only hold on for so long and that I would either have to pull myself up or let go.

Something occurred to me then. Although I had been a property insurance adjuster for several years and had had a few close calls, I had never found myself in a position quite like this: utterly helpless, out on a limb as it were. It reminded me of something I encountered every day. Almost all of the homeowners I have helped over the years have conveyed to me at some point their sense of helplessness when it comes to dealing with their insurance company, that uneasy feeling of being left dangling by a thread, waiting for me or another adjuster to come to their aid and tell them what to do, but also wondering who they can trust. It's no secret among insurance adjusters (and insurance companies) that most homeowners are, to put it kindly, clueless about their homeowners insurance and the claims process in general, something that most insurance companies count on to save them money. This lack of knowledge has created a divide between homeowners and insurers that has tipped the balance of power unfairly in favor of the insurance companies. The truth is, homeowners have as much power as insurers do—most of them just don't know it.

Of course, it didn't take me long to realize there was something I could do about it. As I slowly woke up and (with exaggerated agony) pulled myself to the peak (not that it was hard, but at eight in the morning, everything seems more difficult), it occurred to me that the years I had spent "in the trenches" were an invaluable resource for every homeowner, and that my years of experience and knowledge could be used to bridge the gap between what homeowners know and what they need to know.

Applying the knowledge I have accumulated over the years, what follows is a step-by-step guide that walks homeowners through the stages of a property damage or theft claim. You will learn what you need to know, what to do, when to do it and, perhaps more important-ly, what not to do so that you can arrive at a quick and fair settlement with your insurance company. There *are* secrets to settling homeown-ers insurance claims, there *are* provisions in most homeowners poli-cies that insurance companies would rather you didn't know, there are bureaucratic hurdles and pitfalls that insurance companies place before homeowners. By unravelling these secrets, by shedding light on the labyrinth-like maze of rules, regulation and red tape, by clarifying and making sense of the seemingly arbitrary limitations and exclusions of the homeowners policy, I hope to empower all insured homeowners so that they can avoid an insurance catastrophe and ensure an insurance success.

By the way, after pulling myself up (and vowing that I would start drinking coffee immediately, at which I have failed miserably) I carefully made my way across the rest of the roof and completed my inspection before moving on to the next house. After many years and thousands of houses, garages, sheds, barns and other structures, I am lucky to say I have never fallen off a single roof—not yet, anyway. I fell through a roof once and caught myself on the rafters before hitting the concrete floor below—but that's another story.

Disclaimer

This book does not provide legal advice and is not intended as such. If you need legal advice, please consult the proper authorities or an appropriate legal council. The information in this book is not intended to be and should not be a substitute for your own research with regards to individual or unique policy information, legal advice, and tax situations. The information contained in this book may not be sufficient for your particular needs. Every attempt has been made to ensure that the information in this book is accurate and up to date; however, this book contains only generalized information and does not include specific legal provisions particular to any state, county or municipality. Laws within each state, county and municipality may be unique to that entity and are subject to change without notice. This book does not address homeowners policies unique to specific insurers, nor does it address how individual insurers interpret their own homeowners policies or any particular provisions within those policies. Quarter Sawn Books, the author, and any distributors of this book cannot provide a guarantee or warranty, nor can represent that the guided information is correct for every situation and for every user. In addition, this book is not to be used to commit insurance fraud. Insurance fraud is a very serious crime and is harmful to all holders of insurance policies.

Part 1:

Pre-Game

Chapter 1: The Nutshell

Insurance is a game of chance. You're betting that something will happen and you'll get back some of the money you've been paying to your insurer for years, insurers are betting that either nothing will happen or that policyholders will be too afraid to file a claim or are uninformed enough about their own coverages to know whether something is covered or not. An insurance claim is a game: certain players must do certain things at certain times, some players are not allowed to do some things, very particular steps must be taken at all times, and every phase of the game has a timer on it. Despite a common misconception, the game is not rigged in favor of insurance companies. They must play by the same set of rules as homeowners. The only advantage insurers have over most homeowners is that they know how the game works (they invented it) and they know the rules of the game, mainly because they wrote the rules.

Your greatest tools in this game are knowledge, persistence and diligence. While it may not always seem as though the insurance company is playing fair or playing by the rules (which sometimes happens), I strongly urge all homeowners to play fair and to play by the rules. When everyone plays by the rules, everyone benefits; when no one plays by the rules, everyone loses.

For Homeowners who have never had a claim, this is a brief summary of how it works or how, in a perfect world, it's supposed to work. A loss occurs—there is damage to (or theft of) your property. You inform your insurance company, they issue a claim number and authorize any temporary repairs such as putting a tarp on the roof, covering broken windows, etc. An insurance company adjuster then contacts you and sets an appointment to view the damages (sometimes they attempt to estimate damages over the phone, which, frankly, is stupid). The adjuster inspects the risk (the insured property) and determines if the damage is covered by your insurance and if it is, he writes an estimate, gives you a copy and cuts a check for the damages which, depending on the type of damage and repair methods, represents either part of the total payment or the whole amount. Often the estimate and check are mailed to the homeowner though sometimes an adjuster can write the estimate and the check on the spot. Next you select a contractor, who, as he examines the insurance company estimate, Hmmmms a little bit, scratches his chin and then matter-of-factly tells you it will cost six times that amount, at which point you exclaim, "You gotta be kidding me!" and feel as though you are being given the shaft by your insurance company. In a panic, you call your adjuster and let him known how dissatisfied you are. The adjuster does his best to soothe you and allay your concerns and tells you that this is actually normal. The contactor and adjuster get together and hammer out the nitty-gritty details of what work is to be done and how much it should cost (and lo and behold! it doesn't cost as little as the insurance company said it would!) and the work gets done at the homeowner's behest and the insurance company makes the final payments and everybody's happy—raise a toast, have a laugh and smile until your face hurts.

If this were a perfect world, that's how it would work and you wouldn't need this book.

In case you haven't noticed, this is not a perfect world and things do not always go as planned. Can you say, "Iraq"?

Attempts to reach a quick and fair settlement with an insurance company will make any homeowner a believer that Murphy's Law—that which can go wrong, will go wrong—was coined by a frustrated homeowner who thought that collecting on a homeowners insurance claim would be a quick and easy affair, devoid of loopholes, delays and complications. It will also lead any sane homeowner to believe that insurance, at its core, is a ridiculous farce, an absurdity worthy of the greatest humorist's most witty barbs and vocal lambasting.

The Nutshell is that there is no Nutshell: every claim is different, every claim has its own unique set of complications and setbacks, every claim has its own distinctive path to resolution. But what makes every homeowners claim similar is that the rules, regulations, duties, limitations and restrictions are similar for every homeowner (with minor variations from insurer to insurer).

The Rules of the Games—embodied in the form of the Homeowners Policy—are the same for each player, and regardless of the size of the claim or the size of the insurer, as long as you know the rules of the game you are on a level playing field with any insurance company and can anticipate the effects that the rules, duties, limitations and restrictions are going to have on your claim. Once you set foot on a level playing field, not only does the view change but so does the game.

Chapter 2: Dynamite and Sledgehammers: Busting Myths About Homeowners Insurance

Some writers and homeowner advocates may be satisfied with simply dispelling the elusive and stubborn myths regarding homeowners insurance. Some may find blissful contentment in shining a spotlight on the underbelly of these unfounded rumors. I, on the other hand, do not wish to merely shoot down and bag me a few Myths. Rather I feel a calling to eradicate these false legends and misconceptions with a profound and juicy violence, to incinerate these insidious deceptions with as much gunpowder and horsepower as I can muster. It is time to uncork the proverbial dynamite and blow up some long-held, oft-perpetuated myths about homeowners insurance and filing a claim, it is time to raise that sledgehammer like John Henry and crush some misconceptions straight down to oblivion. This is going to feel very, very good.

"Will filing a claim make my rates go up?" I hear this every day.

"Will they cancel my insurance because I file a claim?" I hear this every *other* day.

"They gonna put the Voodoo on me?" I've only heard this once, but it's worth mentioning to illustrate just how powerful some people perceive insurers to be, as though an insurer could have unforeseen supernatural effects on you or your family.

With the possible exception of the last quotation above, it would be fair to say that most insured homeowners have heard some variation of these statements and have come to accept them as fact. While they may seem plausible due to infinite repetition by friends, neighbors and general busy-bodies; while they may seem like the logical consequences of cause and effect, the reality is that the statements above are myths, preposterous misstatements of the truth like so much American lore: George Washington chopped down a cherry tree and 'fessed up; Paul Bunyan cleared an entire forest with one swipe of his axe; trickle-down economics benefits everyone; and the whole "I didn't inhale" thing.

The reality is that these are myths and distortions. Joseph Goebbels, an infamous Nazi propagandist once said, "The bigger the lie, the more people will believe it." These myths have made homeowners highly reticent, even fearful, of filing claims, dreading unknown consequences. Rightfully speaking, most homeowners ought to be more afraid of "catching" a voodoo curse than filing an insurance claim. It is not at all an exaggeration to say that insurance companies are more than willing to allow the silly and untrue myths of instantly rising premiums and inevitable cancellation to proliferate and penetrate the consciousness of every insured homeowner in the hopes of preventing claims from being filed in the first place and to ensure that they're kept in hay.

To be clear: **your homeowners premiums will not go up because you file a claim. You will not be cancelled because you file a single claim**. Premiums are not determined on an individual-by-individual basis (more on this below). Filing one or more claims every year for several years may result in cancellation; filing fraudulent claims, absolutely will result in cancellation. But simply *using* your insurance when you need it is not grounds for cancellation—or voodoo.

If there is damage to your property, no matter how insignificant it may seem, the answer as to whether or not to file a claim is always YES. Yes, yes, yes, yes. Countless times I have inspected a home for damage only to have the homeowner tell me he wasn't sure if he should've filed a claim because he "wasn't sure it was worth it"—and it turns out he has $10,000.00 (or more) in damages. If there was large hail (golf ball size and larger) in your neighborhood but you don't see any damage, file a claim. If you are unable to determine if any shingles were blown off of your roof after a wind storm but you see shingles in your yard, file a claim. If a tree landed on your house and you are unsure if it actually caused any damage or not, file a claim. Even if you are not sure if the damages are covered, make a claim to verify it. Filing a claim is the surest way to protect yourself from possible financial setbacks or devastation.

There's another reason to file a claim, even if you're sure something's not covered, like flood: if the county or area in which you live is declared a federal disaster area and your damages aren't covered by your homeowners insurance, you will need documentation from your insurance carrier (a letter sating denial of coverage) to receive assistance from FEMA, the Federal Emergency Management Agency.

Filing a claim, most of the time, is easy and free. Aside from being the first step to recovery, it is a resource you are entitled to as a homeowner, one that ought never cause fear or trepidation or even a moment's hesitation. And filing a claim is the surest way to make certain that the protection provided under your homeowners insurance is granted. It is also a sensible and responsible way to retain the value and enhance the appreciation of your property. There are times when *not* filing a claim comes back to haunt homeowners, especially when they find out that they were covered when they thought they weren't and the deadline to file a claim has expired or when they attempt to sell their house and the buyer's inspector discovers previous damage—damages that a seller will most likely have to fix or deduct from the asking price, which I guarantee will cost more than a trip to your psychiatrist to discuss your latent fears of filing an insurance claim.

There is another reason to file an insurance claim when you have damage or suspect you have damage. Insurance companies, it has long been suspected, were the originators of the myths mentioned above and while it may seem like the first and most prominent diversionary tactic to forestall or entirely prevent their paying claims, insurance companies, and this may sound strange, actually want—and yet *don't* want—homeowners to file claims. Insurers want to make it seem like they are fulfilling the obligations under their policies, they want to reinforce the self-appointed perception that they are a "Good Neighbor" or that you're in "Good Hands," that they're the upstanding fellows who'll do what they've promised to do. They *want* homeowners to maintain their property and be happy customers. Conversely, they don't want homeowners to file claims because they're in business to make money and they can't make money if they have to keep paying all those pesky claims. Don't insurance company executives deserve to drive Porsches, too?

To elaborate on that question that plagues me time and time again, each and every day, day after day: "Will filing a claim make my premiums go up?"

This is a trick question. Yes, your premiums are more than likely to go up, but no, your premiums will not go up *because* you file a claim. Premiums go up because they go up *every* year in most places: nationwide, premiums rise an average 7% to 8% each year, though there are many homeowners in hail- and tornado-prone Midwestern cities who would love it if their premiums rose only *that* much each year. Some companies do tack on a nominal temporary "Claim Surcharge" to your premiums for a few months after a claim has been filed, but this is the exception rather than the rule. Premiums keep going up because the price of everything keeps going up: energy, health care, food, office supplies, Porsches, etc.

Premiums are not determined solely on an individual-by-individual, or in this case, property-by-property basis like car insurance: they are determined by a multitude of factors including how much the house is insured for, the zip code or the neighborhood you live in (and the number of claims in that zip code or neighborhood), your credit score, the proximity to fire fighting stations, the type of construction (wood frame, log, concrete block, etc.), and the age of the home; newer, up-to-code homes are generally less prone to damage than older construction and therefore cost less to repair and therefore insure.

For purposes of example, let's say a set of twins, John and Joe Smith, live across the street from one another and have two houses of identical design, age, materials and overall value and are insured by the same insurance company. The properties should be insured for the same amount and if that is the case, they will have the same premium. Let's say Joe Smith is more unlucky than John and has had to file two claims over the course of a year. Which homeowner will have the higher premiums the next year, John or Joe? Neither—they'll still be the same. Simply because you file a claim you will not be financially penalized, other than paying your deductible. You'll be "penalized" whether or not you file a claim at all courtesy of premiums that rise each and every year, you'll be penalized just for having insurance in the first place.

Returning to another myth mentioned above, if you file a single claim you will NOT be cancelled by your carrier simply because you've filed a claim, nor will you need a sacrificial chicken or goat's blood or any other voodoo remedy. Cancellation occurs because of a variety of reasons: an excessive number of claims filed in a short time span (the more expensive you are to keep around, the less they'll want to keep you around); fraudulent claims; homeowners who literally let their property fall to pieces and/or create an on-going safety issue, a liability lawsuit just waiting to happen; homeowners who don't pay their premiums; a property that has been abandoned or factors that are beyond a homeowner's control such as a large number of claims or dollars paid out in your area; or in the case of Farmers Insurance who, a few years ago, cancelled *every* homeowners policy in which the insured property was over a certain age. If you pay your premiums, take care of your property and shy away from insurance fraud, the chances for random and capricious cancellation are rare and the vast majority of responsible, conscientious homeowners have nothing to worry about. On the upside, there is always another insurance company more than willing to take your money.

Another myth is that insurance companies want to take advantage of homeowners.

It's not that insurance companies *want* to take advantage of homeowners, it's that they're more than happy to do so if homeowners let them. If it happens that homeowners are unknowledgeable about certain aspects of the homeowners policy, that's not the insurance company's fault. Insurance companies expect homeowners to know everything about their own homeowners policy without the insurance company actually having to tell the homeowner everything they really need to know and if it happens that an insurance company doesn't go out of its way to advertise in big bright bold letters every little detail of coverage that homeowners are entitled to, well, that's not their fault—you didn't ask, you didn't read the policy closely enough. If *you* don't know what your coverages are, then they're not responsible for you not knowing, for you not claiming something. At least that's the insurance carriers' point of view. To put it another way, if you don't know you're being taken advantage of, they're not going to tell you. Which is why I wrote this book. So yes, insurance companies are inclined to take advantage of you if you allow them to, but they can't take advantage of people who won't let them.

A myth, in the form of a question. Do insurance companies care about you?

Of course they do. More specifically, they care about your money—which is why they've gone to great lengths in the past several years to emphasize that they do care about each and every customer. When you call your agent or show up in his office, you're their most important client. Insurance is like any other business: competition is fierce and one way an insurance company can separate itself from the pack is by providing superior customer service. And naturally, when one insurer raises the bar with better customer service, the others, like the sheep they are, race to match their competition. What you get is a fierce and bloody battle to be the nicest sweetest corporate machine. The result of this bloodbath of kindness has brought about an eagerness to be (to paraphrase a former U.S. President) kinder, gentler insurance companies. Believe it or not, most insurance companies want their policy-holders to be happy, they want them to be satisfied with the service and the resolution of their homeowners claim, even if they can't pay the claim. Okay, okay what they really want is your money—but the best way to keep it is by keeping you, their customer, satisfied and to prevent you from going elsewhere. So yes, insurance companies are more than willing to take advantage of you if you let them—but at least they want you to be happy about it!

Raise that sledgehammer!

Another common myth is that your insurance company will repair your home for you. Many homeowners are under the mistaken impression that some Hercules-like contractor who is always on schedule and under budget is going to miraculously appear at their doorstep the day after damages occur, wave his magic hammer, mumble a few Harry Potter-like incantations and make their house as good as new.

(Excuse me while I fall to the floor laughing.)

There are a very small number of insurers who occasionally dispatch what is called a Preferred Vendor or Preferred Service Provider (a contractor who has previously worked with the insurance company and has agreed to work at prices set by the insurer) after a property damage claim. These contractors can do the work without the usual aggravation of settling a claim and can guarantee the repairs, though this is the equivalent of a health insurance plan that doesn't allow you to choose your own doctor. However, only about 10% of all property damage losses fall under this category. The other 90% of homeowners are in charge of getting their own repairs made.

It is always the option of the homeowner to accept a Preferred Vendor/Service Provider or not. Thus far the track record of these companies has been very good, mainly because the insurance company usually guarantees the repairs, something that costs them a little more money in some instances. It is up to individual homeowners to decide whether they want to take this route or not and this may be the best course for many if not most people if it is available. Of course, there's something else to consider: would you want a company that would gladly take advantage of you fix your house while you're away at work?

Every few days or so a savvy, though unknowing, homeowner attempts to persuade me that their deductible doesn't apply to their loss because it was an "Act of God," and, well, they just don't think they should have to pay for something that wasn't their fault like a wind or hail storm, an earthquake, a forest fire, etc. Obviously these homeowners don't work for insurance companies. Insurance companies have a thing about deductibles: they love deductibles, they worship them, they build great towering monuments to deductibles to demonstrate their profound adoration, they compose amorous poems and performs curiously flamboyant plays in their honor…you get the picture. Deductibles *always apply*. Period. Once in a while, part or all of the deductible can be absorbed or subtracted if the amount of damage is over the limit of coverage—which sounds really cool but in actuality is a bittersweet good news/bad news situation: yes, part or all of your deductible is being wiped away, cleared from the books, but no, the insurance company is not going to give you enough money to cover the actual expenses and/or the full cost of repairs.

Do I smell gunpowder?

Another myth: that any and all decisions made by an insurance company—be it from an adjuster, his supervisor or the supervisor's supervisor—are final and cannot be overturned, that the bucks stops at the first, second or third sign of "No." It is sad to say, but quite often the decisions made by those in the lower (non-corporate) levels of an insurance company are done so to avoid drawing unwanted negative attention. I often get the impression that the fear of making a mistake, of looking bad to one's supervisors or thinking in a way that is outside the rigid confines of the corporate norm are some of the motivating factors for not taking chances or making what may seem like unconventional decisions. Though sometimes it's just a matter of bureaucracy overwhelming a common sense interpretation of a policy.

Insurance companies want their customers to be happy and if a homeowner is not happy with a decision from his insurance company, the homeowner needs to keep going up the corporate ladder until he finds an ear willing to hear his concerns. It may be a slight exaggeration, but until you get a letter from the C.E.O. of the insurance company proclaiming that your case is closed and that any further attempts to collect on a claim will have to be done through the courts, no decision is final.

The final myth: when a homeowner receives a check for property damages, that is the amount the insurer will "allow" for a claim—that that's the most an insurer will pay, period. The claims process is much more fluid than most homeowners think: a claim is never truly closed until the very last repair has been made and the last dollar has been paid. Until that time, a claim is essentially open and there is always room for necessary adjustments, especially when hidden or additional damages are found or there has been a sudden increase in the price of materials due to a lack of supply, which happened in Florida in 2004 after four major hurricanes hit the state (Florida state law dictates that new composition shingles installed on dwellings must be wind rated to a level superior to the requirements of most states, causing a shortage when tens of thousands of homes suddenly needed these special kind of shingles; many homeowners had to wait nine to 12 months just to obtain the specific kind of shingles.) As you will learn in the forthcoming chapters, homeowners with replacement cost are usually issued at least two payments, a first partial payment and a final payment, often with what are called supplemental payments in between. These supplemental payments are the adjustments that can always be made to a claim before the final payments are issued.

Lightning burns at 50,000 degrees Fahrenheit.

The outer surface of the sun burns at 11,000 degrees Fahrenheit.

Lightning is among the top five causes of loss for homeowner claims.

Part 2:

The Rules of the Game

Chapter 3: FZXYROER EDZJUDT (Understanding and Deciphering Your Homeowners Policy)

FZXYROER EDZJUDT"? What the heck is that? A new hair loss formula? The name of a foreign exchange student from some former Soviet Republic? The verbatim transcript of the Iraq post-invasion plan?

No—this is your homeowner's policy; at least that's what I've been told what a policy reads like for most people who have made the brave attempt to actually read it. (Ironically, I've also been told that dyslexics have an uncanny ability to understand their homeowner's policy with pristine clarity.) While your policy may look like an incomprehensible jumble of random letters and numbers whose sole purpose is to vex you until you pull your hair out and need a real hair loss formula, when understood, your homeowner's policy is your greatest weapon in the claim game.

Policies are built upon conditions, restrictions, limitations, exclusions and out and out lunacy. When reading a homeowners policy, you may get the impression that a policy is contradictory in many places and the reason it may seem that way is because they are contradictory in many places. Some things are covered—except when they're not. Some things aren't covered—except when they are. This section will not only give an in-depth "translation" of a homeowners policy, it will also teach you *how* to read a policy. While most policies are similar to the one below, all policies have variations unique to the company issuing it; my goal is to help readers make sense of the nuances of their own policy by giving insight into how insurers think and what they mean by what their policies say.

As this book covers only **property damage**, building damage and personal property damage, liability issues and coverages will not be addressed.

The policy that follows is representative of the most popular and current homeowners policy, what is called an "open peril" policy, a peril being something that causes loss or damage—wind, hail, fire, burst water pipe, theft, that dump truck parked in your living room. The policy below, however, is only open peril for structural items, not for personal property items. Most new policies issued today are open peril for both building and personal property items, however there are still a large number of policies that offer open peril on building items only. There are still older policies that are "named peril" for both building and personal property items, which means they are much more restrictive in what they cover a note will be made of the differences between the older policies and their current versions.

The policy below is a replacement cost policy, the most common type. A replacement cost policy means that an insurer is required to pay the full cost to repair or replace damaged items when the cause of damage is covered. If your policy is an Actual Cash Value policy, your insurer is only required to pay the depreciated value of the items damaged.

A note on letters: for some policies, there may be a difference in how sections are lettered. For example, the policy below labels all buildings (house, garage, fences, etc.) "Coverage A", personal property Coverage B and loss of use Coverage C; some policies only call the primary structure (the dwelling) Coverage A, all other structures (detached garages, fences, sheds, etc.) Coverage B, and personal property Coverage C, with loss of use getting a "D."

Sample Policy

Coverage A - Dwelling
1. We cover:
    a. the dwelling shown in the declarations used primarily as a private residence. This includes structures permanently affixed to the dwelling.

2. Dwelling Extensions. We cover other structures on the residence premises that are not permanently affixed to the dwelling but are permanently affixed to the ground. Structures attached by fencing, utility lines or other means to the dwelling are other structures.

We do not cover other structures:
    a. not permanently affixed to the ground that comprises the residence premises;
    b. used for business; or
    c. rented, unless rented as a private garage.

3. Except as indicated in **Section I - Additional Coverages, Land**, we provide no coverage for land. This includes land which supports any Coverage A property. We provide no coverage for any costs to replace, stabilize, rebuild, or otherwise repair the land, including techniques designed to reverse or undermine land stability.

Coverage B - Personal Property
1. We cover personal property located anywhere in the world, provided it is owned or used by an insured. This includes structures not permanently affixed to the ground that comprises the residence premises. We cover personal property owned by others while the property is located on the residence premises. We cover personal property owned by a guest or a residence employee that is located at the residence premises when the insured is also living there.

We cover personal property not located at an insured's residence for up to $2000 or 10% of the Coverage B limit, whichever is greater. This limitation does not apply to personal property located at a new principal residence for the first 30 days of moving property there. If the residence premises is a new principal residence, personal property in the formal principle residence is not subject to the limitation for 30 days after the inception of this policy.

Special Limits of Liability. The limits of Coverage B are not increased by the following special limits of liability. The total limit for each category below is for each individual loss that occurs within that category:
    a. $500 for paper money, bank notes, coins, medals and other valid currency;
    b. $2000 for property used for business purposes, including merchandise while on the residence premises. This does not include electronic data processing equipment or the storage media used with that equipment;

c. $5000 for computer equipment and the storage media used with that equipment There is no coverage for computer equipment or media storage used with it while not located at the residence premises except when removed to be repaired or serviced. An insured student's computer equipment are covered while at a residence away from home;

d. $1500 for manuscripts, tickets, passports, securities, accounts, deeds, evidences of debt, letters of credit, notes other than bank notes, coupons and stamps;

e. $1200 for all types of watercraft, including outboard motors and their trailers, furnishings and equipment;

f. $1200 for non-watercraft trailers;

g. $3500 for loss of firearms when caused by theft;

h. $3000 for loss of silverware or goldware when caused by theft;

i. $1,000 for:
   (1) the legal obligation of an insured due to the theft or unauthorized use of credit cards or debit cards. If an insured fails to comply with all terms and conditions by which the cards are issued, we will not cover the use by an insured or anyone else;
   (2) loss caused by forgery or alteration of any paper or electronic check; and
   (3) loss to an insured caused by a good faith acceptance of counterfeit United States or Canadian paper currency. No deductible applies to this coverage. We will pay no more than the above stated limit for forgery or alteration committed by any single person or entity. This limit also applies when one or more instrument of forgery or alteration are involved in the same loss.; and

j. $6000 for any single article and $12,000 total for any rug, non wall-to wall carpet, tapestry, wall-hanging or other similar article when the loss is caused by theft.

Special limits for jewelry, watches, fur garments and garments trimmed with fur, precious and semi-precious stones, gold other than goldware, silver other than silverware, and platinum can be found in **Section I - Additional Coverages**.

2. **Property Not Covered**. We do not insure for loss against:
   a. articles covered by any other insurance or separately described in this insurance;
   b. domesticated pets and livestock, including all animals, fish or birds;
   c. any motor propelled vehicle, including their parts, designed to move across land. We do cover machines not licensed for highway use which are:
      1. used exclusively to service the residence premises; or
      2. assist the handicapped;
   d. sound recording devices or instruments permanently affixed to a motorized machine or vehicle, including any tapes or medium, wiring, or medium used with these devices while located in the vehicle;
   e. property of residents not related to an insured, including but not limited to, roomers, boarder and tenants. We do cover property of roomers, boarders and other residents provided they are related to an insured;
   f. aircraft and all parts, including instruments, whether functioning or not;

g. property rented to others by an insured. This exclusion does not apply to an insured's property located in a room rented to others.

h. property rented to others while located away from the residence premises;

i. any citizens band radios, radio telephones, radio transceivers and transmitters, radar detectors, antennas and any equipment used with them located within or affixed to a motor propelled vehicle, whether attached or not;

j. accounting books, abstracts, drawings, card index systems and other records, not including file, tape, disc, drum, cell and other digital and magnetic storage media for electronic data processing. We will cover the cost of blank books, cards or other blank material and any labor cost of incurred for transcribing or copying these records into the books; or

k. obsolete media for storing or recording electronic data that otherwise cannot be replaced with other of like kind and quality on the current retail market.

Coverage C - Loss of use

1. Additional Living Expenses. When the residence premises become uninhabitable due to a Loss Insured, we will cover the expenses to maintain your standard of living while living elsewhere. Payment will be for the shortest amount of time required to repair or replace the premises or for you to settle elsewhere, not exceeding 12 months. The expiration date of this policy does not limit the period of coverage.

2. Retail Rental Value. When the part of the residence premises rented to others becomes uninhabitable due to a Loss Insured, we cover its retail rental value. Payment is for the time required to repair or replace the part of the premises rented, not exceeding 12 months. The expiration date of this policy does not limit the period of coverage. Retail rental value does not include expenses that stop while that part of the residence premises rented remains uninhabitable.

3. Prohibited Use. When a neighboring property is damaged by a Loss Insured and civil authorities prohibit the use of your dwelling, we cover any resulting Additional Living Expense and Retail Rental Value for up to two weeks.

We do not cover loss due to cancellation or voiding of a lease or agreement.

Section I - Additional Coverages

1. **Debris Removal**. When a property is damaged by a Loss Insured, we will pay all reasonable expenses for the removal of covered property debris. This amount is included in the limit of liability for the damaged property. When a tree damages Coverage A property we will pay no more than $500 in the aggregate per loss to cover the reasonable expenses to remove tree debris from the residence premises.

2. **Temporary Repairs**. When a property is damaged by a Loss Insured, we will pay the reasonable and necessary expenses for temporary repairs to the covered property so that the property is protected from further damage or loss. This amount is included in

the limit of liability for the damaged property.

3. **Fire Department Service Charge.** We will pay up to $500 for fire department charges when a Loss Insured requires the fire department to save, protect or salvage property covered under this policy. This amount may increase the limit of liability for the dwelling. The deductible does not apply to this coverage.

4. **Trees, Shrubs and Other Plants.** When damaged by fire or lightning, explosion, riot or civil commotion, vandalism, aircraft, vehicles not owned by an insured, malicious mischief or theft we cover outdoor trees, shrubs, plants (including lawns), located on the residence premises. Including the removal of debris, the limit of this coverage is five (5) percent of the dwelling limit, with a $500 limit for any single outdoor tree, shrub, plant or lawn. This amount may increase the limit of liability for the dwelling. Property grown for business purposes is not covered.

5. **Removed Property.** When threatened by a Loss Insured, all covered property is insured against any accidental direct physical loss that may occur in the removal of said property from the residence premises. This coverage is available for up to 30 days while removed. Any reasonable expenses to remove and/or return covered property is also included in this coverage. This coverage is included in the limit of liability for the damaged property.

6. **Credit Card, Bank Fund Transfer Card, Forgery and Counterfeit Money.**
   a. Losses caused by the dishonesty of an insured or from business interests are not covered.
   b. Defense:
      (1) We will investigate and settle any claims or lawsuit that we deem appropriate. When the limit of liability is met, our requirement to counter lawsuits or claims ends.
      (2) We will provide defense when a lawsuit or claim is made against an insured for liability under this coverage. We shall have the option of choosing our own attorneys and will pay any expense up to the limit of liability.
      (3) At our option and expense, we will defend an insured against any suit sought for payment under the Forgery coverage.

7. **Power Interruption.** Power interruptions from a Loss Insured which occur on the residence premises are insured for accidental direct physical loss caused directly or indirectly by a change of temperature. Power to the surrounding homes, area or neighborhood must remain intact. This coverage is included in the limit of liability for the damaged property.

8. **Refrigerated Products.** The contents of refrigerators and deep freezes located on the residence premises are covered for loss resulting from mechanical failure of the unit or a loss of electricity. Reasonable measures must be taken to prevent further damage when loss is caused by mechanical failure or power loss. Power failure or mechanical

failure does not include removing the plug from the electrical outlet or switching off of the unit unless this is the result of a Loss Insured. The deductible does not apply to this coverage. There is a limit of $750 per unit per loss when caused by a Loss Insured.

9. **Land**. There is $12,000 available for when a Loss Insured causes damage to the dwelling and results in the instability of land. The land that sustains the loss must support the portion of the dwelling damaged by a Loss Insured. This limit is for all costs to stabilize, repair, rebuild and replace land, including engineering fees, permits and removal of existing land. This is an extra amount of insurance.

10. **Jewelry and Furs**. Jewelry, watches, fur garments and garments trimmed with fur, precious and semi-precious stones, gold (other than goldware), silver (other than silverware), and platinum are insured for accidental direct physical loss or damage. Loss by theft for any of the above items is limited to $3,000 in the aggregate and $1,000 for any single item. Loss by any other Loss Insured shall be the policy limits stated in the Declarations.

Loss resulting from mechanical breakdown, wear and tear, deterioration, insects, vermin, inherent vice or seizure or destruction under quarantine or customs regulations is otherwise excluded.

11. **Arson Reward**. There is up to $1,500 available for persons providing information leading to a conviction for arson to the property covered by this policy. This coverage may increase the dwelling coverage limit. The $1,500 limit is aggregate for all persons claiming reward.

12. **Volcanic Action**. Direct physical loss resulting from a volcanic blast and/or airborne shockwaves, lava flow and volcanic ash and/or particulate matter is extended to covered buildings. Contents within a fully enclosed building are covered only if damage is sustained to the building. Coverage B items not in an enclosed building or in a carport are included in this coverage.

Coverage for the removal of volcanic ash or particulate matter is also extended to buildings and to contents within buildings provided the buildings sustain direct physical damage from ash or particulate matter or volcanic blast and/or airborne shockwaves or lava flow. Volcanic eruptions occurring within 48 hours are considered one loss. This coverage is included in the limit of liability for the damaged property.

13. **Collapse**. We cover direct physical loss to buildings and their contents when caused by collapse. Direct physical loss to covered property involving the collapse of a building or any part of a building must be caused by one or more of the following:
    a. perils described in **Section I - Losses Insured, Coverage B - Personal Property**. These perils apply to Coverage A and Coverage B items for loss by collapse;
    b. unknown and unseen decay;
    c. unknown and unseen insect or vermin damage;
    d. weight of snow, ice, sleet, rain or hail upon a roof. This applies only to Coverage

structures.

e. weight of people, contents, tools, instruments or animals; or

f. use of defective material or construction methods, remodelling or renovation provided the collapse occurs during the course of construction, remodelling or renovation.

Loss to dwelling extensions such as fences, pavement, swimming pool, underground pipe, flue, drain, cesspool, septic tank, and loss to patios, pavements, foundations, retaining walls, bulkheads, piers, wharfs or docks are excluded under items b., c., d., e., and f. unless the collapse of a building causes the loss directly. Settling, cracking, shrinking, bulging, or expansion are not considered collapse.

This coverage is included in the limit of liability for the damaged property.

14. **Locks**. When keys to the locks of exterior doors are part of a covered loss due to theft, we will pay the reasonable expenses to re-key locks on all exterior doors of the dwelling located on the residence premises. The deductible does not apply to this coverage.

15. **Temporary Living Expense Allowance**. There is $3,000 available to maintain your standard of living should the dwelling become uninhabitable due to earthquake, flood, landslide, mudslide, sinkhole, volcanic explosion, earth movement, or should civil authorities declare your dwelling uninhabitable due to earthquake, flood, landslide, mudslide, sinkhole, volcanic explosion or earth movement. The **Section I - Losses Not Insured** references to earthquake, landslide, flood and volcanic explosion do not apply to this Additional Coverage. This is an extra amount of insurance.

Report Increased Values

You must notify us within 90 days of the start of any new buildings, renovations or additions valued at $5,000 or more. Payment for a loss Insured will not exceed the existing limit of liability applying to the building if you fail to notify us within 90 days of said new buildings, renovations or additions being completed. See **Section I - Conditions, Loss Settlement** for additional provisions.

Section I - Losses Insured

Coverage A - Dwelling

We provide coverage against accidental direct physical loss for all Coverage A items. All losses under **Section I - Losses Not Insured** are otherwise excluded.

Coverage B - Personal Property

We provide coverage against accidental direct physical loss for all Coverage B items caused by the following perils, unless otherwise excluded in **Section I - Losses Not**

Insured.

1. **Fire or lightning.**

2. **Windstorm or hail.** Loss to personal property in a fully enclosed building from rain, snow, sleet, sand, dirt or dust is otherwise excluded unless wind or hail damages the building and creates an opening through which rain, snow, dust, sand, sleet or dirt enters and causes loss to the property.

3. **Explosion.**

4. **Aircraft.** Rockets, missiles, unidentified flying objects and spacecraft are included in this category.

5. **Vehicles.**

6. **Riot or civil commotion.**

7. **Smoke.** Smoke damage which occurs or a period of time is excluded.

8. **Vandalism or malicious mischief.** Purposeful and deliberate damage to or destruction of property by someone who is not an insured is included.

9. **Theft.** This also includes loss from an attempted theft. The following are excluded:
   a. loss of a precious or semi-precious stone from its setting.
   b. theft:
      (1) committed by an insured or by persons who habitually reside at the residence premises. Property of a student is covered while located at a residence away from home, provided the theft is not committed by an insured;
      (2) to a dwelling under construction, including the material and supplies for use in the construction provided the dwelling is unoccupied; or
      (3) of Coverage B items from the portion of the residence premises rented to others:
         a. perpetrated by a tenant, a member of the tenant's household, or the tenant's employees;
         b. of paper money, coins, bank notes, currency, medallions and medals;
         c. of securities, checks, including paper and electronic checks, cashier's checks, traveler's check, money orders and other legal tender, accounts, deeds, evidences of debt, letters of credit, notes other than bank notes, manuscripts, passports, tickets, coupons, vouchers and stamps; or
         d. of jewelry, fur garments and garments trimmed with fur, watches, precious and semi-precious stones, bullion, gold, goldware, silver, silverware, pewterware, and platinum.
   c. theft that occurs at a location other than the residence premises of:
      (1) property while at another residence owned, permanently rented to, or occupied by an insured. The property of a student who is an insured is cov-

ered while residing away from home;

(2) watercraft of every type, including any furnishings, equipment and out-board motors which complement or belong with the watercraft; or

(3) trailers and campers designed to be conveyed by or on a vehicle.

Property in a former principal residence is not considered property away from the residence premises for the first 30 days after the inception of this policy.

10. **Falling Objects.** Loss to property within a fully enclosed building is otherwise excluded unless the falling object causes damage to the exterior of the building before damaging the contents within. Damage to the falling object itself is not included unless the object is damaged by a loss insured.

11. **Weight of ice, snow or sleet.** Loss to property within a fully enclosed building is otherwise excluded unless the weight of ice, snow or sleet creates an opening through which melted ice, snow or sleet causes damage to the property contained within the building.

12. **Sudden and accidental discharge or overflow of water or steam.** Direct physical loss from water or steam escaping from a plumbing, heating, air conditioning or automatic fire protective sprinkler system, or from within a household appliance is covered.

This does not include loss:

a. to the system or appliance which discharged the water or steam;

b. from freezing;

c. from water from outside the plumbing system that enters through sewers or drains or which enters from or overflows from within a sump pump well or a similar system designed to remove subsurface water from beneath the foundation area; or

d. from seepage or leakage of water or that occurs over a period of time which results in deterioration, corrosion, rust, mold, or wet or dry rot.

13. **Sudden and accidental tearing asunder, cracking, burning or bulging.** Direct physical loss from water or steam from a steam or hot water heating system, an air conditioning or automatic fire protective sprinkler system, or an appliance for heating water in which there is sudden and accidental tearing asunder, cracking, burning or bulging of that system is covered.

This does not include loss:

a. from freezing; or

b. from seepage or leakage of water or steam over a period of time which results in deterioration, corrosion, rust, mold, or wet or dry rot.

14. **Freezing.** Direct physical loss from the freezing of a plumbing, heating, air conditioning or automatic fire protective sprinkler system, or of a household appliance is covered. This peril is excluded if the dwelling is vacant, unoccupied or being con-

structed, unless you have taken reasonable measures to:

    a. maintain sufficient heat in the structure; or

    b. turn off the water and drain the water from all appliances and systems.

15. **Power Surge.** We cover accidental direct loss to electrical appliances, devices, fixtures, electronic systems and wiring from a change in artificially generated electrical current. The limit for each damaged item from this loss is $1,200 per item.

16. **Breakage of glass.** We cover accidental direct loss to personal property caused by the breakage of glass which is a part of a building on the residence premises.

Section I - Losses Not Insured

1. Any loss to Coverage A property caused by the following are specifically excluded, regardless whether the loss is the result of one event or occurs over a period of time, causes isolated or comprehensive damage or is the a result of any combination of the following.

    a. collapse, except that which is indicated in **Section I - Additional Coverages, Collapse;**

    b. freezing damage to a building that is vacant, unoccupied or being constructed. Any direct physical loss from freezing to a plumbing, heating, air conditioning or automatic fire protective or to a household appliance, is excluded; any direct physical loss from freezing that causes discharge, leakage or overflow from within a plumbing, heating, air conditioning or automatic fire protective system or appliance caused by freezing when a dwelling is excluded. This exclusion only applies when a building is not occupied, under construction or otherwise is vacant, provided reasonable measures have been taken to maintain heat in the building and to turn off the water and drain the water from all appliances and systems.

    c. freezing, thawing, pressure or weight of water or ice, on a fence, pavement, patio swimming pool, foundation, retaining wall, bulkhead, pier, wharf or dock, regardless if it driven by wind or not;

    d. if the dwelling has been vacant for 30 days or more before a loss, any acts of vandalism or malicious mischief or breakage of glass and safety glazing materials is excluded. A dwelling under construction is not considered vacant.

    e. theft to a dwelling under construction, including materials and supplies used in the construction, until the dwelling is completed and occupied.

    f. continuous or repeated discharge or leakage of water or steam over a period of time that results in deterioration, corrosion, rust, mold or wet or dry rot from any of the following:

        (1) heating, air conditioning or automatic fire protective sprinkler system;

        (2) dehumidifiers or other household appliance; or

        (3) plumbing systems, including any area surrounding a shower stall, shower,

bath, tub installation, toilet, faucet or other plumbing fixture, including damage to any walls, ceiling or floors that results from this loss;

If the loss is caused by water or steam not otherwise excluded, we will cover the cost to tear out and repair or replace any part of the building necessary to return the system or appliance to the condition it was in before the loss. We do not cover damage to the system or appliance the water or steam escaped from.

g. wear, tear, marring, scratching, deterioration, inherent vice, latent defect, mechanical breakdown, corrosion, electrolysis or rust;

h. mold, or wet or dry rot;

i. contamination, pollution;

j. smog, industrial or agricultural smoke or smudging;

k. cracking, settling, shrinking, bulging, expansion or deterioration of pavements, patios, foundation, walls, floors, roofs, in-ground pools or below-ground water collection installations; or

l. domestic animals, birds, vermin, rodents, insects, or wild animals. We cover glass breakage or breaking of safety glazing material when caused by birds, vermin, rodents insects or wild or domestic animals.

Unless the resulting loss is a Loss Not Insured as indicated in this section, we cover accidental direct loss from items a. through l.

2. We provide no coverage for the following losses that occur, regardless of the cause of the loss and the extent of the damages, whether other causes occur simultaneously, concurrently, in combination with or occur in any order with the losses below. These losses are excluded whether the events take place suddenly or over time, rise from natural sources, or are the result of a combination of any of the following:

a. **Earthquake.** Direct physical loss is covered when earthquake causes loss by fire, explosion, theft, or breakage of glass or safety glazing materials, provided the resulting loss is a Loss Insured.

b. **Nuclear Hazard.** Nuclear Hazard includes a nuclear reaction of any type, radiation or radioactive contamination from any source, all whether controlled or uncontrolled. Loss caused by nuclear hazard is not considered loss caused by fire, explosion, or smoke. However, we do insure for fire when it is a direct result of a nuclear hazard.

3. We provide no coverage for the following, regardless of the cause of the loss and the extent of the damages, whether other causes occur simultaneously, concurrently, in combination with or occur in any order with the losses below. These losses are excluded whether the events take place suddenly or over time, rise from natural sources, or are the result of a combination of any of the following:

a. **Ordinance or Law.** Unless provided elsewhere under this policy, the enforcement of any ordinance, statute or law overseeing the construction, repair or demolition of a building or other structure is not covered.

b. **Earth Movement.** Earth movement includes sinking, rising, shifting, expanding, contracting or sudden or gradual upheaval of earth, whether occurring concurrently with water or not. Earth movement includes but is not limited to landslide, mudflow, sinkhole, subsidence and erosion. This exclusion also includes volcanic explosion and lava flow, except as specifically provided in **Section I- Additional Coverages, Volcanic action.**

We do insure for accidental direct loss by fire, explosion, theft, or breakage of glass or safety glazing materials that arises from earth movement, provided the resulting loss is a Loss Insured.

    c. **Water Damage,** meaning:
        (1) flood, surface water, subsurface water, tidal waves, waves, overflow of a body of water, or spray from any of these, regardless of its source or if it is propelled by wind or any other natural external source including pressure, osmosis or transference;
        (2) external water from without the plumbing system that enters the dwelling through sewers or drains, or water which enters into and overflows from within a sump pump, sump pump well or any subsurface water removal system which drains water from the foundation area; or
        (3) water from below the surface of the ground which exerts pressure on, seeps or leaks through a building, sidewalk, driveway, foundation, swimming pool or other structure.

Direct physical loss from fire, explosion or theft resulting from water damage is covered, provided the loss is itself is a Loss Insured.

    d. **Neglect.** This includes deliberate and wilful neglect that results in loss or further loss, including but not limited to, an insured's failure take reasonable steps to protect and preserve property before, during and after a loss or when property is threatened by a continued loss.

    e. **War.** War is defined as any declared or undeclared war, civil war, insurrection, rebellion, terrorism of a domestic or international source, revolution, actions of militias or anarchists, warlike acts by a military force or military personnel. Any destruction, damage, theft, appropriation or use for a military purpose by a military force, including militias, terrorists and anarchist is excluded. Resulting loss from any of the above are excluded. Explosion of a nuclear device is considered a warlike act even if accidental.

4. The losses indicated in paragraphs 1., 2., and 3. above are excluded regardless of whether the following contribute or aggravate the loss or occur in any sequence with the above losses or any other cause of loss:
    a. conduct, actions, inactions, or decision of any person, group, organization or governmental body whether intentional, wrongful, negligent, or without fault;
    b. inherent defect, weakness, inadequacy, fault or unsoundness in
        (1) design, specifications, workmanship, construction, grading or compaction;

(2) planning, zoning, development, surveying or placement;

(3) construction materials; or

(4) maintenance and upkeep;

This applies to all covered property, including but not limited to land, structures, contents or improvements whether located on the residence premises or away from the residence premises.

Direct physical loss resulting from items a. and b. are covered under this policy unless the resulting loss is also a Loss Not Insured included in this Section.

5. If a loss is caused by a peril that is not specifically excluded, we provide coverage for direct physical loss. However, this provision does not apply to the losses indicated in paragraphs 1., 2., 3., and 4. above, for which there is no coverage.

Section I - Conditions

1. **Limit of Liability and Insurable Interest.** Our limit of liability is the amount indicated in the declarations, the amount indicated in this policy or the amount for which the insured is liable, regardless of other persons or entities who may have an interest in the covered property. We will pay no more than our insured's portion of a loss.

2. **Your Duties After Loss.** Following a loss, you are required to perform the following duties:

a. notify us when a loss occurs. If the loss is caused by theft, you must notify the police; if it is a credit card or debit card loss, you must notify the credit card issuer or bank;

b. prevent further loss by protecting the property, meaning making required temporary repairs and maintaining a record of repair expenses;

c. inventory all damaged or stolen personal property. Provide a description, age, place of purchase, serial numbers (if applicable), quantity, and replacement cost for each item. Include any receipts or documents that substantiate the figures in the inventory;

d. as frequently as we reasonably request:

(1) display the damaged property or provide clear photographic evidence of damaged items that have been disposed of;

(2) in a timely manner, give us any and all documentation we request and allow us to produce copies of these documents;

(3) provide us with recorded statements and official statements taken under oath while all other insureds are absent;

(4) allow us to take official statements under oath of any employees, members of the insured's household or any persons having knowledge of the events of a loss, provided the insured has the capacity to do so; and

e. within 180 days after the loss provide us with a signed, sworn proof of loss indicating:

(1) the date, time and cause of loss, if known;

(2) your interest and the interest of all others in the property involved and any entailments placed upon the property;

(3) any known alterations of title, deed, ownership, interest or occupancy of the insured property;

(4) any other insurance that may provide coverage for the loss;

(5) documentation of loss to any personal property items, including but not limited to an inventory of all damaged or stolen property and any blueprints or other suitable specifications of damaged buildings and, if available, detailed estimates to repair any damaged building(s) or personal property item;

(6) records of expenses for claim made for additional living expenses paid and records which substantiate the retail rental value loss;

(7) records, recorded statements under oath which substantiate a claim for a loss under the Credit Card, Debit Card, Check, Forgery and Counterfeit Money coverage, indicating the validity of a claim, the cause of the loss and the amount of the loss.

3. **Loss Settlement**. The following sets forth the settlement of covered losses:

a. At the time of loss we will pay actual cash value for the following:

(1) items that are deemed irreplaceable with what is available on the current retail market, including antiques, fine arts, painting, sculptures, and statues.

(2) items in which the age, history or significance substantially contribute to their inherent value above and beyond the current retail value of the object itself, including, but not limited to, memorabilia, souvenirs and collectibles;

(3) property which is used for something other than its original or intended purposes.

b. We will pay the following for Coverage A and Coverage B property damaged by a Loss Insured:

(1) any damage to covered property claimed, reported or not repaired or replaced within one year after the loss will be settled on an actual cash value basis;

(2) we will pay the lowest amount of the following:

(a) the actual cost to replace damaged items at the time of loss;

(b) the actual cost to repair damaged items at the time of loss;

(c) any special limits of liability indicated in this policy; or

(d) the Coverage A or Coverage B limit of liability that may apply.

c. We are required to pay only the following to repair or replace Coverage A structures and Dwelling Extensions, subject to these conditions:

(1) we will pay for construction of like kind and similar quality of the damaged items;

(2) until the damaged structure or structures have been repaired or replaced, we will pay the actual cash value at the time of loss up to the policy limits, provided all incurred expenses have been accounted for and the cost to repair the damaged structures do not exceed the cost to repair the same structures;

(3) any claim for replacement cost payments exceeding the actual cash value must be made within one year from the date of loss. All payments are restricted to

what is actually and necessarily spent to repair or replace the damaged portion or portions of the buildings or other structures with the same construction for the equivalent use on the same premises.

(4) we are not required to pay any increase in cost due to state or local ordinances, statues or laws for the repair, replacement, construction, remodelling or demolition of a structure or building, unless indicated elsewhere in this policy.

4. **Loss to a Pair or Set**. When there is loss to a pair or set, at our option we will:
   a. repair or replace that part of the pair or set that will restore the pair or set to its value before the loss; or
   b. pay the actual cash value of the pair or set as it was before the loss minus the actual cash value of the pair or set after the loss.

5. **Appraisal**. When there is a disagreement on the amount of a loss, you or we can request that the valuation of the claim be determined by appraisal. When the request for appraisal is made, each party will select their own appraiser and notify the other party within 30 days of receiving notice of appraisal of their selection of an appraiser. The two appraisers will then determine the amount of the loss. If agreement on the valuation of the loss is reached, this will be the amount of the settlement. Should the appraisers not reach agreement within 30 days, the appraisers will then select an impartial umpire, who will determine the valuation of the loss. Each party will pay the expenses incurred by the appraiser they select; any additional expenses, including but not limited to umpire fees and expenses will be shared equally by you and us.

6. **Other Insurance**. When other insurance covers any loss covered by this insurance, we will pay our portion of the loss or the applicable policy limit, whichever is less.

7. **Lawsuit Against Us**. All legal action against us must commence within one year from the date of the loss and can only be brought after all policy conditions have been met.

8. **Our Option**. When there is a payable loss, we reserve the right to repair or replace the damaged property with like kind and quality items or materials. All property for which we pay becomes our property and at our option we will assume possession of that property. However, we are not required to accept any damaged or abandoned property.

9. **Loss Payment**. All losses will be adjusted with you. Unless there is another person, persons or entity named in the policy, we will pay you for the loss. All losses will be paid within 30 business days once:
   a. you and us agree on the amount of the loss;
   b. a final judgement has been rendered; or
   c. an appraisal decision has been determined by the process indicated in number 5. above.

10. **Mortgage Clause**. All mortgagees and trustees have a payable interest in all Coverage A damages. This clause does not apply to Coverage B property.

    a. Should a mortgagee be listed under this policy, all payable losses will be paid to you and to the mortgagee as their interest may appear. Should more than one mortgagee be listed, the mortgagees will be ordered by the precedence of the mortgagees.

    b. Should a claim be denied, any valid claim made by the mortgagee will be paid provided the mortgagee:

        (1) informs us of changes in the title, deed, ownership, occupancy or significant alterations to the property which is insured.

        (2) at our request, issues payment for the premiums due under this policy when you fail to pay said premiums; or

    c. Should this policy be cancelled by us, we will notify the mortgagee at least 15 business days before the cancellation date.

    d. Should we deny payment to you and pay the mortgagee for losses incurred under this policy:

        (1) our rights and duties will be assumed by those of the mortgagee provided under the mortgage contract; or

        (2) we reserve the right to pay the mortgagee the balance of the mortgage principal. Should we exercise this option, we assume all rights of the mortgagee and any collateral assigned to the mortgage debt.

    e. The mortgagee retains all rights to their portion of claim payment of a valid claim against this policy, regardless of any subrogation of the claim.

11. **Intentional Acts**. Any deliberate damages caused by any insured with the intent of collecting payment will void this policy and no payment will be made to you or to any other insured.

Coverage "A"

Coverage A means building items: the dwelling and dwelling extensions. The dwelling includes the building and all building materials inside it—electrical wiring, plumbing, wall to wall carpeting, cabinetry—basically anything that's attached or nailed or screwed down permanently that you wouldn't take with you if you moved, including built-in shelving that is attached to the walls or floor. Most policies also state that this includes building materials that happen to be lying about.

Dwelling Extensions are buildings and items that are permanently connected to the ground but not structurally attached to the dwelling. Detached garages, fences, gates, sheds, gazebos, in-ground swimming pools, driveways. If you have a small shed that isn't sitting atop a permanent (concrete) foundation—if it was just plunked down in the yard on top of the grass or dirt—it is considered personal property.

The dwelling and dwelling extensions each have separate, unique policy limits. These coverage limits are listed on your Declarations page. Typically the Dwelling Extensions limit is 10% of the Dwelling limit; if 10% for Dwelling Extensions is not sufficient, this amount can be raised.

What is Covered

Under **Section I – Losses Insured**, an open peril policy states simply, "We provide coverage against accidental direct physical loss for all Coverage A items. All losses under **Section I - Losses Not Insured** are otherwise excluded." What this means for Coverage A is that any sudden, one-time damage that occurs to your property is covered—unless it is specifically excluded somewhere else. If your policy has a statement like the one above, you have an open peril policy. In older "named peril" policies, the Losses Insured section will list the specific causes of damage/loss for which the policy insures; in this case, these are the *only* coverages afforded under that policy.

For an open peril policy, most damages that occur slowly over time are not covered, like deterioration, long-term seepage of water from pipes, corrosion of surface materials, ordinary wear and tear, wet or dry rot—if it takes a long time to occur, it more than likely isn't covered. The few exceptions will typically be found under **Section I – Coverages, Additional Coverages**, which in the policy I'm using provides coverage for collapse caused by hidden decay and hidden insect and vermin damage.

When insurers want to determine whether or not damages are covered, they look for the Proximate Cause—the root cause of the damages. More often than not this is easy to determine—wind blew shingles off the roof, causing rain to leak into the house and damage the drywall or wallpaper. In this case, wind is the root cause of all of the resulting damages and since wind is not specifically excluded, all damages would be covered. In some cases, something that may be specifically excluded may actually be covered if the Proximate Cause is something that is covered. For example, a violent windstorm causes a large tree limb to land on a retaining wall, collapsing the retaining wall, causing the earth the wall was holding back to give way; the ground that gave way also happened to support a deck, which then collapses. If the retaining wall had collapsed for no reason, moving the ground it was holding back and making the deck fall, nothing would be covered—earth movement and collapse not caused by hidden decay are specifically excluded. In the absence of the tree limb damaging the retaining wall, nothing would be covered in this example; since wind caused the tree limb to fall onto the retaining wall, which caused the earth to move, which caused the deck to collapse, all of the damages should be covered.

Determining Proximate Cause is the cause of all disputes about whether something is covered or not. After hurricane Katrina, Proximate Cause became a highly contentious issue when it became unclear what caused the damage to some homes—did the storm surge cause the damage (ground water = not covered) or was it the Category 3 winds (covered)? In some cases, it was determined that the storm surge caused some of the damage but that the wind also caused some of the damages, too—but some insurers didn't want to pay for what engineers determined to be wind damage—in the case of State Farm, one claims manager hired a series of structural engineers until she could cherry pick the report that suited her decision not to cover the losses. Naturally that got State Farm into a wee bit of trouble in the form of a series of lawsuits, many of which they lost in spectacular fashion. Funny how trying to save money can be really expensive.

There is some extra coverage available to Coverage A property, found under Section I – Coverages – Additional Coverages. Some of these items are self-explanatory, some require a dash of interpretation. Each of these has their own little set of rules, conditions and restrictions.

Debris Removal. As long as the debris was put there or caused by a peril that is covered, insurers pay the "reasonable" expenses to haul that debris away. Most policies indicate that the debris must be from the dwelling or dwelling extensions listed under the policy, but in the real world, when windstorms like a tornado or hurricane blow debris into your yard from other houses, the removal of this debris is also covered. Any expenses for debris removal are applied toward the policy limits—which means unlike some items below, it does not have it's own special limit, that any money spent toward debris removal is included in the tally for the damages to the property damaged, whether it is the house or dwelling extensions. Also, if a dwelling is a total loss and the amount to rebuild *and* remove the debris are above the policy limits, there is an extra 5% of the policy limits available for debris removal. For example: for a dwelling with limits of $200,000.00, once the cost to rebuild goes over $200,000.00, you have an extra $10,000.00 available just for debris removal. This amount is paid on an "if incurred" basis, which means it's only paid when it is actually needed. This extra 5% also applies to dwelling extensions (which, again, have their own limits separate from the dwelling) and, as you are about to learn, tree debris removal. For more on debris removal, see Part IV, Common Losses and Issues, Chapter 26: General Debris Removal.

Tree Debris Removal. Everyone seems to want to go green lately—but what happens when green wants to go right into your living room? Tree debris removal is one of the most misinterpreted and misunderstood parts of the policy. Here's the basics: if a covered type of loss causes a tree or tree limbs to damage the dwelling or dwelling extensions (house, fence, shed, gazebo, etc.), insurers must pay any reasonable amount to lift or cut the tree (or tree limbs) off the damaged Coverage A structure(s) and place them on the ground. Once the tree or tree limbs that damaged the dwelling or dwelling extensions are on the ground, there is a separate limit of $500.00 to have any and all of the trees that caused damage to Coverage A structures to be cut up and hauled away. If it costs more than $500.00 to cut up and haul away trees or limbs that caused damage, there is an additional 5% of $500.00—a whopping $25.00!—that can also be used to pay for the cutting up and hauling away of tree debris. These only apply to Coverage A items—it does not apply to personal property items like lawn mowers or birdbaths. Also, these coverages don't apply to trees that land out in the middle of the yard and don't damage any Coverage A property—the $500.00 sublimit (as it is called) to cut up and haul away tree debris is only for trees that damage structural property. Any expenses for tree debris removal are applied to the Coverage A policy limits. Like "regular" debris removal, if a large tree totally destroys a dwelling and the amount to lift the tree off the house (and place it on the ground) and the cost to rebuild the dwelling go over the policy limits, that extra 5% of the policy limits for debris removal can be used to pay for the tree to be lifted off the dwelling and placed on the ground—but the $500.00 limit to cut up and haul away the debris once it is on the ground is still in effect. For more on Tree Debris Removal (and boy, is there more!) see Part IV, Common Losses and Issues, Chapter 23: Tree Debris Removal.

Temporary Repairs. When a type of loss that is covered causes damage to any Coverage A structure, insurers must pay any and all reasonable expenses to protect the property from further damages, regardless of whether this work is done by a professional or a homeowner. Some types of temporary repairs include putting a tarp on a roof after wind blows shingles off to prevent leaking; boarding up a window or door that was blown out; propping up a deck or porch that was weakened or loosened by a tornado or hurricane. The amount spent for temporary repairs gets applied to the policy limits for the items damaged. What the policy *doesn't* say is that if you or members of your family spend time to make the necessary temporary repairs, you can be reimbursed for your time.

Trees, Shrubs and Other Plants. "You mean my ficus is covered? Hooray!" Well, *maybe* it's covered. Including your lawn, these items are only covered for the following types of losses: fire, lightning, explosion, riot, civil commotion, aircraft, vehicles other than your own or driven by someone who lives at your dwelling, vandalism, malicious mischief, and theft. Also, anything damaged must be located **outdoors**; indoor house plants, shrubs or trees (yes, people do grow trees inside their house—my mom has a small palm tree growing in her house) are not covered. The total amount to remove and replace all trees, shrubs, plants or grass damaged by the above named perils is 5% of the dwelling limits (for a house insured for $200,000.00, the limit is $10,000.00 for all trees, shrubs, and plants.) But it's actually more restrictive than that: there is also sublimit of $500.00 per tree, shrub or plant (a lawn is considered one plant), which also includes the removal of any debris. If the entire dwelling and extensions are total losses caused by one of the listed causes above, the amount available for trees, shrubs and plants is not applied toward the building policy limit—it's an extra amount on top of that.

Power Interruption. If a type of covered loss causes you to lose electricity at your house while none of the houses surrounding yours lose their electricity, you are covered for most types damages that result, some of which are excluded elsewhere in the policy. The most common example would be freezing of plumbing pipes.

Land. In the "Proximate Cause" example above about the windstorm that felled a tree limb, which broke a retaining wall and caused the land to give way, we learned that land is covered when a covered type of loss causes land to become unstable. The catch with this particular provision is not just that a covered type of loss must cause the land to collapse or become unstable but that the land must support the dwelling or part of the dwelling such as the deck mentioned above. Land that is out in the middle of the yard or is supporting a fence, shed, doghouse, birdbath or detached garage is not covered, regardless of the cause of the land loss. On the upside, there is $10,000.00 available to replace, rebuild, restore or stabilize the land—an extra amount of insurance that, in the case of a total loss, provides money that is above and beyond the policy limits that would normally apply. This sublimit also includes any engineering costs associated with the restoration of the land.

Volcanic Action. The good news: the volcano next door that finally erupted and blew out half your windows, then spewed ash inside the house which damaged the furniture and then caused lava to burn away the corner of your garage is covered by your homeowners insurance. The bad news: your flock of pink flamingo lawn ornaments made extinct from the lava is not covered. If your precious fake plastic birds had been inside your house or garage when damaged they would have been covered. Coverage A items are covered by the force of the blast, ash and lava; personal property items are only covered by these three troublemakers if they're in a fully enclosed building (a carport is not a fully enclosed building). Also, any eruptions that happen within a 72-hour period are considered one event, with one deductible; any other eruptions that occur outside the 72-hour window are considered a separate event, with another deductible applying—drats!

Collapse. *The* classic example of the "It's covered unless it's not covered" syndrome. And also the classic example of where the title of this chapter came from. There is a whole laundry list of specific causes where collapse is covered. However, item d., "weight of snow, ice..." etc., means that only the collapse of a *roof* is covered by the weight of ice, snow, sleet or rain, and not anything else. All the others would cover the collapse of part or all of a building.

Of course, there are exceptions to the specific items listed above: "Loss to dwelling extensions such as fences" etc. What this means is that if only a *part* of a building collapses—the roof, for example—then those items are not covered—the *entire* building must collapse for the listed items to be covered. To add further insult to injury, "Settling, cracking, shrinking, bulging, or expansion are not considered collapse." Of course, what it doesn't say is that if a covered type of collapse causes any of those things to happen—cracks in stucco from wind blowing a tree against the side of a house—then they *are* covered.

To sum up collapse: it is never covered unless the specific causes above cause the damage. And certain things (awnings, etc.) are only covered in certain instances. If the proximate cause of the collapse is covered, then any exclusions are overridden.

When reading a section in a policy like the one above, first tell yourself that this type of damage is never covered; then work back from there; read the section once or twice and sort out (if you're able to) which causes actually *are* covered; whatever is mentioned as being covered, it overrules any exclusions.

Locks. Simple: if someone steals your keys, the insurance company will pay the "reasonable" expense to re-key the locks on the doors of the dwelling. The good news: with most insurers, no deductible applies. The bad news: it has to be a "covered theft" which means if your pissed off teen—or anyone else who lives in the dwelling—steals the keys and tosses them in a random garbage bin, it's not covered.

There are several additional coverages that some insurers include that are not in the sample policy, like the following.

Mold. Most policies have been amended to include special provisions for mold. This additional coverage states that the mold must be caused by a type of damage that is covered. For example, if wind blows shingles off a roof and wind blows water into the house and the water causes mold, the mold would be covered. Most insurers place strict dollar limits for the total amount they will pay for the detection and remediation (the finding and removal of mold), which is inclusive for structural and personal property damages.

Grave Markers. There is normally a dollar limit for the coverage of grave markers. Some policies state that the grave markers must be located off the residence premises.

Inflation Protection. This additional coverage provides homeowners with additional coverage should the actual cost of repair or replacement exceed the policy limits for a structural item. Some insurers provide this coverage for personal property also. Some insurers tie the percentage of this additional cost to the Residential Building Cost Index.

Loss Assessments. For homeowners who live in a development with a homeowners association or similar entity, some insurers provide this extra amount of insurance to cover loss assessments charged to you due to a type of damage covered under your policy. There is normally a set dollar limit, like $1,000.

Pollution Removal. When a covered type of loss causes a covered piece of property to be exposed to pollution or turns covered property into pollution, some insurers provide this extra amount of insurance, usually a fixed amount, to cover the costs to extract pollution or clean property of pollution.

What isn't Covered

The items in this section refer to **Section I – Losses Not Insured**. It could be entitled Exclusions, but losses not insured sounds nicer somehow.

The good news about exclusions? For an open peril policy, with Coverage A property, unless a sudden one-time occurrence is specifically excluded, it's actually covered. And the better news: the doctrine of proximate cause reigns supreme over most exclusions—that is to say, something that is excluded in the sample policy above, such as mold, is actually covered if the root cause is something that is covered: for example, if wind damages a roof and causes leaking and the leaking causes mold, in this case, mold is covered because wind is covered—the proximate cause is wind. There are exceptions to this, such as the Water exclusion, which brings me to the bad news about exclusions: they are very broad and tend to be interpreted broadly, leaving little wiggle room or forgiveness when it comes to paying claims.

If you have a named peril policy, for Coverage A, you are only covered for what is listed under **Section I – Losses Insured**, and any additional exclusions under Section I - Losses Not Insured clarify which instances covered losses overrule exclusions and which exclusion take precedence over covered losses.

Most exclusions are fairly straight forward, but there are some that aren't listed in the sample policy and some that need a little clarification.

Business/Rental. This is not listed in the sample policy, but most policies have some variation on this. If any part of a dwelling or dwelling extension is used for business or is rented out, any damage to that structure is not covered—*unless* it is a building that is rented as a private garage, then it may be covered. Most insurers have additional endorsements available that will cover losses for home businesses.

Collapse. This *again*? Yes—unless the collapse is caused specifically by any of the causes from the lengthy list above, then it is not covered. Basically, what this means is if something collapses for no reason or because something is old and wasn't properly maintained—or for any other reason then the ones named, it isn't covered.

Freezing. This is what this exclusion means: if a dwelling is unoccupied (no furniture or people; vacation doesn't count) or under construction, any freezing of the plumbing pipes, heating or air conditioning system, fire sprinkler system, or appliances is not covered. If, however, the house *is* occupied and you have made a "reasonable" attempt to maintain heat inside the property and/or have drained the water from water heaters and appliances, then freezing of plumbing pipes, heating or air conditioning system, fire sprinkler system, or appliances would be covered.

Freezing, thawing, pressure or weight of water or ice. Wait—wasn't weight of water or ice covered above? Why, yes it was—to *roofs* only. Freezing, thawing, pressure or weight of water or ice to fences, pavement, patios, swimming pools, foundations, retaining walls, bulkheads, piers, wharfs and docks is never covered, no exceptions.

Theft in or to a dwelling under construction. Theft of construction materials at a dwelling are covered—as long as the house is not under construction. Picky, picky, picky. Of course, if a house is being remodelled or repaired, then theft of construction materials would be covered.

Vandalism or malicious mischief to a vacant property. Apparently insurers have something against mayhem. The good news here is that "vacant" means not inhabited (again, no furniture, no people = vacant) for more than 30 days. If you've vacated a house for 30 days and it is vandalized, you're covered. If you've vacated a house for 31 days and it is vandalized, you're not covered. If you're on vacation for two months in Europe, you're fine; if your house is under construction, you're covered. To sum up, if your dwelling is under construction and someone steals a box of nails it isn't covered, but if someone hammers a box of nails randomly into the drywall, it is covered. Does that sounds arbitrary? Naaaaw...I'm sure the people who came up with these exclusions weren't suffering from any kind of mental defect.

Continuous or repeated discharge or leakage of water or steam. Okay, we get it—if something happens over an extended period of time, it's not covered. But the tricky thing with this exclusion is not just that long-term leakage/seepage from your plumbing, heating or air conditioning system, fire sprinkler system or appliances and any damage it causes is excluded; any resulting wet or dry rot, mold, deterioration, corrosion, or rust is also excluded. To take another trip down Arbitrary Street, if it's determined that a leak *is* covered, insurers will pay to repair any areas damaged by the leakage—drywall, plaster, flooring, etc.—but they *won't* pay to repair or replace the system that caused the leak.

Wear, tear, marring, scratching, deterioration, inherent vice, latent defect or mechanical breakdown. With the exception of scratching and mechanical breakdown, all of these fall under the "takes a long time to occur" umbrella. Scratching, though in some cases, *is* covered, if the root cause is covered: wind damage from tornado and hurricane-propelled objects that scratch or gouge roofing, siding or doors is covered.

Corrosion, electrolysis, rust, mold, wet or dry rot, contamination. If any of these items spring up on their own—if mold just appears one day out of the blue—then they are not covered. But, once again, proximate cause overrules exclusions: if any of these *are* caused directly by something that is covered, then these exclusions are covered. Example: if hail causes a leak in a roof and the moisture that infiltrates the interior of the dwelling causes mold, then that mold would then be covered because hail is covered.

Birds, vermin, rodents, insects or domestic animals. These are not covered, with two notable exceptions: hidden damage from insects or vermin that then causes collapse; and breakage of glass from any of the animals listed above. Naturally, if a tornado rips a hole in your roof and then hurtles a raccoon into your attic and the force of the raccoon being violently flung into your attic damages—well, *anything*—then whatever is damaged should be covered. Whoever said raccoons can't fly? There has been a debate over the years over what constitutes "vermin." This will likely be an area where an insurer applies the broadest definition possible in order to not pay a claim.

There is a statement at the end of Loses Not Insured - #1: "Unless the resulting loss is a Loss Not Insured as indicated in this section, we cover accidental direct loss from items a. through l."

Huh?

What this means is that if a covered type of loss causes of any of the exclusions listed under number one, then the loss is covered. For example, if wind blows shingles off a roof and the wind blows water into a house and the water that infiltrated the house spurs the growth of mold, the mold would then be covered. This concept applies to most of the exclusions under Losses Not Insured, but not all.

Earthquake. Earthquake, strangely enough, is where insurers get generous and toss Proximate Cause out the window: if an earthquake is the root cause of a fire, explosion, theft or breakage of glass to a dwelling, then those would be covered. Note that this sample policy specifies dwelling; not dwelling extensions. If your policy doesn't say dwelling *and* dwelling extensions, you're guaranteed that they're only going to cover the dwelling and not your detached garage, gazebo, fence or shed. The catch with this provision is that the only secondary effects of an earthquake that are covered are the ones listed. If an earthquake causes water pipes to break, the breaking of the pipes would be excluded and so would any mold that grew as a result of the water that was released. Earthquake itself is only covered with a specific endorsement (see below).

Nuclear Hazard. Scary prospect. Nuclear hazard includes any type of damage caused by radiation or radioactive materials, man made or not. When it comes to nuclear hazard, insurers are a little stingier about proximate cause coverage for specific damages: if a nuclear hazard is the root cause of a fire, the fire is covered, but nothing else is.

Ordinance or Law. This means a couple of things. First, if local building code requires that upgrades be made to a home after a covered loss, then the insurance company isn't necessarily going to pay for any forced upgrades because of those codes: the policy states in Section I – Conditions that they pay to replace like with like and they cannot and will not be held responsible for codes beyond their control. Secondly, if a building is damaged by a covered loss and is then condemned by local authorities and the property is ordered to be torn down, it doesn't necessarily mean the insurance company will agree to pay for the demolition of the property. This is a *very* unlikely scenario, but insurance companies reserve the right to not be forced to spend money for things that are beyond their control.

Earth Movement. In the "Section I – Additional Coverages," the policy states that it insures for the "loss of land stability" caused by a covered type of loss. Earth movement is the shifting, rising, sinking, contracting of land on its own, including earthquake, landslides, mudflows, sinkholes, subsidence, and erosion that **occurs on its own**. As in the example of the tree limb that damaged a retaining wall and caused a deck to collapse because the land gave way, if a covered loss causes the earth movement, then any damage to a dwelling should be covered—but only the dwelling and items attached to it are covered. For another example a fire on a hillside above a home burned all the trees and shrubbery and before any shrubbery could grow back, heavy rain caused a landslide and caused damage to the dwelling. It was determined that the proximate cause was fire and the damage was covered. Also, if land movement causes a fire, explosion, theft or glass breakage, then these specific damages are covered. In Florida, there are state laws that allow some sinkholes to be covered. For sinkhole losses in Florida, check with your insurer or local authorities concerning the laws and policy provisions or endorsements that may cover sinkholes.

Water Damage. There's a saying in insurance about water damage and whether or not it's covered: "Once water touches the ground, it's out of bounds," meaning if water enters a house or dwelling extension from ground level or below, it's not covered. The vast majority of exclusions I've dealt with over the years were from water damage. This includes flood, surface water, tidal water, waves, overflow of a body of water or spray from any of these, **whether driven by wind or not**. The words in bold are important because wind-driven water means that, according to insurers, surface water is still the root cause—without the water, the wind could not have blown the water and caused the damage. Once water is on the ground, no matter how it damages a home or other structure, it is not covered. Water damage also includes water that enters a dwelling through the drains or sewer line or pushes up through a sump pump or any type of system that is supposed to drain the water from or around the foundation; and water that seeps from below the ground's surface.

Water damage is one of the instances where the exclusions override most covered types of losses. For example, if lightning damages a sump pump and causes it to fail and water enters the basement through the sump pump hole (known as a crock) the resulting structural damages would be excluded. What would be covered is the lightning damage to the sump pump itself.

Neglect. This includes failing to make temporary repairs, the failure to do so resulting in more damage; not sweeping up broken glass before the neighbor's kids play in it like it's sand in a sandbox; not putting up a warning sign/tape or cordoning off a giant hole caused by an uprooted tree felled by wind. A homeowner's failure to protect his property from further damage can result in that additional damage being denied.

War and Terrorism. After September 11, 2001, insurers revised their policies to make sure that terrorism was considered an act of war or otherwise specifically not covered. To insurers war and terrorism can have very broad definitions, including an accidental discharge of a nuclear weapon, another civil war, or a hijacked plane shot down by the military. This exclusion also includes any property that is commandeered by a military force or terrorist and is subsequently damaged.

Conduct/Acts. "Conduct, actions, inactions, or decision of any person, group, organization or governmental body whether intentional, wrongful, negligent, or without fault" is not covered. In other words, if someone else's decision or actions or neglect cause the loss, then insurers wash their hands of it. This is the most broad and vague exclusion in the policy; if they wanted to, insurers could use this provision to exclude theft—or anything else caused by any human being who completes an action or makes a decision that causes a loss. But they wouldn't do that—*would they?*

Weakness and Defect. Another broad stroke by the geniuses who brought you "collapse." Basically, if anything is defective or has an inherent weakness in its composition, construction, planning or isn't properly maintained, it's not covered. If they wanted to, insurers could use this provision to exclude virtually any and every claim they wanted to: the reason that tree fell through your house was because the construction of the house was defective—it wasn't built to withstand a tree crashing through it so we're not going to pay for it. If insurers were really truly evil, they would do that, but they wouldn't do that—*would they?*

Coverage B

Coverage B is personal property—basically anything inside or outside a house that belongs to you and isn't screwed or nailed down or otherwise *permanently* affixed to the dwelling, garage, shed or gazebo or any other Coverage A structure. (Note: some policies label personal property Coverage C) Years ago, when I first started out, I was given a good definition of what is considered Coverage B: if you were to move, could you take it with you? This would include drapes and blinds, area rugs and that little shed in the back yard that is nestled in the grass or on the dirt; it doesn't mean you *would* take it with you, just that you reasonably could, like your stove and refrigerator, which many people don't take with them. Your personal property is covered if it is lost, stolen or damaged anywhere in the world, though usually with monetary limits, and like many Coverage A items, many Coverage B items have specific limits. Each insurer has its own monetary limits for items under the "Special Limits of Liability" (Section I – Coverages, Coverage B – Personal Property) and some insurers have additional items listed separately with specific limits, such as tools and computer equipment; if there are specific limits to a particular category of personal property item, it will be found under Section I – Coverages, Coverage B. What is not specifically noted in some policies is that the possessions of a child or dependent who is away at summer camp, summer school or college are also covered—naturally, most policies put limits on the amount of damages that can be collected.

I'm occasionally asked why the Coverage B Limits listed in the Declarations Page seems like a completely random number—most homeowners don't specifically request a particular limit, though you can.

Unless a different amount is requested, the Coverage B Limit is always a set percentage of the Coverage A limit. With some insurers, it's 60%, some it's 65%, some it's a different percentage altogether. Thrilled to learn that, aren't you?

What is Covered

If you have an open peril policy that is open peril for contents/personal property, you are provided with the same coverage as building items, any sudden one-time occurrence is covered unless specifically excluded. For policies like the sample policy above, the types of losses covered are the exact opposite of what is covered under Coverage A. For personal property damage, your property is not covered for anything except for what is specifically listed. The doctrine of Proximate Cause still applies to types of loss/damage that are listed and as long as the root cause of loss is covered, most exclusions are overridden.

Under **Section I – Coverages, Coverage B – Personal Property**, there are a few particularities about the items under **Special Limits of Liability**. These limits do not increase the overall policy limits for Coverage B—they are included in the total policy limits.

In the examples below taken from the sample policy, you'll notice a pattern: if something has a limit for a specific type of loss, it will mention it in this section. Policies often get misinterpreted when it is inferred that the limit for a particular item or category of items applies to all types of damages and loss. For example, in the sample policy item g., firearms have a limit of $3,500 for loss by theft; this doesn't mean that there is a total limit of $3,500 for loss of firearms, but that there is a $3,500 limit in case the firearms are stolen. When a policy mentions a limit for a specific type of item (for example, e., $1,200 for water-craft) but doesn't mention a particular type of loss, that means there is $1,200 limit for all types of covered losses.

Property away from home. If you accidentally drop your cam-corder into the Grand Canyon while recording its majestic hole-y-ness (I mean, come on, it's a *hole in the ground!*) most policies limit the amount homeowners can collect to $2,000.00 or 10% of the Coverage

B limits, whichever is greater. Some policies don't have a specific limit if the property is lost, damaged or stolen in the U.S., while some policies have specific limits about property that is taken out of the country. If a policy has this particular limit, it will be listed in Section I – Coverages, either under the heading Coverage B – Personal Property, Special Limits of Liability or in the Additional Coverages.

Business Property. There are usually two limits listed here: business property located at home and that which is damaged elsewhere. Some policies exclude electronics that are used for business, like the sample policy; if your policy does, it will say it here or in Additional Coverages.

Boats and Trailers. When it comes to watercraft and trailers (which does not include travel trailers/RVs), what it *doesn't* say in this section is that a boat (including a canoe) or any of their parts and accessories must be inside a fully enclosed building like a garage or a shed that is set upon a permanent foundation. If it's sitting outside or under a carport, it's not covered under most homeowners policies for any type of damage. If a canoe is hanging on the outside wall of a garage (which is a handy place to store one) and the wind lifts it off its brackets and rams it into a tree, bending it in half, it's not covered. However, if that same canoe is *inside* the garage and the tornadic forces of wind sucks the overhead door out and then pulls the canoe from the inside of the garage and rams it into a tree, bending it in half, then it is covered. A (non-travel) trailer not used with watercraft can be setting outside and still be covered. Most policies do not cover RVs, requiring a separate RV policy.

Firearms. The $3,500 limit in the sample policy is only for firearms that are *stolen*. If your firearms burn in a fire or are damaged by another type of covered loss, then the loss of firearms are applied toward policy limits for personal property and the $3,500 limit does not apply.

Silverware or Goldware. This $3,000 limit does not include gold or silver or jewelry—they have their own limits, too! As with firearms, most policies specify that silverware or goldware must be *stolen*. Again, if the silverware or goldware is damaged or lost by any other covered type of loss, then the amount of damage comes out of the total policy limits for personal property.

Computer Equipment. Insurers *hate* replacing computer equipment, mainly because they become out of date or obsolete so quickly and the parameters of what is a top level, mid level and lower level computer change from year to year—a computer that was top of the line three years ago may have the features and capacity of a mid or low level computer today. The limits found here includes back up hard drives, recordable media (CD-ROMs, DVDs, etc.). The good news is that a student's computer while he's away at school is covered, but with the same limit.

Rugs, Tapestry, Wall Hangings. As with firearms and goldware and silverware, most policies specify that limits only apply in the case of theft.

In **Section I – Coverages, Additional Coverages**, many of the items listed apply to both Coverage A and Coverage B and some are little-known coverages that most folks are surprised to learn they have. In this section, if there is no explicit limit mentioned for an item or type of loss, then the regular policy limits for personal property apply, as does the regular deductible. Some policies will include breakage of glass in this section (the sample doesn't) and will tell you whether or not the deductible applies. Some items will state the deductible doesn't apply; that means it doesn't apply to that type of loss for a particular item only. For example, the sample policy indicates no deductible applies for the re-keying of locks if a set of house keys are taken in a covered theft—the deductible won't apply to the re-keying of locks, but if other items are stolen, the deductible will apply to those items.

Debris Removal. Like with building items, Coverage B also includes coverage for debris removal. Also like Coverage A, in the case of a large or total loss, if the expense to remove the debris and the cost to replace the personal property items goes above the Coverage B limits, there is an extra 5% of the Coverage B limits available to remove the debris. NOTE: tree debris removal does NOT apply to personal property. If a tree or large tree limb lands on personal property and nothing else, there is no coverage to have the tree or limbs removed, cut up or hauled away.

Property Removed. If a covered type of loss threatens your home—a wildfire, for example—any Coverage B items that you move or attempt to move to protect them from being damage or destroyed, any damage that occurs to these items is covered. Any limits applying to these items are still in effect—computers, for example.

Refrigerated Products. While this one is self-explanatory, most people are completely unaware that if their electricity goes out for a duration long enough to cause food or medicine to spoil, the contents of their refrigerators and freezers are covered. Some insurers do not charge a deductible for this type of loss if it is the only kind of loss sustained. Some insurers limit the dollar amount per freezer and/or refrigerator unit. This section of the additional coverages should state whether or not a deductible applies or if there is a per unit limit.

Jewelry and Furs. To sum this coverage up, unless the items are stolen, there are no predefined policy limits for loss of jewelry and furs. For theft, there is a strict limit of $1,000 per item or $3,000 total, however you can buy an endorsement to increase this amount to suit your needs. What it doesn't say here is that precious or semi-precious stones that are taken from their settings are not covered for theft—someone must steal the entire ring or bracelet or necklace or whatever for the stones to be covered.

Volcanic Action. Any personal property items damaged by volcanic action, ash, dust or lava, must be inside a fully enclosed building for it to be covered. The building does not necessarily have to sustain damage.

Collapse. If you're sensing a pattern about personal property coverage, then you can guess that any personal property damaged by a collapse must be inside a fully enclosed building. Some policies also state that the entire building must collapse in order for personal property items to be covered.

Let's look at **Section I – Losses Insured**. When reading a Losses Insured section that has exclusions built into what is covered (this is, after all the Losses Insured section not the Losses Not Insured), if you see something that says it isn't covered, look through **Section I – Coverages, Additional Coverages**. If that item is not listed under additional coverages, it truly isn't covered. If it is listed under Additional Coverages, then it actually is covered despite what it says under Losses Insured, though there may be limits to the coverage and there may be instances when only some types of loss are covered. For example, Theft is covered in this section; Jewelry and Furs are covered in Additional Coverages, but theft of a precious or semi-precious stone from its setting is not covered for theft.

Fire or Lightning. Or fires started by lightning or electrical fires or grease fires—you know, fire. This also includes any damage as the result of putting out the fire, such as smoke, water damage or in the case of our house fire those many years ago, the broken window the firefighters caused when they dumped my brother's smoldering mattress into the snow from the second story.

Windstorm or hail. The "catch" with wind and hail is that in order to cause covered damage to indoor personal property the wind or hail must actually "create an opening" in a fully enclosed structure and then cause damage to personal property. Wind or hail (or objects driven by wind) must physically damage a building in some way: break glass, open up the roof, punch a hole in the wall—and allow rain, snow, sleet, sand, dirt, snert (mix of snow and dirt) or dust to enter the fully enclosed building and then damage the personal property. If a roof leaks for no apparent reason and water drips onto your leather sofa and ruins it, the sofa would not be covered. If a tree limb punctures the roof and water leaks into the house and onto your sofa, your sofa would then be covered. If rain blows through an open window and damages your leather sofa, it would not be covered. If wind tosses a piece of debris and breaks a window and rain blows into the house through the window and onto the sofa, it would be covered. Some insurers are very picky about whether or not an "opening" has been created. Some insurers insist it must be a *visible* opening, not a theoretical opening, such as damaging hail that causes a roof to leak when the roof hasn't leaked before, while others are more flexible. This is an area where you can challenge an insurer who denies a claim.

Personal property stored outside (or outside an enclosed building or under a carport) is covered when damaged by wind or hail. That means your bird baths, bird houses and that flock of plastic pink flamingos standing guard over your front lawn are covered should wind or hail damage or disfigure them.

Theft. Theft is covered unless and with exception to and without the presence or absence of...AIIIGGGH! This is one of the sections of the policy that make reading it an exercise in self-torture. For example, the sample policy says loss of a precious or semi-precious stone from its setting is not covered. The problem is that in **Section I – Coverages**, **Additional Coverages**, number 10, Jewelry and Furs, it is covered up $1,000 per article or $3,000 total—except for theft, which #10 doesn't say. If a piece of jewelry is stolen, the thieves must take the whole piece and not just the stones for it to be covered. Item c. under Theft, means the belongings you take with you that you intend to bring home are covered when you are at a second home (including a short- or long-term rental), but the items that you own that are stored at a rental home or vacation home are not covered if they are damaged—if you own a vacation home, your insurer wants you to buy a separate policy to cover that place and its contents.

Falling Objects. Just like with wind or hail, in order for there to be coverage for personal property damage, the property has to be inside a fully enclosed building and the falling object must first cause damage to the building—it doesn't have to "create an opening," it just has to *damage* the building. For example, if the neighbor's boys launch large rocks from a catapult (been there, done that) and the force of a rock crashing against the side of your house knocks an expensive clock off the wall and breaks the clock, there *is* going to be damage to the outside of the house, even if the "repair" consists of cleaning off the scuff marks.

Weight of ice, snow or sleet. Once more, the personal property must be inside a fully enclosed building—but unlike wind and hail, there doesn't have to be an opening created by the ice or snow build up, it just has to be damaged directly by the weight or the melting of ice, sleet or snow.

Sudden and accidental discharge of water or steam/tearing asunder, cracking, burning or bulging (numbers 12 and 13 of the sample policy)…of water or steam from plumbing, heating system, A/C system or fire sprinkler system when caused by freezing is not covered. If the overflow or discharge of water comes from outside the house and/or plumbing system through the drains or sewer line, it is not covered. If the sudden discharge or overflow or sudden and accidental tearing asunder, cracking, burning or bulging of water or steam from plumbing, heating system, A/C system or fire sprinkler system occurs over a long period of time (for example, weeks or months), it is not covered. If your water pipes just suddenly burst one day for no apparent reason, any personal property items the water damage is covered. Though, oddly, the repairs to the plumbing, heating, A/C or sprinkler system would not actually be covered.

Freezing…of a plumbing, heating, air conditioning, sprinkler system or household appliance. Um, *wait*. Didn't it just say this *isn't* covered if they freeze? Yep, that's what it said. But how…? But why…? You see, freezing *is* covered for these systems. This provision provides the coverage not allowed in items 12 and 13, provided you maintain heat in the building and/or drain the water from systems or appliances. If you're wondering why this particular item would be listed under personal property but gives the impression of not providing much coverage for personal property if, say, a pipe were to freeze and burst and cause water to damage your stuff, then you're beginning to understand why I say these policies were written by deranged individuals. Of course, it does cover the fridge, freezer, washing machine, window A/C unit and other appliances should they be damaged by freezing.

Power surge. Of course, most policies don't *say* "power surge," it says damage "from a change in artificially generated electrical current." Which is exactly what a power surge is. Most policies have strict monetary limits to this coverage—some have limits for particular items, some have a blanket limit.

Breakage of Glass. This may seem like an odd thing for personal property, but it can be very useful in some circumstances. If a tree limb crashes through a window and the glass from the window becomes embedded in a cloth couch or chair, that cloth item should either be replaced or reupholstered—this doesn't apply to leather. This also applies to blankets, most types of mattresses and pillows, etc.

What isn't Covered

With the sample policy, what isn't covered is easy to figure out. When it comes to types of losses, everything isn't covered unless it specifically *is* covered under **Section I – Coverages, Additional Coverages** or **Section I – Losses Insured, Coverage B – Personal Property**. These are the only causes of loss for which your personal property is covered. To make sure folks really get it, (and to add insult to injury) all of the items in **Section I – Losses Not Insured** are also types of losses for which your personal property isn't covered. Apparently, when it comes to personal property causes of loss, this section is sponsored by the Redundancy Department of Redundancy.

When it comes to specific categories of property that isn't covered, one need only look to **Section I – Coverages, Coverage B – Personal Property**, item #2 **Property Not Covered**. There you'll find a very specific a list of what particular property items are not covered, from birds and fish to motor vehicles and airplanes.

The way to interpret coverage for personal property is simple. If you have an open peril policy for personal property, you are covered for any sudden one time occurrence with the exception of those that are excluded in Losses Not Insured. If you have a named peril policy and you're trying to discern whether or not a type of loss is covered, first tell yourself nothing is covered, then look through the **Additional Coverages** section of your policy (as mentioned earlier, some items are for both Coverage A and B) and then look under Losses Insured, Coverage B. If your type of loss isn't mentioned there or specifically noted as not being covered, your type of loss is excluded.

If you're trying to determine whether or not a particular item or category of items is covered, it's the opposite: everything is covered unless it is ruled out under **Property Not Covered**.

Coverage "C"

Loss of Use, as it is called, is perhaps the least known coverage under the homeowners policy and the least understood. "Loss of use" means your dwelling becomes uninhabitable after a covered type of loss. Under coverage C is also "Market Rental Value" (also called Loss of Rents) which is loss of use of a part of a property that is rented to others when damaged by a covered type of loss or when civil authorities prohibit the use of your property due to a covered loss that damaged a neighboring premises or a covered loss that is threatening your home directly—a wildfire or when an area is under a mandatory evacuation due to a hurricane.

Unlike Coverage A and B, there are no hard dollar limits for Coverage C—insurers must pay the actual cost of the loss of use. Instead of a hard dollar limit, they put a time limit, usually one year, though this varies. **Section I – Coverages, Coverage C – Loss of Use** will state the time limits. When property owners are forced to evacuate due to an impending peril, there is a time limit on how long this coverage applies (the sample policy states two weeks, which also varies from insurer to insurer), unless the home or rental property is also made uninhabitable by the peril that threatened the property in the first place, then the regular time limit applies.

For homeowners whose house is made uninhabitable by an insurable loss, Coverage C pays the everyday living expenses to live elsewhere while a house is being repaired—be it a hotel, an apartment or renting rooms from a friend or relative. This type of coverage is referred to as ALE—Additional Living Expenses—and pays everything above and beyond what is normally spent to live: if you have to drive farther to work while living in your temporary quarters, you can claim the additional gas expenses; if you have to take your clothes to a Laundromat instead of doing it at home, you can claim the expenses above and beyond what you normally would have spent. Insurers do not like paying ALE and will often fight not to pay it unless it is obvious that they have to or if it absolutely necessary. In many cases, ALE is doled out on a case by case basis and there have been instances where the damages to a dwelling did not warrant ALE but the extent of the repairs did.

With some insurers, they also provide short-term ALE—but *not* Loss of Rents/Market Rental Value—when an earthquake, landslide, flood or volcanic explosion make a home uninhabitable or if civil authorities force you out of your home because of an earthquake, landslide, flood or volcanic explosion. This is the ONLY coverage homeowners will get for these types of losses—unless a homeowner also has Flood insurance or an endorsement that provides earthquake coverage. This coverage is usually very limited—if it is available at all—and as stated above, does not cover Loss of Rents. If your policy has this, typically no deductible applies.

Before a hurricane strikes, if an area or county is put under a mandatory evacuation, insurers are *supposed* to pay for temporary lodging if you decide to evacuate (for up to the limit, two weeks in the sample policy) however, most insurers will only reimburse your expenses to evacuate if there is damage to your home or property from the hurricane.

For more on ALE and Loss of Rents, see Chapter 22, Additional Living Expenses and Loss of Rents.

Conditions

The good thing about the Conditions portion of Section I of the policy is that 90% of it is actually written in English and not insurance-ese and needs a minimum of translation. What's important about the conditions of a homeowners policy is that when it comes to actual claims, the conditions portion of the policy are the most overt references to how claims are actually handled and settled and when these are understood by homeowners—which I can personally attest does not happen often—it goes a long way toward levelling the playing field when it comes to property damage claims.

Beginning with "Your Duties After Loss," the conditions listed here are basic and mostly common sense, although in all the years I've handled insurance claims the only situations where homeowners have been forced to fill out a sworn proof of loss is after a theft. The most important articles in this section are b., protecting the property from further damage after an insured loss, and d., displaying the damaged property. After hurricane Katrina, another adjuster was assigned a claim filed by an officer of the law who declared that he wasn't going to allow the insurance company come to his house and inspect the damages from the wind, that the insurance company was going to have to take his word and use his contractor's estimate to pay the claim. The claim was denied. I never found out what happened after that, but it serves as a good example of how the conditions can work for or against a homeowner. As will be discussed in greater depth in the next chapter, *not* protecting a property after a loss can result in any additional damage not being covered.

The 10% of the conditions section that flies over the head of most policyholders is the section on Loss Settlement. Right off the bat, the first questions arise: "At the time of loss we will pay actual cash value for the following..." Actual Cash Value? What the dickens is that? Actual Cash Value (or ACV) is the present value of an item: for building components or personal property items that decrease in value over time, ACV is the new/full replacement cost minus depreciation; for items that actually appreciate over time (some fine art, etc.), ACV is the current market value. There is much more on ACV in the Chapter 7, Getting Paid: a Crash Course on Insurance Company Math.

Item b. of loss settlement indicates the time limit for collecting damages; this policy indicates the time limit is for personal property and some other specific items, but most policies have a very strict time limit for getting any and all items repaired or replaced, regardless if they are structural items or personal property items. What items b. and c. mean is that the insurance company is going to make a partial payment (the Actual Cash Value as opposed to the full replacement cost) of the damages for your loss unless and until you actually complete the repairs or replace the damaged items and that they're only going to pay the actual cost of repair or replacement or pay the policy limits, whichever is smallest. This may sound like no big deal, but as you will learn in Chapter 9, Settling Your Claim: What Insurance Companies Don't Want You to Know, this is actually the key to getting the policy to work for you during the claim settlement process. In item c., number 3 it says a policyholder only has one year to collect the full payments for structural damages. Most policies state in this section that after your property is damaged and the insurance company makes a partial payment for damages, you have a period of time (usually two years to six months) to tell the insurance company that you're actually going to complete the repairs/replacement and therefore be eligible to collect the remainder of the payment for your claim. Of course, in 11 years, I've only ever received one letter stating this—in the real world, this generally is not required.

The second most important article in the Conditions section is article 9, Loss Payment. The insurance company promises to make payment for a claim within 30 days—which usually isn't a problem unless it is an extremely large, complex claim requiring engineers or any other special loss assessments or if there is an extremely high claim volume and the insurer can't keep up—but it also says that in order to make a payment you and the insurer must be in agreement. If you don't agree with their assessment or the monetary settlement amount, then you are under no obligation to accept their settlement offer.

Special Attention should also be paid to article 10 Mortgage Clause. Technically what this item says is that if you have a mortgage on your structural property, then your mortgage company or mortgagee must be a co-payee for all structural damage claims—their name is going to appear on all checks for damages along with your name. This does not apply to personal property checks, just building items. In the real world, the vast majority of mortgage companies don't want the nuisance of dealing with the paperwork that this entails and they have made agreements with each individual insurance companies that their names should only appear on claims over a certain amount, which varies from insurer to insurer, from $5000 to $7500 or more. It should be noted that some mortgage companies do require that their name appear on each and every payment beginning with dollar one. The insurance company should tell you if your mortgage company is going to be named on the checks for payment. Chapter 7 also has specific instructions for handling checks with the mortgage company name(s) on them.

Additional Coverages/Endorsements

At the back of every policy is a list of additional coverages and special endorsements that increase policy limits for specific items that can be purchased for an additional fee. This is where policyholders can "customize" their policy to suit their needs or provide that extra coverage for situations that may be typical of their home or their lifestyle. Endorsements by their nature must follow all tenets of the policy, all the same conditions and time restrictions, although some endorsements exist to modify the limits and coverages stated in the policy so that that specific item or type of coverage is increased or becomes available. In addition to the items listed below, virtually any type of structure can be insured for an additional amount above and beyond the normal policy limits. For example, if you have an unusually large detached garage, you can get extra coverage for it. Also, if you have particularly valuable personal property, you can get it scheduled so that special limits apply to that item or a group of items—if you just happen to have an original Picasso painting, for example, you'd probably want to have that scheduled separately, just in case it's worth more than everything else you own. The following are some of the more typical and popular endorsements available.

Replacement Cost. Some policies provide replacement cost coverage for structural but not personal property; some older policies don't provide replacement cost for either but you can often buy into replacement cost if you don't feel like upgrading to a more current policy. This endorsement doesn't actually increase policy limits. There is one exception to being able to purchase replacement coverage: mobile homes are not usually replacement cost policies and with most insurers you can't actually buy replacement cost coverage.

Sewer and Drain backup/Sump Pump Overflow. If you have a finished basement or area of the home that is below the level of the ground, you should have this endorsement. Correction: you *need* this endorsement. This endorsement provides coverage for a type of loss that is ordinarily excluded. A sewer and drain backup/sump pump overflow endorsement gives coverage to structural damage and, depending on the insurer, some or all personal property items. When water or waste water (it happens) enters through the drains from the city's sewer/drainage system and back ups into your house or water backs up through the sump pump or if the sump pump stops working (due to a power outage or mechanical failure) and external water enters the house, this endorsement provides coverage.

Business pursuits. There are various endorsements that increase the coverage limits for specific types of businesses and types of coverage. Some endorsements provide extra liability coverage to providers of home day care; some increase the **Special Limits of Liability** found in **Section I – Coverages** for specific business equipment for persons who work at home or bring their work home and need extra coverage for their supplies or equipment. Some simply increase the amount of personal property coverage for business equipment.

Earthquake. You can buy an endorsement that specifically covers earthquake in almost every state—in California, some insurers don't offer this endorsement and customers who want earthquake coverage can buy a CEA (California Earthquake Authority) policy through their insurer. All earthquake endorsements come with a percentage deductible, which means the deductible is a percentage of the total policy limits. Most insurers have a catch with this endorsement: separate deductibles for structural items and for personal property items. For example, if you have structural limits of $100,000.00 and your earthquake deductible is 5%, you have a $5000.00 deductible. If you have a $60,000.00 personal property coverage limit and a 5% deductible, you have a separate $3000.00 deductible for personal property damage due to earthquake. If you have structural and personal property damage, both deductibles would apply. The percentage of the deductible is going to be listed in the declarations page of the policy. The actual percentage varies from insurer to insurer, but it can range from 2% to 15%.

Jewelry/Furs. Depending on the insurer, this coverage can increase the amount you can claim on jewelry, watches, and furs when they are stolen. Some policies automatically provide this extra coverage, but most make you buy it. As with any type of item, you may want to have especially valuable items scheduled—engagement rings, for example, which are often worth many times more than what policy limits are in the first place.

Firearms. Who doesn't love the smell of gunpowder in the morning? If you're a gun enthusiast like my brother and my mom's neighbors, this endorsement is for you. It increases the amount of coverage available for firearms in case they are stolen.

Other Structures. This increases the coverage for detached structures such as garages, workshops and that gold-plated gazebo you've always dreamed of having in your back yard.

Additional Premises. If you have a guest house or there just happens to be a second home on your property or if you're building your dream house next to your existing home and want to have coverage for both once the new one is done, this provides additional coverage.

Computers. As stated above, insurers *hate* replacing computers and almost always put limits on computers and related equipment. Typically what is in most policies is more than enough but if you have special equipment—like an Avid machine, which is what Hollywood uses to edit 35mm films (the software alone costs more than $25,000.00)—then you'll want this extra coverage or if you have a specific piece that needs even more coverage, you may want to consider having it scheduled.

Clouds are floating pods of condensed water vapor.

The average cloud weighs 25 tons.

Cumulonimbus clouds, which bring thunderstorms and lightning, can weigh up to 10 million tons.

Part 3:

The Game

Chapter 4: From the First Moment: Homeowners' Duties and Responsibilities

It may surprise many to discover that insurance companies place numerous responsibilities for a homeowner's insurance claim on homeowners. While most of these duties and responsibilities are common sense, many are also requirements of your policy and all of them are vital to a successful claim settlement. As with the myths of suddenly exploding premiums and "claim and you're cancelled," insurance carriers quite often don't trouble themselves to inform homeowners as to the particularities of these duties and responsibilities and how they can best be fulfilled, mostly because if a homeowner does everything he is supposed to do the way he is supposed to do it, it usually costs the insurance company more money, and as we all know, insurance companies are not tax-deductible charitable organizations. Worse than that, not knowing what to do can result in a claim being denied, in part or in whole.

The most critical time for a homeowner to act are the hours and days following damage to your property, especially if the damage is substantial or creates an opening into which water or animals or the neighbor's kids can enter. A homeowner's action, or inaction, can be what makes or breaks a claim and what defines the parameters of what will be covered and how much time and money it is going to cost you—or how much it is going to save you. Many of the following duties and responsibilities apply to every type of claim; some, the first for example, may not apply in every case. Whatever the scenario and regardless of the extent of the loss, the following are crucial steps in the path to restoring your property once it has been damaged.

Safety

While you're pondering the probability of a voodoo curse and pins sticking in your side, there is one aspect of damage to your property that cannot and should not be ignored. Before you call your agent, before you start picking up debris or taking pictures, there is one thing you must do: make sure no one gets hurt. If there is glass inside your home or out on the sidewalk, clean it up; if it looks as though the roof is going to fall in where that giant oak tree landed, get out. If there is a gutter dangling from the roofline, swaying precariously each time the wind blows, take it down or tie it up. Preventing anyone from getting hurt—you, your family or anyone else (curious or helpful neighbors for example)—is not just common sense, but according to your insurance policy, it is your first duty as a homeowner when a loss occurs. It may be a matter of cordoning off the effected area or putting up a warning sign or calling the power company to reattach electrical wires, but whatever it is, it is your first priority. If you are unable to take the necessary safety precautions, then call someone who is: a relative, a neighbor, a tree service, a qualified repairperson, a restoration company, etc. If the situation is too dangerous—writhing electrical wires, an inaccessible roof—then call a professional who is equipped and qualified to handle the situation.

Not securing your property after a loss may result in a denial of coverage by the insurance company to anyone who may be injured—a liability claim—leaving you to foot the bill. The justification for a denial in this instance is that the injury was not caused by whatever damaged the property but by the negligence of the homeowner who failed to secure the safety of the premises. If safety is a concern, a homeowner must, at the very least, *attempt* to make an area safe or safer. Alas, this is one of the most important homeowner duties that, for various reasons get overlooked by homeowners—and sometimes insurance agents or their assistants—simply due to unfamiliarity with the procedures of a loss. Ensuring the safety of the premises will go a long way in ensuring not only peace of mind but also that all coverages are extended to you and that you are protected in case any harm comes to anyone who could make a liability claim. Note: if you or a member of your immediate family is injured by the after effects of a loss your homeowners insurance is not going to cover your medical bills or time lost from work; a homeowner can't make a liability claim against himself.

Since most policies state that safety precautions must be taken in the event of covered damage, the insurance company can and should pay for these emergency measures, whether it is your time and expenses (more on that later) or that of a professional. However, an insurance company won't reimburse homeowners for any expenses if the damages themselves are not covered: groundwater, flood, water seeping into a basement, etc., or if no damage has actually occurred: for example, if a wind storm causes a large tree limb to hang suspended over your house, an insurance company will not pay to have the tree limb cut down, even if it is directly above your house, even if it is an enormous limb that may take out half of your home. From the insurance company's point of view, since nothing has happened yet, it is a homeowner's problem that the homeowner must address—that is, until the tree limb actually falls and causes damage to your property, then it becomes an insurance company problem. In other words, an insurance company would rather pay $20,000.00 to repair a house *after* a tree limb falls on it in order to avoid paying $1000.00 to remove the tree limb in the first place.

It should be noted that if a homeowner is aware of an imminent threat to his property, he is required to take "prevent further loss by protecting the property, meaning making required temporary repairs," which is item number two of Section I - Conditions.

Reporting Damages

So something has happened to your property: a tree branch has punctured your roof, some siding has been stripped away, there are water stains on the walls and ceilings, an earthquake has leveled your garage. You've taken a look around, remedied any safety concerns and have finally resigned yourself to the fact that you are more than likely immune to chicken blood and voodoo curses. The next thing to do is to report the damages. While this is perhaps the easiest part of a claim, as insurance companies are wont to do, there are restrictions imposed upon homeowners even for this most unremarkable of tasks: most policies state that homeowners have 60 days from the Date Of Loss (DOL) to inform their insurance company of damages, which is usually not a problem unless of course you get *really* bogged down on your psychiatrist's couch examining and re-examining the roots of your preternatural fears of filing a claim. Despite this inane restriction, most insurance companies are actually reasonable, fair, and flexible when it comes to the deadline, especially if it is a hail claim and the homeowners had no idea they had damage to their roof.

When you call your agent or your insurance carrier's claims hotline and advise them that you have damages and want to make a claim, a claim number will be established—sometimes you will be given it right away, sometimes later. When you are given a claim number, write it down and—this cannot be understated enough—*DO NOT LOSE IT!* Your claim number is *very* important, perhaps the most important set of numbers you may ever encounter save for 911 or winning lottery numbers.

When you report damages make sure you are specific about what has occurred. The more severe the damage, the higher the priority the claim and the more information available to the insurance company the better they will be able to serve you. In addition, make sure your carrier has the correct address and phone number(s) for you, *especially* if an event has made your home unliveable and especially if your only number is a cell phone. A helpful tip is to tell them the best time to reach you and at which number. It may sound surprising, but many claims are delayed simply because the information the insurance company has is either missing, incorrect or not up to date. Typos, old phone numbers, even wrong addresses are disturbingly common in insurance files and it's always a good idea when filing a claim to double check the insurance company's records to make sure all contact information is correct and up to date. Often, with hundreds or even thousands of claims pouring into an agent's office, these little details understandably get overlooked by overwhelmed agents and office workers and unnecessary delays ensue.

One other thing. A pet peeve of mine. If you file a claim, there is one very important thing that you should *not* do immediately after filing your claim: GO ON VACATION. To put it another way: if you're planning a vacation and you experience a loss that is not severe and does not require the immediate attention of an insurance company, by all means, go—relax, enjoy yourself, try to find that lost shaker of salt in Margaritaville, whatever—but wait until you get *home* to file a claim. Going on vacation right after you file a claim is the ideal way to get lost in the shuffle and to make sure that your claim slips through the cracks and unless you like being ignored and overlooked, it is a good idea to wait to file a claim until after you get home.

Temporary Repairs

Temporary Repairs are the pragmatic cousins to taking safety precautions. And like securing the premises, it doesn't apply to every situation. If a large patch of shingles are blown from your roof, if a door or window gets blown out, or a water pipe bursts—not only is making any and all temporary repairs to prevent further damage common sense, but according to your policy, it is a requirement. When you call in your claim, most of the time the person you speak to will "authorize" you to make temporary repairs, which is hilarious since they're authorizing you to do something you MUST do: if wind blows numerous shingles off the roof, exposing wood, creating the potential for a leak, you MUST do something about it, cover it with a tarp or call a roofer to temporarily cover it or patch it; if a window gets blown out, cover the opening with plastic or plywood or whatever is available; if a pipe bursts, turn off the water and try to sop up as much water as possible; if a portion of your siding has blown off, cover the exposed area—if it's small, plastic trash bags and duct tape work reasonably well—to prevent moisture from penetrating wood sheathing or stud walls as well as the growth of mold. If having to make temporary repairs puts you in an unsafe situation, if you have a steep or high roof or damage in an area that is difficult to access, and you have any doubts or reservations about doing something yourself, then by all means call a trained professional to take care of it. As with safety measures if the loss is one that a homeowner is insured for, the insurance company will reimburse you for the expenses to make temporary repairs, including any materials you have to purchase and your time involved in making the repairs or the materials and labor of a professional.

The objective of making temporary repairs is simply to prevent further damages, to prevent a small loss from turning into a big loss or a big loss into a total loss. The insurance word for preventing further damages is mitigation. Which rhymes with litigation. Which is what could result if mitigation is not taken: if a homeowner is negligent in not making temporary repairs, any further damages resulting from that negligence may be excluded from coverage: if you don't cover the area of your roof where the wind blew the shingles off and it later rains and your ceilings collapse, your insurance carrier will ask you if you made temporary repairs and if you didn't, they may decide that your negligence was the cause of the ceiling collapse and opt to only cover the shingles that blew off in the first place. If a door gets blown in or out and you don't seal it off and a herd of deer charge through your living room and throw a kegger (you know, party animals), your insurance company may decline payment for damages resulting from not sealing the doorway. When an insurance company issues a denial of coverage and/or payment due to a homeowner's negligence, it's not fun for anyone, including the insurance companies because denials are the most frequent source of lawsuits against them. By making necessary temporary repairs, you are not only being a good homeowner and policyholder, but you're protecting yourself against an unnecessary denial, the cost of having to make repairs yourself and the possibility of a lengthy lawsuit.

Documentation

Documentation is the Holy Grail for any homeowner who has an insurance claim: not only will proper documentation help substantiate any loss, not only will it solidify your position when making a claim against your insurance, not only will it save you time, money and aggravation, but proper documentation has actually been proven to prevent hair loss—okay, maybe that's stretching it, but documenting every aspect of your claim can mean the difference between a fair and satisfying settlement and getting left holding the bag. There's a saying in claims adjusting: if it isn't documented, it never happened; if there's no proof, it doesn't exist. Proof—of damages, of work performed, of expenses paid—is the cornerstone of every claim, the one aspect of a claim that homeowners actually have total control over: you can't control mother nature or providence, you can't control the actions or mindset of an insurance company, but you can make sure that there is a paper trail that verifies your claim and assures that at least the foundations for a equitable settlement are set. And naturally, not only is documenting your loss common sense, but according to your homeowner's policy, it is your duty and responsibility.

Anything related to your claim, no matter insignificant it may seem, SAVE IT.

In insurance, there is no such thing as an insignificant detail: insurance is *all* detail and the more thorough your documentation, the more protected you are. Immediately put all documents into a file or a folder—and put your file or folder where you're *not going to lose it.* Even after the very last repair has been made, I advise homeowners to not throw anything away: if you have to sell your house or if you are unlucky enough to have another claim, diligent documentation on your part will ensure that any doubts or questions can be substantiated quickly and easily.

Bills and Invoices

So you've been a good homeowner and secured the safety of your property and made any necessary temporary repairs. But you had to call a professional service/contractor to help out and now they've given you a bill; or your house was made unliveable and you've had to stay in a hotel and eat meals at restaurants; or you've had to buy some plywood to prevent those pesky party animals from throwing a toga in your living room. Do you now:

    a. Use the receipts to line the bottom of a birdcage

    b. Make paper airplanes out of them and light them on fire and pretend you're being "shot down"

    c. Put them in your claim file or folder.

(If you truly don't know the answer, seek help. Dr. Phil kind of help.)

But the most commonly overlooked receipt or bill is the one that homeowners *don't* receive—the one they don't ask for or don't even think about. If a neighbor or a family friend charges you for any temporary repairs or similar work—tree debris removal, patching your roof, or hauling damaged items to the curb—and you've paid them, it is reimbursable. In this situation, ask them to write you a receipt with their name, date, address and phone number on it so you are able to claim it. A cancelled check in this instance is usually not sufficient: the insurance company will want to know if the check was for claim-related activities, snow removal, trimming your hedges or that mountain of smoked salmon in your freezer. Innumerable times, I've encountered homeowners who've had a friend or neighbor make temporary or even permanent repairs. When I ask for a copy of the bill or receipt, they tell me, "Oh, don't worry about, it was just a couple of bucks." Of course, when they receive their estimate from the insurance company and see that their deductible has been viciously sucked out of the total amount, I invariably receive that "Is it too late to put that bill that I got from so and so in the estimate?" phone call. Lucky for them, and every homeowner, it's almost never too late but if there's no documentation, then no payment can be made until a receipt is given to the insurance company.

Any invoices and receipts that you receive make copies and give the *copies* to the insurance company. Always keep the originals for your own records—this goes for *any* form of documentation. An insurer may ask for the originals, and if so, make sure you have a copy. If a claim goes to trial, the validity and authenticity of an original document can never be doubted, unlike a photocopy. But also, in a large insurance office, sometimes things simply disappear; sometimes faxes and documents sent by mail vanish mysteriously, slipping unnoticed into a black hole, never to be seen again. In a large busy office this happens with startling regularity and unless you want to take the chance that your only copy of a paid $10,000.00 bill for the repair of your house won't get vaporized in the furtive inner workings of a bureaucratic nether world, make a copy and give the copy to the insurance company.

In addition, some contractors—especially restoration services (who specialize in smoke/fire, water and mold damage)—send bills directly to the insurance company so that the insurance carrier can pay them; while this may be more expedient for the contractors, always insist that they send you a copy as well, so you can make sure that the numbers add up and that nothing was left out.

Photos/Video

Unlike eyewitness accounts, photos and video don't have memory gaps, they don't rearrange history, and more importantly they don't lie—unless you're good at Photoshop. Photos and videos often make the most dramatic and indelible impression; they tell the story of your loss by framing the damages and resulting repairs into a discernable context and temporal sequence, they provide essential details and general facts that are as integral to a claim as any other form of documentation and often can substantiate and verify other documentation, especially if you've had to make temporary repairs. It goes without saying, but if you do make temporary repairs, you'll want to take photos of the effected area(s) *beforehand.*

You can never take too many photos. It always helps to have a variety of angles and perspectives—up close and from a distance—and naturally, make sure the damages actually show up. Interior damage can be especially difficult to document: water stains on walls or ceilings can literally evaporate before your eyes (though more typically when you *aren't* looking), so photographing them immediately is crucial. Also, take photos of *everything* that is damaged: inside the dwelling, outside, garages, sheds, fences, decks, anything *inside* a garage or shed, anything that may have been sitting out—lawn furniture, etc. If you haven't caught onto digital photography, have the photos developed (making sure to get duplicates) and write the date, time and a brief description on the back of each photo and give the copies to your adjuster or insurance company representative. If you have digital capabilities, I recommend printing a few select photos (printing on plain paper is acceptable) with dates, times and descriptions and keeping the rest—but make sure you have a backup for the photos; I strongly recommend burning all photos onto a CD or DVD and putting the disc in you file. Unless the insurance company asks for it specifically, keep all videos for your own records. By the way, insurers don't reimburse homeowners for film and the cost of developing/printing pictures; while homeowners are duty-bound to provide Proof of Loss there is nothing in the policy that states homeowners must photograph or videotape their loss in order to prove it, therefore the insurance company is not required to pay for it.

While taking pictures of damages just after they occur is important, it is just as important to take photos when permanent or final repairs are being made and after they have been completed. Full photographic documentation, aside from making an interesting conversation piece and a dandy slide show, bolsters any paper records of a loss and the recovery process. Though it is exceedingly rare, should an insurance company request visual verification that the repairs have actually been completed (final repairs bills are usually sufficient), having photos of repairs in progress and after they have been completed will erase any doubts the insurers, real estate agents, potential home buyers or their home inspectors may have concerning the completion of repairs.

It may sound strange to some, but often the most important photos or videos a homeowner may ever take is *before* any damage occurs: in a case of a total loss—fire, hurricane, tornado, earthquake—or even a smaller loss, having numerous photos and/or videos showing undamaged building and personal property, interior and exterior structural details, the materials used in construction and the overall layout of your dwelling as well as any outbuildings can expedite your claim, answer any questions that may arise and aide you in the unbearable task of remembering every little detail of your house and what was inside it. While most homeowners never think of taking photos or videos of a home for the sake of general documentation, it is something that every homeowner needs to do. But taking pictures and videos aren't enough: make sure that copies of any photos or videos are stored in a fire-resistant safe, a safety deposit box or a secure on-line server.

Damaged Property

So you have this pile of stuff that used to be attached to your house and you're not quite sure what to do with it. Instinct says pitch it, lob it onto the curb and wait for the siding and shingle undertaker to do what you wish he could do with the rest of your problems and make them disappear. Instincts are wonderful, instincts work, instincts are right—most of the time. This always gets people: when I call up a homeowner and ask the usual questions, ("Is your house single story or two story? Is the roof steep? What kind of siding/exterior is on the house?") and we get around to talking about the heap of leftovers cluttering their lawn and debasing their property, they always seemed to get disturbingly annoyed when I emphatically insist they not throw anything away until I inspect their property.

Santa Claus has it right: make a list, check it twice, though we can forgo the naughty or nice part, 'cause everyone's a little naughty some of the time. Once you've secured the premises, made temporary repairs, and taken pictures, take out paper and pencil and begin to list everything that was damaged—*everything*—not just roof, siding, gutters, carpet, etc., but look around and see if your patio furniture, flower pots, bird houses, anything outside or inside, was damaged: furniture, blankets, pillows that may gotten stained or soiled when your ceiling or walls leaked. Except for your lovely plants and trees (which if you were paying attention, are only covered in certain circumstances), it's all covered and needs to be documented. If possible, list building/structural and personal property items separately.

Many people are hesitant to claim personal property items, that is until they realize they have a large deductible to pay and every little bit helps. If it's covered, it is in your best interest to claim it, no matter how insignificant, and if it's covered, list it and photograph it. And again, it's not just a good idea to list all damages that you're aware of, it's required by your policy, though in my experience a homeowner *not* making a list has never become an issue or a reason to deny a claim—in fact, very, very few homeowners make a list unless asked to do so by an agent or adjuster. For structural items, if you know how old the items are, the manufacturer (most windows, for example, have a small brand-name stamp on the interior panes), note that beside each item. For personal property items, record the age, place of purchase and original purchase price—if known—for each item. While most adjusters typically take note of all house/structural damages, not every adjuster will be cognizant of—or interested in—seemingly insignificant personal property items and may not ask about them (though it should be noted that good adjusters will ask about *everything*), so presenting a copy of your list to an adjuster and going over it with him is the best way to make sure your adjuster is aware of all the damages and that you'll be covered for everything for which you're entitled.

Homeowners have a duty to prove their loss and under most policies they are required to display the damaged property at the request of the insurance company. In other words, regardless of how you feel about the recently formed Mt. Saint Debris fouling your yard, if you can help it, don't throw anything away—but more importantly, don't have a contractor or other person make permanent repairs before the insurance company inspects the damages. Even if you've taken photos, even if you have a sworn affidavit from a Supreme Court Justice—even if you *are* a Supreme Court Justice—do not permanently repair or replace anything until your insurance carrier has verified that it was damaged due to a covered loss. While this may sound excessive or even obsessive, keep in mind that insurance companies have been "burned" by fraudulent claims in the past and are ever vigilant about catching and stopping any kind of fraud. Most homeowners know enough about insurance and have enough common sense to know that they need to prove a loss to their insurance company if they wish to make a claim. Unfortunately, I have encountered far too many situations in which homeowners made permanent repairs before I could inspect a loss and had to inform the homeowner that the insurance company was not going to pay for any of the repairs.

There are exceptions to having to "exhibit the damaged property." If wind blows a personal property item away (a lawn chair, a bird house, clothes on the clothes line) obviously you can't exhibit it—but be ready to supply some sort of verification that it actually existed: a receipt, a photo, a neighbor who remembers seeing it. Also, if you lose electricity for an extended period of time and the food in your refrigerators() and freezer(s) become spoiled, it is okay to dispose of these items (unless, of course, you *like* a smelly kitchen)—but be sure to take an inventory of what you throw away, the prices of the items (if you know them) and where you purchased them. If it is an especially large food loss (be aware that some policies have limits on this coverage) the insurance company will most likely want to verify that there is at least *room* for the items lost, which usually means an adjuster looking at any and all refrigerators and freezers. Food loss, from my experience, is one of the most under-reported types of loss—and obviously one that insurance companies don't go out of their way to advertise—but one that many homeowners are relieved to discover is available to them, especially since some insurance carriers (American Family for example) don't apply the deductible to this type of loss.

Your Time and Expenses

"You mean my insurance company is going to pay *me* for work I did?"

Damn right! Any work you or your relatives perform due to an insured loss—temporary repairs, safety measures, tree or other debris removal—and which is not part of routine maintenance, upkeep, and cleaning—can be claimed. Most of the materials purchased for these tasks can also be claimed, but with limitations. The general rule is if the materials are applied directly to the damaged property/area, they can be claimed. For example: if a tree branch punctures your roof, the tarp used to cover the hole, as well as nails or screws to attach the tarp can be claimed—but not the ladder you had to buy to access the roof. If wind blows out a window, the plywood and nails to cover the opening can be claimed, but not the wet-dry vacuum to clean up the leaves and rain that entered the house; some insurers will pay for rental equipment, but ask before actually renting. If wind blows numerous trees onto your garage and damages it in several places, expect to be compensated for your time to remove the trees from the garage and for the removal of the remainder of the trees from your yard (up to the $500 policy limits once tree debris is on the ground), but not for the chainsaw you had to buy; you should be able to claim the gas used to power the chainsaw or the cost to rent one. Also, don't expect to be reimbursed for your time to go to Home Depot to buy tarps or plywood or hurricane fencing—only the actual work done directly to the insured structure can be claimed.

The key to getting paid, naturally, is documentation. If there is occasion for you to perform necessary labors such as temporary repairs and debris removal, start a Log in your claim file or folder and list out the dates and number of hours hours each person worked and note what general task they performed. The more specific you are as to what each person did and when he did it and how much time he spent doing it, the quicker your claim will be resolved. For a free downloadable Work Log, go to Forms at the end of this book or to the Red Tape Lounge area of www.ClaimGameBook.com.

Sample Work Log from a windstorm for John and his brother Bill:

	5-11-09	5-12-09	5-13-09	5-14-09	Total
John, brace & cut oak tree off house:	4.5hrs.	3hrs.	2.5hrs.	0	10 hours
John, cut up oak tree & haul away:	0	0	0	8	8 hours
John, patch roof where oak tree hit:	2	0	0	0	2 hours
Bill, cut pine trees off shed:	1.25	3.75	0	0	5 hours
John, cut up pine tree & haul away:	0	2	0	0	2 hours
Bill, reset fence:	0	0	3	0	3 hours
				TOTAL:	30 hrs.

Note that times are rounded up to the nearest 15-minute increment. Insurers love detail and the more detailed your account, the better.

As stated with the other examples above the work must be done for a loss that is actually covered by your insurance. For example: if your basement gets flooded from water seeping through the foundation and you spend two days cleaning and hauling damaged items to the curb, your insurance company will not pay you for your time as this is not a loss that is covered by your homeowner's policy. If wind blows down several trees in your yard but the trees don't damage anything that is an insured building item (house, garage, shed, fence, in-ground pool), any work done to cut up and remove the tree is not covered and won't be paid for by the insurance company. If wind blows trees over and they only damage personal property items (gas grill, swing set, birdbath, etc.) the expense to remove the tree would not be covered. As with any form of documentation, present a copy of your Log to your adjuster and go over it with him. If you're planning to do any permanent or final repairs yourself, please see Chapter 10.

While homeowner's policies do not specifically mention homeowner compensation for claim-related work, insurance companies are duty bound to pay *any* expenditures for labor that are a direct result of an insured loss, whether the work is performed by a homeowner or a professional—and, frankly, most insurers would rather pay homeowners than professionals because it saves them money: insurance companies, at their leisure, set the rate of pay for homeowners, typically a portion (usually about 1/3 to 1/2) of what professionals charge for the same work, generally $8 to $30 dollars an hour, depending on the rates in your area and the trade involved, though some companies have one flat "Homeowner rate" for any work performed, regardless if it involves securing the premises, making temporary repairs or permanent repairs. If you're dying to know how much you'll get paid for boarding up your blown-out window, ask your adjuster or insurance company representative.

Contact with Your Insurance Company

Of all the forms of documentation, keeping track of whom and when you spoke with at an insurance company can be the most challenging, especially with busy schedules and the advent of cell phones—but it can also be one of the most important. Insurance companies require adjusters to keep Activity Logs that detail communications and actions (inspections, research, Faxes sent), not only for legal purposes (a lawsuit, for example) but for practical reasons: if the claim needs to be reassigned to another adjuster or if the original adjuster forgets what he did and when he did it, there is a record of his actions and conversations. Most homeowners, however, don't keep such records, putting them at a distinct disadvantage with the insurance company should any disagreements or litigation arise. I don't know about you, but if an attorney asked what I did and said exactly three years, two months and 16 days ago—which seems about how long it takes for cases to come to trial—I think I'd have a little trouble remembering without the assistance of a log.

While the vast majority of claims do not end up in litigation, keeping a Communications Log (yes, *another* log, also available in Forms or for free download at www.ClaimGameBook.com/RedTapeLounge) detailing contact with your insurance company is one of the most effective means of protecting yourself should a claim proceed to the courts or arbitration. Verifiable, written documentation—knowing to whom you spoke (*always* get the name of the person you spoke to), when you spoke and what was discussed—will not only fortify your position in case of a dispute, but will also help *you* remember the sequence of events so there is no doubt, even with yourself, as to who said what and when it was said. Aside from legal protections, maintaining a detailed phone log also helps homeowners keep track of some of the most important information that can be imparted to them by an adjuster or other insurance company representatives: claim numbers, adjuster phone numbers, appointment dates and times. You can also use a communications log to keep track of your doings with a contractor, especially if the contractor fails to do what he says or if your dissatisfaction leads to litigation against him.

The most important elements of a Communications Log, alluded to above, are the dates and times of your conversations, with whom you spoke and a brief description of what was discussed. The best way to maintain a detailed and accurate phone log is to arrange to speak to an adjuster (or anyone involved in your claim) at the same location/phone each and every time you call or they call you, thus allowing you to keep your phone log in one place and not have to transport it with you everywhere you go. One of the first questions I ask homeowners is when the best time to reach them is: evenings after 7pm, at work, etc. It is well within your rights to ask an adjuster, insurance representative or contractor to call you at a specific time and location—in fact, it tends to simplify the sometimes arduous communication process: many times in the past I've had to set up an appointment with a busy homeowner just to *call* them so we could discuss their claim. And if you're like most people and quickly tire of playing "Phone Tag," setting an appointment or having a fixed time and/or location to call or be called at is one of the most effective means to streamline communications and make sure you get through to each other. Anything a homeowner or an adjuster can do to simplify the process of establishing and maintaining communication will make a claim go more quickly and smoothly and sets a positive tone for the remaining facets of a claim.

Chapter 5: That Exhausted, Sweaty Person Who Shows Up on Your Doorstep: the Adjuster

Definition, please: Adjuster, *ad just er*, noun: a person who determines the validity of insurance claims for insurance companies and authorizes payments for repair, replacement or liability concerns.

A claim has been flied, you've made temporary repairs and/or taken precautionary safety measures, you've made copies of all receipts, invoices, and photos and have been given a claim number and told that an adjuster or claim representative (same thing) will contact you soon, anywhere from 2-7 days, depending on the insurance carrier. For the moment, the next move belongs to the insurance company, specifically the adjuster who is assigned to your claim.

I won't lie to you: insurance adjusters are, on the whole, an odd lot. What else can you say about people who see nothing at all peculiar about risking their lives on a daily basis, hauling themselves up wobbly, over-used ladders as they scale terrifying heights and shimmy across treacherously steep roofs to take pictures where no sane person would dare to tread, much less examine closely. What else can be made of people who revel in the fact that while most people work 40 to 60 hours a week, in a particularly restful week they will *sleep* 40 hours and work, often in ghastly heat and humidity, more than 100 hours a week (and sometimes do so hundreds or thousands of miles away from home for weeks or months at a time, especially after a hurricane or earthquake). How else are we to take a class of citizenry who get strangely excited by a little board-on-board action (a style of siding) and whom you may overhear declaring, "Nice Rack!" only to discover they are referring to a place to store a ladder?

Despite these peculiarities (and there are more, boy are there more), the vast majority of adjusters are honest, hardworking, honorable professionals who conduct themselves with integrity and objectivity. Adjusters are the "face" of the insurance company, they are who the insurance company relies upon to present a human representation, someone who embodies their standards and principals, someone who projects the core ideals and concerns of the insurance company and to ensure, if possible, that homeowners are satisfied with the service they've received and made to feel as though the recovery process was fair and went as smoothly and painlessly as possible. Customer service should be always be the top priority with adjusters. Adjusters are there to answer any questions homeowners have, to listen to the concerns of homeowners, to guide homeowners through the claims process and to work with the contractor(s) the homeowner selects to make the repairs and iron out the details of the repairs and get the claim settled. Sometimes adjusters have to be more: sometimes they are a hand to hold in the face of devastation, a voice of reassurance in a time of hopelessness, when the walls and ceilings are literally falling on top of you. Sometimes they actually care about the people they help and it shows.

By necessity, adjusters have a wide range of construction knowledge and/or experience: adjusters need to know more than the average human about every aspect of a building, from the foundation to the roof, though only a few adjusters are *experts* in any single construction area like plumbing, electrical, heating and cooling, structural engineering. More often than not, when it comes areas of specialization that do require advanced knowledge and training, adjusters will defer to experts for opinions on repair or replacement.

There are two primary types of property adjusters: company adjusters and independent adjusters. The principal difference between a company adjuster and an independent adjuster is simply that company adjusters work directly for the insurance company while independents are "sub-contracted" out to the insurance company, either on their own or through what is called a vendor. The insurance company pays the vendor a pre-arranged fee and the vendor then pays their adjusters. Independents do not work for the insurance company, which in some cases can be a bonus for homeowners: independents often have less exposure to institutionalized company dogma and in some case can be slightly more objective than their company counterparts. Conversely, the benefit of a company adjuster is that they often know the system so well that they can more efficiently and effectively circumvent red tape and resolve questionable or problematic claims more quickly. But in the end, it is—or should be—the objective of all adjusters to be as professional, objective and fair as possible. There is a third type of adjuster, the quality control/reinspector whose job is exactly what it sounds like: to reinspect the claims of other adjusters and to evaluate the accuracy of the inspection and the overall customer service and/or satisfaction provided by that adjuster. Reinspectors are usually the most experienced and jaded adjusters, people who have seen and heard almost everything and if your adjuster missed anything, more than likely, they're the ones who are going to catch it.

Aside from being the face of the insurance company, adjusters are, at least partly, investigators, though they're told never to use that word with homeowners. They inspect a loss to determine if there is, in fact, damage, and if there is damage, what is the proximate cause and evaluate whether or not the damage is covered under your Homeowners Policy. In many cases, this is not an issue but if an adjuster indicates that you are not covered for a loss and you are denied coverage and you disagree, please see Chapter 11. Also, adjusters keep an eye out for suspicious or fraudulent losses. But mostly they are collectors of information: what happened, when it happened, what was damaged, how old the items are, how much time the homeowner spent doing temporary repairs and/or securing the area, but also noting if the homeowner didn't do these things. As stated in the previous chapter, when an adjuster comes to your property to do an inspection of damages, give him copies of all your documentation.

The "what, when, why, and how" mentioned above is usually achieved in two different ways: the account by the homeowner of what happened, to the best of his knowledge, and the inspection of the adjuster. Together, these items tell the story of the loss. The information collected by an adjuster comprises what is called the Scope of Loss, which becomes the Scope of Repairs, the basis for the estimate the adjuster will write.

There has been a trend in the last few years by insurers to attempt to adjust property damage losses over the telephone, which is an absurd way of attempting to adjust property damage claims. Unless it is a personal property damage only claim (which can be settled over the phone easily enough) or an extremely simple claim (the definition of this will vary from homeowner to homeowner, but one example would be a pre-fabricated/pre-built shed destroyed by wind) *insist* that an inspection be done in person. To give just one example from personal experience as to why a phone adjustment is not acceptable: after hurricane Katrina, homeowners who had roof damage and fence damage had a phone adjustment done and the total estimate for damage was under $1000.00. After I showed up and did a thorough inspection, I discovered additional damages (including personal property damage) and wrote an estimate for over $8000.00. Insist on an in-person inspection.

Why You Need to be Present During an Adjuster's Inspection

Many homeowners may find it appealing to be present during an adjuster's inspection simply because it is one of those rare chances in life to meet an actual in-the-flesh crazy person, an individual so devoid of the common sense that prevents sane people from scaling treacherous heights and ignoring the tremendous risk to their person—and doing so just for the sake of helping other people—in other words, the irresistible opportunity to meet a sort of deranged Superhero.

Once an adjuster has received a claim, he/she is typically required to contact a homeowner/policyholder within 24 hours. If you've made sure the insurance company has your correct phone number(s) and you are not silly enough to go on vacation after you've filed a claim, this is usually not a problem. Some adjusters will want to set up a time to inspect your property with you when it is convenient for you; but if there is no damage to the interior of the dwelling, some may try to convince you to let them inspect it anytime, whenever they're in the neighborhood, and while this is not an indicator that the adjuster is a bad adjuster (quite the opposite in many cases) it is imperative that a homeowner be present during an adjuster's inspection, regardless of the extent of damages. Simply request an appointment and most adjusters will be more than happy to accommodate you and work around your schedule, though if have to take time off from work it is not an expense you can add onto your claim.

Aside from the unique opportunity to meet someone with more than a few screws loose, it is vital for a homeowner to be present during an adjuster's inspection for several reasons: to ensure that an adjuster sees everything you've put on your list of damaged items (though 9 out of 10 times an adjuster will point out things a homeowner missed or didn't think about at); to make sure an adjuster actually receives all of your documentation and it doesn't get lost in the mail or in cyberspace, which does happen; so that the adjuster can answer your questions; so you can answer the adjuster's questions about what happened and when, what you did about it, how old the siding (or roofing or lawn furniture) is, how much you paid for that giant bird house that had its roof blown off. While good adjusters look at *everything*, every nook and cranny, every little blemish on your house (quite possibly to your chagrin, having convinced yourself that your castle was flawless) and usually know if damage is storm related or not, there are occasions, some usual, some unusual, when an adjuster needs to know if a heretofore undiscovered imperfection is loss-related or not: did the hail or flying debris cause that window pane to crack or was it an errant baseball courtesy the neighborhood kids? A strong wind storm can bedevil the best adjuster and homeowner alike: it can deposit odd things like flower pots and kittens in your yard, it can plaster your siding with lily pads and escaped laundry. (I've seen these firsthand.) Flying debris can also leave marks on your house that may seem as though they were made by aliens or street gangs. In these instances, being able to tell an adjuster what is loss-related damage and what isn't will make your claim go more smoothly and eliminate any silly and unnecessary delays. It goes without saying, but don't try to pull a fast on the insurance company or the adjuster—unless, of course, you *like* cellmates: most adjusters are savvy and jaded enough to know when they're being sold a bill of goods and every adjuster is trained to spot and report fraud or anything suspicious. Every insurance company has a department dedicated solely to investigating fraud.

Mostly, though, it is imperative for a homeowner to be present so that the adjuster can simply answer your questions and make sure you understand the intricacies of your insurance company's claims process: the exact time limitations, your duties and responsibilities from this point on, which payments are forthcoming and which will be deferred until repairs have begun or are completed and whether or not you and the adjuster agree upon what was damaged and what repairs are necessary or recommended and which items need to be replaced. From my experience, homeowners who are present during an adjuster's inspection understand and comprehend the copious amount of information conveyed to them during an inspection much better than homeowners who are informed of everything over the phone and when problems with your claim arise, a homeowner can and will benefit from the face-to-face contact with an adjuster, having established a person to person relationship that will go a long way toward settling disagreements.

How to Handle an Adjuster, i.e., Don't Pull a Gun on Him

Several years ago I was working as a lowly clerk in a "Catastrophe" office when a company adjuster, let's call her J., stumbled into the office looking frazzled and stunned, the tracks of recent tears on her cheeks. In between sobs and cries of disbelief, she told her supervisor what had happened. When she arrived for a pre-arranged appointment, the homeowner, a grizzled old man, swaggered onto his front porch with a pistol in his hand and loudly told her to get the you-know-what off his property. Momentarily stunned, she didn't know what to do but then cried out, "But I'm here to give you money!" which didn't seem to carry much weight with him and he once again demanded she leave. Before she could even take a step back or say "Yes, sir, right away sir!" he fired a shot over her head, sending her scrambling into her car and on her way. (Makes you wonder what he does to *uninvited* guests who *aren't* there to give him money.) Understandably, the adjuster was shaken up and unable to do much work the rest of the day. Unfortunately, for reasons beyond the understanding of modern psychoanalysis, this is not an isolated incident. Like urban legends, tales of homeowners pulling guns on adjusters for no other reason then they show up when they're supposed to flourish in every insurance office, though unlike most urban legends, these stories are all too real.

No adjuster is perfect: even the best miss something once in a while, even the best make silly or dumb mistakes. (I usually have to double-check my math calculations.) Nor is every adjuster the cream of the crop: some adjusters are "green" and have little experience, some have attitudes that just aren't conducive to helping others, some are border-line civil, some are borderline human, some are nearly competent, some need to power trip on an hourly basis, and some have grown overly accustomed to the taste of blood. Like all people, adjusters have bad days and like many folks out there, they are constantly overwhelmed. But regardless of an adjuster's proficiency or emotion or psychological bent, there is one thing I urge upon all homeowners: *don't pull a gun on him.*

This will not help your cause.

As stated above the vast majority of adjusters are professionals and the best advice on how to "handle" an adjuster is quite simply to treat him as a professional. Doing so will go a long way in getting an adjuster on your side and make him more receptive to the problems and issues that routinely occur. Most adjusters do care about your loss and are genuinely (or at least try to be) sympathetic to your position and having a sympathetic advocate in the bureaucratic quagmire of an insurance company is an invaluable resource. While insurance companies don't typically encourage it on the part of the adjuster, building a rela-

tionship with an adjuster—it may just be a professional relationship—
does a homeowner more good than anything else.

While it never hurts to offer an adjuster water or soda on a hot day
or coffee on a cool morning or even lunch (though it is not necessary
to do so), offering a bribe (cash or other gratuity) to an adjuster is not
only a bad idea because of the awkwardly-fitting jumpsuits (or so I've
been told) that come with a trip to jail or prison, but, to me at least, is
an offensive gesture toward an adjuster, a way of saying that you don't
respect an adjuster's professionalism or integrity. A small gesture—water, coffee, snack—is not considered a bribe, nor will it, in most cases,
influence an adjuster one way or another with regards to your claim,
but it never hurts to be nice. Don't be surprised if an adjuster turns
down your invitation to lunch: adjusters often have to turn down generous offers simply because of a lack of time, though once, in Maryland, I was offered a delectable slice of German Chocolate cake, which
at three in the afternoon can really boost sagging energy levels, and yes,
I sat down at their dinner table and ate that delicious cake.

Bad Adjuster? Get a new one!

If you happen upon a bad adjuster—one who seems to have a chronic
and severe allergy to the word "professionalism," or one who refuses
to listen to you or refuses to let you in on what's happening with your
claim (as though it's a state secret or something) or one that simply
seems to have gone AWOL, telephonically or mentally—it is well
within your rights to ask for another adjuster. Some insurers, not to
name names (okay, State Farm, but you didn't hear it from me), will put
up resistance to sending a second adjuster to inspect the same claim,
simply to save money. Most insurers value good customer service as
much as the bottom line and will gladly fulfill your request.

However, if your insurer decides it isn't in *their* best interest to send
another adjuster to reinspect your property, here's what to say: "I will
be unable to agree to any terms of settlement based upon the current
situation of my claim." (Feel free to use your own words.) If you will
remember, in the Conditions section of the policy, item number 9,

Loss Payment, an insurance company can't settle and/or pay a claim unless the insurer *and* homeowner are in agreement. An insurer can't simply impose their will on a policyholder and force them to agree to the terms of settlement. If you indicate that you will not under any circumstances agree to settle your claim without the necessary requested change, they have no choice but to do something to correct this. In the long run, it is going to cost an insurance company a lot less to send another adjuster to do a reinspection then it will to drag a claim out indefinitely, possibly even into court or appraisal—and it doesn't hurt to remind them of this.

As long as what you tell your insurer has a foundation in the policy, the insurance company will be in no position to refuse. They *must* follow their own policy; they may have their own interpretation of the policy, but as long as what you say is derived directly from the contract between you and them (and the policy *is* a contract) then you put yourself in a position that is, if not superior to the insurer's, at least on equal footing.

And if that doesn't work, call up a local TV station or newspaper and talk to them. Seriously, this works. Bad press to insurers is what Kryptonite is to Superman.

Chapter 6: How to tell the Difference Between a Stone Tablet from God and an Estimate from your Insurance Company

S o, how *do* you tell the difference between a stone tablet from God and an estimate from your insurance company? Very simple: insurance company estimates are written on paper. In ink.

The first and most important thing a homeowner needs to know about an estimate from an insurance company is that it is not set in stone, it is not the word of God chiseled on granite tablets and handed down from a mighty mount by some hairy figure recently returned from an extended meditation. It is an *estimate*; if you need additional assistance with this word, please crack open a dictionary. An estimate from an insurance company is just what it sounds like, a close approximation, a general idea of what needs to be done and how much it should cost. But by no means is an estimate the final word. So many homeowners fall into the trap of thinking that an estimate from an insurance company is what the insurer will *allow* for a claim. An estimate is not an allowance, it is the first offer in what may turn out to be a lengthy negotiation.

The second thing a homeowner needs to know about an estimate from an insurance company is that any and all payments for a claim cannot be issued unless and until the homeowner and insurance company agree, as stated in **Section I, Conditions**, number 9, Loss Payment, item a. agreement with you. As stated in the previous chapter, no insurance company can force you to accept their valuation of a claim or any settlement based upon that valuation.

The Scope of Repairs

The scope of repairs is the precursor to the estimate, an industry term that simply means the findings of an adjuster's inspection or survey of the damages: what needs to be repaired, what needs to be replaced, where it is located, how it was damaged, the quantities needed for repair or replacement, the quality or grade of materials damaged (aluminum or steel siding, for example), and additional items that may need to be included like scaffolding, dumpsters, charges to move non-damaged items out of the way, etc. Your list of what has been damaged is the beginning of your own scope. An adjuster can and should take a close look at any and all damaged areas and items—and often at areas that may not be damaged for comparison—and take measurements, pictures, notes, and ask a litany of loss-related questions, such as how old the roof, siding, windows, etc. are, what happened and when, what temporary repairs that were made.

The scope of repairs is usually organized by area: exterior—including the roof if applicable and the elevations—interior, garage, outbuildings, fences, and so on. After an adjuster makes a thorough inspection, he goes over the scope of repairs with the homeowner, telling the homeowner what he noticed was damaged and what repairs are recommended or what items need to be replaced. Repair versus replacement can be a point of contention between a homeowner and an insurance company and the more expensive an item, the more vigorous the disagreement can be: roofs, siding and carpeting, for example, are usually the sources of long drawn out battles when it comes to whether to repair some or all of the areas that *weren't* damaged.

While adjusters are given guidelines to work from and for the most part stay within these fairly strict boundaries, they are also required to use their judgment. Sometimes an adjuster will write an estimate for the repair of an item when replacement is also an option. For exam-

ple, if the vacuum from a tornado or hurricane dislodges a front door
so that it is no longer plumb in its frame—a gap has formed so that
daylight can be seen where daylight shouldn't be seen—but the door or
the frame are not physically damaged, more than likely the first thing
the adjuster will suggest is to attempt to have the door reset/repaired
by a carpenter or door specialist and not replaced—and then add that
if the carpenter or door expert says it can't be repaired, then the insurance company will pay to have it replaced at that time. Naturally, the
next question is, "Why not just replace it now?" Money. Money money
money. It costs less to repair most things than to replace them and the
insurance company doesn't want to have to pay to replace something
unless it *has* to. This little Mexican hat dance is at the center of claim
resolution and can often take place with numerous damaged items:
anything that has the *potential* to be repaired but also the *possibility* of
being replaced, the first thing the insurance company will want to do is
pay to repair it. In other words, minor disagreements with an adjuster's
scope of repairs are a normal and natural occurrence in the claims process and will work themselves out in the ensuing stages; major disagreements—whether an entire roof needs be replaced when there is damage
to only one area of a roof—are more problematic and will be addressed
in Chapter 9, Appraisal/Arbitration.

There is one aspect of the scope of repairs that is helpful and benefi-
cial for homeowners: the Continuation or Line of Sight rule. This rule
states that for items in an area being repaired or replaced, there is to be
uniformity of materials or surfaces in a continuous area. An example
would be if water damages the drywall in your ceiling and the walls are
painted the same color as the ceiling, the scope of repairs will include
repairing the damaged ceiling drywall and painting the entire ceiling
(as opposed to just the damaged area) and *all* the walls to match, even
if the ceiling or walls run continuously into an adjoining room or into
five or ten rooms, as long as the walls or ceiling continue uninterrupt-
ed. In the case above if the walls are a different color than the ceiling,
the scope would only including painting the ceiling. The same goes for
wall-to-wall carpet: if water leaked around a window and saturated the
carpet and the carpet cannot be dried without stinking (and wet carpet

is one of the most vile odors), the entire carpet should be replaced, not just patched, regardless if it runs into another room or several rooms. If there is a seam or a doorway most insurers will stop at that point. Insurance companies can be picky about this rule, however, especially when it comes to more expensive items like roofing and siding. If wind pulled a single panel of aluminum siding from one side of your house and bent or twisted it, some companies will want to replace the entire side of siding, some will replace the siding on the entire house and some—the cheapest and stingiest—will pay to repair only the damaged piece, regardless of the glaring color mismatch that will result in having one new panel mixed in with sun faded panels. Each insurance company has its own guidelines and it is very important to ask your adjuster about your carrier's guidelines on Line of Sight/Uniform Appearance. Some states have laws governing Line of Sight; consult your adjuster or state or local officials for further information.

When it comes to sets or pairs of items—high quality lawn furniture for example—most insurance companies will usually *not* pay to replace an entire set if only part of the set is damaged as stated in the policy in **Section I – Conditions**, number 4, Loss to a Pair or Set, a principle which has held up in court over the years.

As stated above, using his scope notes, the adjuster prepares an estimate for the damages.

Using a computer program with a self-contained price list he inputs the quantities and sizes of the damaged items and generates an estimate with the quantities and dollar amounts listed beside each item. Every insurance company makes their own price list, deriving their own figures for each and every item on the list from their own private method. Most companies have pricing specialists whose sole job is to research the price of each and every item in the list, people who are magically able to figure out exactly how much it costs to remove a square (100 square feet) of 30-year asphalt shingles and exactly how much it costs to put the shingles back on—without having to go to Home Depot. Some companies survey the contractors in their area and use the median price while others use the "prevailing rates" of the area.

As noted above, some insurance companies allow their adjusters to write an estimate on the spot and give it to the homeowner (and sometimes write a check, too), while most require the adjuster to submit their estimate to management for review and then mail it to the homeowner.

The Estimate

At first glance, an insurance company estimate can seem painfully confusing, especially the first few pages, which summarize the payments and enlighten a homeowner as to just how little time the insurance company will give you to complete the repairs. While every insurance company offers a different format, all insurance companies are required to put front and center the same legal disclosures about when and how to make claim for payments not yet received. (More on this in the next chapter.) There are three vital pieces of information on the first page (which sometimes extends onto a second page): a statement that the insurance company can only pay the limits of your policy according to the amounts described in the declarations page issued each year at the policy renewal period; the amount of time, which varies from insurer to insurer, a homeowner has to make a claim for the full cost of repairs; and lastly, and most importantly, the estimated amount of money that you have coming to you after the initial payment for damages is made. Once again, when you receive an estimate for damages the check that comes with it (provided that you don't decline this payment or someone forgets to put it in the envelope) is a partial payment of the damages to your property. Outrageous! Contemptible! How dare they! How do they get away with it—well, it's in the policy. The insurance company intends to pay you the least amount of money possible, which comes in two sleek and stylish alternatives: 1) the amount *they* estimate it costs to make all repairs; or 2) the actual costs of repairs. In other words, if you get an estimate from a contractor that is *lower* than your insurance company's estimate (although exceedingly rare, it has been known to happen during blue moons and leap years) the insurance company is going to pay you *based upon your contractor's estimate*—the actual cost of repairs. But "the actual cost of repairs" can also mean that if the final costs are *more* than what the insurance company estimates, they are obliged to pay this amount—but, of course, they're not going to *tell* you this because they want to reserve the right to approve all payments before repairs begin and also because they don't want to be taken advantage of or be given the shaft—giving the shaft is *their* job.

Line Items

It would be an understatement that the saying, "The devil is in the details," applies to the line items of an insurance company estimate. Line items for a property damage claim are the details of an estimate, the fine print, and while you won't need a magnifying glass to read them, a sharp eye and an attention to detail are helpful—as is a familiarity with construction and materials. Like the scope, most estimates are organized into discernable areas: roof, exterior, interior. The line items for each area lists the item/materials, quantities and cost of each item that will be used to make the repairs for that area, sometimes put fourth in a cost-per-unit format. In most cases, when an item is listed, the labor to remove and/or install is also included, as in the estimate for a roof replacement due to a hailstorm listed below, though most roofing estimates break out the removal cost from the replacement cost, adding waste to the replacement quantity.

Room: Roof Total area: 10,000 Square Feet

Item	Quantity	RCV	Depreciation	ACV
Remove 3-tab 20 year comp shingles	10 SQ	$ 300.00	($ 150.00)	$ 150.00
Replace 3-tab 20 year comp shingles	11 SQ	$2280.00	($1140.00)	$1140.00

NOTE: The items in this section are to replace the dwelling roof. Roof is 10 years old and in average condition. Based upon a life expectancy of 20 years, final depreciation is 50%.

TOTALS:		$2580.00	($1290.00)	$1290.0

In the example above, the line items for roof replacement are

Continued on page 110

American Standard Insurance Company
123 Anywhere Place
Any Ol' Town, USA
88-Dont-Call

Cause of loss: hail   Claim Number: 00112233445566
Date of loss: 5-15-09   Policy Number: ASI-1234-55-78
Insured: Sample, Estimate   Agent: Goodfellow, I.M.
Insured Location: 321 Whereany Pl.
                  Any Ol' Town, USA

Summary for HAIL

Line item totals	$8400.00
Adjustments for Base Service Charges	$ 200.00
Material Sales tax	$ 0.00
Subtotal and Replacement Cost Value	$8600.00
Less Depreciation	($2454.00)
Actual Cash Value	$6146.00
Less Deductible	($1000.00)
Net Actual Cash Value	$5146.00
Total Recoverable Depreciation	$2454.00
Net Claim if Depreciation is Recovered	$7600.00

In order to receive payment on a replacement cost basis, you must
first repair or replace the lost or damaged items within one year of the
date of loss. Once final invoices have been received by us, we will pay
the lesser of the following amounts: 1) the replacement cost minus
the applicable deductible; or 2) the actual cost of repair minus the
applicable deductible.

Page 1

Room: Roof Total area: 10,000 Square Feet

Item	Quantity	RCV	Depreciation	ACV
Remove 3-tab 20 year comp shingles	10 SQ	$ 300.00	($ 150.00)	$ 150.00
Replace 3-tab 20 year comp shingles	11 SQ	$1650.00	($ 825.00	$ 825.00
Remove and replace T-vent	3/EA	$ 120.00	($ 60.00)	$ 60.00
Remove and replace Drip Edge	120 LF	$ 180.00	($ 140.00)	$ 140.00
Additonal charge for 2-story roof	11 SQ	$ 330.00	($165.00)	$ 165.00

NOTE: The items in this section are to replace the dwelling roof. Roof is 10 years old and in average condition. Based upon a life expectancy of 20 years, final depreciation is 50%.

TOTALS: $2580.00 ($1290.00) $1290.00

Room: Exterior Area: Siding Total area: 1380 Square Feet

Item	Quantity	RCV	Depreciation	ACV
Remove & replace aluminum siding	1380 SF	$5520.00	($1104.00)	$4416.00
Ladders and jacks	2/EA	$ 200.00	($ 40.00)	$ 160.00
Disposal – small dumpster	1/EA	$ 100.00	($ 20.00)	$ 80.00

NOTE: The items in this section are to replace the all of the siding on the home. Siding is 10 years old and in average condition. Based upon a life expectancy of 50 years, depreciation is 20%.

TOTALS: $5820.00 ($1164.00) $4116.00

Estimate Totals	RCV	Depreciation	ACV
	$8400.00	($2454.00)	$5946.00

Base service charges
Roofing contractor	$100.00
Siding contractor	$100.00
TOTAL:	$200.00

Page 2

comprehensive, including preparation, installation and additional accessories like drip edge and roof vents. Typically, however, the minor accessories or components are broken out into individual items, like in the example on page 105, an estimate for the same roof with individual components separated.

Some estimates can be a page or a few pages long, some can be the size of a short novel. Regardless of length, one must have a highly conscientious eye when reviewing an estimate and a knowledge of construction to know what may be missing. If you don't know much about construction, either find an objective (read: not the contractor you will be hiring for the job) person who knows what they're looking at or prepare yourself for a crash course on j-channels, geometry and pipe jack flashings. The primary goal is simply to make sure that everything that should be there is there, that all the line items and "extras" add up: repairing water-damaged drywall in a vaulted ceiling may require scaffolding; a small dumpster or an equivalent charge would be needed if removing carpeting, drywall and cabinetry; if there is a large amount of furniture in a room that is to be painted, additional charges for moving the furniture may be necessary; if a door needs to be replaced, it may also need to be stained or painted and the lockset will need to be removed from the old door and reset in the new one; a steep or two-story or more roof calls for additional charges. If you think something is missing or don't know if it is included in a different line item, ask your adjuster.

Minimum Charges/Base Service Fees

Hidden at the back of an estimate you'll often find something like the following.

Base Service Charges	
Roofing contractor	$100.00
Painting contractor	$100.00
Drywall contractor	$200.00
Carpet installer	$100.00
Siding contractor	$100.00
TOTAL:	$600.00

For every trade involved in a claim, most insurers tack on what are called Minimum Charges or Base Service Fees. These are the fees plumbers, electricians, drywall installers (on and on and on) charge for simply making a trip to do a repair, above and beyond the billable hours for the actual work performed and the materials used. These fees can often add hundreds or even thousands of dollars to an estimate and relieve the foreboding sensation that construction-savvy homeowners get when they review an estimate and begin to sense that the line items listed simply aren't going to be enough to cover everything, or at least give the perception that they're getting a little something extra—which is exactly the purpose of these little gems, to make you feel like you're getting more than you are even though the total estimate is likely much lower than what the final costs will be.

Chapter 7: Getting Paid: a Crash Course on Insurance Company Math (or Why the Check You Get Seems so Tiny)

Hark now and observe the miracle of insurance company math: even though your adjuster says you have $8,600.00 in damages, he hands you a check for $5,146.00—how is this possible? Is this not a mistake? Where did all that money go?

Brrrrrrring! Class is now in session! Gather 'round one and all and witness a momentous occasion, your one and only chance to learn about the secrets behind the mathematical formulas that allowed NASA to go to the moon—yes, that's right, you're about to enter a realm seldom seen by those without pocket protectors and calculators the size of paper back books; you are about to discover the well-kept secret that the foundations of rocket science—yes, the very ability to reach for the stars—were built upon: the formula to determine how much (or how little) homeowners actually get paid for a claim.

Understanding an estimate is a struggle of numbers and words. Words like Actual Cash Value crop up, large numbers in parenthesis with the word Depreciation make appearances (even though the house has *appreciated* three fold since you bought it 30 years ago), strange combinations of letters that spell out Overhead and Profit perch curiously near the margins—what does it mean, what does it *mean*!

Is it sleight of hand, does some unspeakable force allows these numbers to appear seemingly from out of nowhere? Holy crap, is it voodoo? According to most policies, after a loss the settlement owed home-owners is the Actual Cash Value, which represents a *partial* amount of the total damages. Note: some states require full replacement cost payment up front. Once repairs have been made, the funds a homeowner hasn't yet been paid are then released so that, in the end, a homeowner has been paid the total amount of the repairs minus the deductible. Sounds simple enough, right? But of course, like all aspects of a claim, it's never as simple as it sounds.

Naturally, not all estimate Summary Pages are alike. The following, from the sample estimate above, is the simplest version of a Summary Page.

Summary for HAIL		
Line item totals	$8400.00	Line 1
Adjustments for Base Service Charges	$ 200.00	Line 2
Material Sales tax	$ 0.00	Line 3
Subtotal and Replacement Cost Value	$8600.00	Line 4
Less Depreciation	($2454.00)	Line 5
Actual Cash Value	$6146.00	Line 6
Less Deductible	($1000.00)	Line 7
Net Actual Cash Value	$5146.00	Line 8
Total Recoverable Depreciation	$2454.00	Line 9
Net Claim if Depreciation is Recovered	$7600.00	Line 10

Line 1: Line item totals: this is the dollar amount of structural/building damages.

Line 2: Adjustments for Base Service Charges: these are additional amounts for each "trade" (roofing, siding, etc.) added to the estimate.

Line 3: Material Sales Tax: some estimates will have this, some won't. This one does not.

Line 4: Subtotal and Replacement Cost Value (RCV); this is the total amount of your claim before all the nasty stuff happens to it.

Line 5: Less Depreciation: this amount is the total of the depreciation of all the line items and gets deducted from the replacement cost.

Line 6: Actual Cash Value. This is the replacement cost minus the depreciation.

Line 7: Less Deductible. Evil things.

Line 8: Net Actual Cash Value: this is the amount of the first payment from the insurance company. Not very impressive, this number. Most people look at this and exclaim, "I can't fix the house for this much! I can't even buy the materials for this amount!"

Line 9: Total Recoverable Depreciation: this is the amount you can get back once repairs are completed.

Line 10: Net claim if Depreciation is Recovered: this is the Replacement Cost minus the Deductible; the total amount you can claim once the deductible has been taken out and the repairs have been made.

The insurance company giveth, the insurance company taketh; then giveth back again. The depreciation that gets taken out is also known in some circles as the Replacement Cost Benefits. Replacement Cost Benefits are exactly what they sound like: once the repairs have been made, once the damaged items that have been depreciated have been replaced or repaired, this is the amount that is due a homeowner. This amount is the ACV plus the depreciation.

However, insurers don't just *give* Replacement Cost Benefits away. Replacement Cost Benefits are not automatic. You have to earn them, in more ways than one. First of all, if a homeowner doesn't make the repairs, if he doesn't replace the items for which he is being paid, he is not going to receive any additional payments. Secondly, as stated above, an insurance company is only ever going to pay the actual cost of repairs. If it happens that the actual cost of the work is *lower* than what the insurance company estimated, you are going to receive the actual cost of repairs. For example, if you receive an estimate from a contractor to make all the repairs in the estimate for $8,200.00, then you would receive that amount minus your deductible, or $400.00 less.

Thirdly, if you want your Replacement Cost Benefits, you have to submit a final bill from your contractor(s) for the items that have been repaired or replaced. You don't have to wait until all repairs are completed. For the Sample Estimate, which has roof and siding items, if the roof was replaced first, you would send in the final invoice for the roof (or have your contractor do it for you) and you would then receive the depreciation amounts for the roof only.

ACV and RCV

What would big business and the military do without acronyms? I mean really...

ACV means **A**ctual **C**ash **V**alue.

RCV mean **R**eplacement **C**ost **V**alue.

ACV is the full Replacement Cost Value minus depreciation (RCV – Depreciation = ACV).

ACV can be thought of as the E-Bay (or garage sale) price of an item, the present value of a used piece of material like roofing, siding, or an item like a gas grill. ACV is not a reflection of overall property values, it is only a reflection of the individual components of a structure.

RCV or Replacement Cost Value is the "brand new" price of an item or what it would cost to replace an item.

Most Replacement Cost homeowners policies state that homeowners are owed ACV after a loss unless and until the homeowner makes the repairs to his property or replaces the damaged item(s)—if you don't make the repairs, you get nothing beyond the ACV. Naturally, one might ask, why do insurance companies only pay *part* of the total damages up front? (Which I have been asked many many times.) The dumb answer is because the policy says so—and because the insurance company wrote the policy that way.

But why did they write it like that?

Three reasons. Remember, an insurance company will take advantage of you if you let them and who else but someone who wants to take advantage of another person would not want themselves to be taken advantage of? Yes, there is a certain paranoia to paying homeowners only part of what they are owed at the outset—insurers are afraid that you're going to pocket the money and use it to take a trip to Jamaica or the Bahamas and not fix your property. (Which happens more often than one might think.) Which means the insurance company is not getting what it paid for, a repaired property, which in the long run could cost them more money.

But for less hyper paranoid/Dr. Strangelove reasons, insurers also make partial payments up front to avoid overpayment, which is a rarity and usually only happens when a homeowner does the repairs himself or if he changes materials. For example, if a homeowner has aluminum siding that gets damaged (on all sides of a house) and he elects to put vinyl siding on instead—aluminum siding is almost twice as expensive as vinyl—and he is paid all of the money upfront, the homeowner may actually profit from the repairs. If this same homeowner only receives a partial payment for the damages and submits a final bill for repair, unless the final bill is fraudulent, he is only going to get *some* of his Replacement Cost Benefits/Depreciation back—in this case, the actual cost to replace his alumium siding with cheaper vinyl. Of course, if a homeowner decides to do the work himself and the first payment covers the cost of all the materials, often a homeowner who does the work himself won't file for any additional payments. Even though a homeowner is entitled to be reimbursed for his time to make any final repairs on his own property, (by submitting a written log of the hours he worked) most homeowners don't and won't do that—primarily because insurers don't tell homeowners they can. The last line of some Summary Pages will say in place of "Net Claim if Depreciation is Recovered" something along the lines of "Total amount of claim *if incurred*" (my italics). Notice it doesn't say, "We guarantee to pay you this much." An insurer is only going to pay what they believe they owe and if a homeowner doesn't say otherwise, that is all that will be paid.

Lastly, insurers don't want to pay more than they have to for a claim. If a homeowner happens to have a highly refined sense of procrastination and never calls the insurance company to claim the Replacement Cost Benefits, the insurance company chalks up another win. If an insurer can get away with taking advantage of procrastinators who don't make a claim for any additional funds owed to them, they will do so—with zeal. It is surprising just how many people don't bother asking for the remaining money to be released to them—and insurance companies count on these homeowners' apathy, only encouraging insurers to continue to hold back part of the full payment of damages.

Overhead and Profit

As they say in those annoying infomercials—but wait, *there's more!* You've almost completed your crash course. The Summary Page above is the most simple of the species, an "ordinary" claim without a tremendous amount of damage, hail damage to a roof and some siding damage. Let's put this estimate on steroids.

Summary for HAIL		
Line item totals	$8400.00	Line 1
Adjustments for Base Service Charges	$ 200.00	Line 2
Material Sales tax	$ 0.00	Line 3
Subtotal and Replacement Cost Value	$8600.00	Line 4
Less Depreciation	($2454.00)	Line 5
Actual Cash Value	$6146.00	Line 6
Overhead – 10%	$ 614.60	Line 7
Profit – 10%	$ 614.60	Line 8
Subtotal with overhead and profit	$7375.20	Line 9
Less Deductible	($1000.00)	Line 10
Net Actual Cash Value	$6375.20	Line 11
Recoverable Depreciation	$2454.00	Line 12
Overhead – 10%	$ 245.40	Line 13
Profit – 10%	$ 245.40	Line 14
Total Recoverable Depreciation	$2944.80	Line 15
Net Claim if Depreciation is Recovered	$9320.00	Line 16

Using the same figures, the Summary of Payments above adds what is called overhead and profit to the estimate, the customary and usual charges paid to a General Contractor for coordinating the efforts of subcontractors to build or repair a property. If you can follow the example and understand it the first time around, you get an "A" in your crash course on insurance company math.

You'll note the first few lines are the same: total amount of damages, total amount of damages plus taxes, depreciation and ACV. But this is where it gets interesting.

On Lines 7 and 8 Overhead and Profit (a.k.a. O & P) actually *add* 10% and another 10%—a total of 20%—back into the ACV.

The ACV with O & P gets subtracted by the deductible.

Line 11, the net ACV is higher with this claim, which means the first payment is also higher.

But that's not all. O & P make a comeback: Overhead and Profit are each multiplied by the amount of the Depreciation—10% times the amount of Depreciation once (for Overhead), 10% times the amount of Depreciation again (for Profit)—and the sums of both of these are then added to the amount of "regular" Depreciation to get the "Net Claim if Depreciation is Recovered," (a.k.a., Replacement Cost Benefits) which is significantly higher in this estimate than in the "normal" estimate. The total amount of claim if incurred is, like the first example above, the Net ACV (Line 11) plus the Total Recoverable Depreciation, (Line 15) which in this case is actually *higher* than Line 4, Subtotal and Replacement Cost.

The insurance company giveth, the insurance company taketh; then giveth back again.

Depending on locality, O & P is usually 10% each for Overhead and Profit, though in some places 15% profit is customary. These amounts get added to an estimate to make it much more financially substantial and bolsters a claim's bottom line, making settlement a little easier. Not every claim is eligible for O & P: as a general rule, if three or more trades (roofing, windows, doors, drywall, framing, painting, etc.) are involved in the repairs of a damaged property, then it usually qualifies for O & P, though every insurer has it's own standards. An example of a claim that would typically qualify is if hail damaged the roof, gutters, siding, windows and doors of a home. For most insurers, this would qualify for O & P.

Also, not every contractor is eligible for O & P: typically it is only paid to a licensed General Contractor, though sometimes an insurer will pay O & P to a non-general contractor provided that he has to coordinate with one or more subcontractors—which is why most people feel more comfortable hiring an experienced, licensed General Contractor, since they frequently do just that. Most insurers will resist paying O & P for contractors who only do one job—if only the siding is damaged, for example—though rare exceptions have been made to this.

The catch with O & P and insurance companies is that sometimes what may seem like three trades is not always considered three trades: roofing and guttering are often considered one trade, since many roofers also do gutters and for the example above, if the only damage was roofing, gutters and siding, the claim may not qualify for O & P. The other catch is that with some insurers O & P is not paid until it is actually incurred, that is until a General Contractor submits a bill for it (once again, insurance companies don't want to pay for something unless and until they have to)—which prevents homeowners who do their own repairs from unethically collecting money they are not and should not be entitled to, although if a homeowner is a General Contactor, his *company* may submit an invoice for O & P.

O & P is one of the things that insurance companies or adjusters often don't tell homeowners about, mostly because the money goes to the contractor and not the homeowner. While O & P is usually not an issue for most homeowners, it is something for homeowners to look out for in their estimate—and if it's not there, it may be a bargaining chip that can be used in negotiations. By the way, O & P only applies to Coverage A items, never to personal property.

How Not to Get Depressed Over Depreciation

Depreciation is the deduction of an item's worth due to its age and/or condition.

With homeowners insurance, deprecation is applied only when items are *replaced*; depreciation should not apply when an item is being *repaired*. An example of repair versus replacement: if wind blew three shingles off one side of a roof, an insurer would pay to repair the roof with three new shingles where the old ones blew off; if wind blew more than half the shingles off one side of a roof, most insurers would pay to remove the remaining shingles on the damaged side of the roof and replace the shingles on that side of the roof. The repair with three shingles would not a have a deduction for depreciation; a replacement of an entire side or slope of shingles would.

Some homeowner get so depressed over depreciation that it nearly makes them homicidal toward their property adjuster (which I can attest to and recommend against). Once again, depreciation taken on a claim is not a reflection of the overall value of a property. Which leads to one of the most frequently asked questions: why do insurance companies deduct depreciation if a property has actually *increased* in value over time? How can you depreciate a part of something if the whole has gained in value over time?

The insurance company answer: *you* wouldn't pay a new car price for a used car, so why should they? The individual components of a house lose value as they age and in doing so lose their usefulness, even while the structure as a whole may gain in value.

Depreciation is determined on a component-by-component basis and has nothing to do with the overall value of a home and the land it sits upon. Just as the individual parts of a home are priced separately—roofing, siding, paint—they are also depreciated differently due to their varying lifespans and rates of deterioration. Depreciation is determined by two main factors: age and condition/appearance. Sometimes an item can be very old but look good and is subject to less depreciation. Conversely, an item can be newer but appear to be in poor condition and is subject to more depreciation.

Depreciation comes in two forms: *straight* deprecation and *adjusted* depreciation. Straight depreciation is the age of an item over its life expectancy without deduction or enhancement for age and appearance. For example, five year-old carpeting that is expected to last 10 years would be depreciated 50%, (5/10). Adjusted depreciation takes into account the age of the item and includes any adjustments for its physical appearance. If five year-old carpet that is supposed to last ten years looks like it's seven years old could be depreciated 70%, (7/10).

Every insurer has depreciation tables that list the expected lifespan of different items. These values can vary dramatically from insurer to insurer. In the Appendix, you'll find a depreciation table that I have culled from my years of experience.

As stated above, depreciation is only taken on items that are being replaced, not when they are *repaired*. Another example: if water damages the ceiling of a room and a 1-foot by 1-foot patch of drywall needs to be cut out and new section inserted, the entire ceiling will have to be repainted (for this example, the ceiling is a different color than the walls). In this case, cutting out and putting in a new piece of drywall is considered a repair and no depreciation would be taken for the drywall; however, the paint would be subject to depreciation as it is considered an *entire replacement* as all the paint on the ceiling is being replaced. A good rule of thumb is if all of a component in a continuous line of sight is being replaced, it will most likely be subject to depreciation, like the roof example above—even though the entire roof is not being replaced, all the roofing in the continuous line of sight on the damaged side is being replaced.

While it may seem like the depreciation taken on damaged property is an arbitrary figure whose sole purpose is to provide an insurer the opportunity to avoid paying an entire claim upfront, the reason it seems like that is because that's exactly what it is: insurance companies want to avoid even the slightest possibility of overpayment and they want to ensure that repairs get done.

The Dreaded Deductible

There's no getting around it: deductibles suck. Literally: they suck money out of your claim—especially if you live in a hurricane zone and have to pay a hurricane deductible (either 2%, 5% or even 10% of the property's insured value: for a $200,000.00 home with a 5% deductible, that's $10,000.00 per hurricane) or have earthquake coverage (a 2% or 5% deductible per earthquake)—no $250.00, $500.00 or $1000.00 deductibles there. Obviously, the purpose of a deductible is to reduce the amount of money insurers have to pay on a claim but another function is to discourage homeowners from filing smaller claims that they think won't be above the deductible, which sometimes they are, though sometimes they're not.

The most important thing to note about the deductible as it pertains to an estimate is that you don't have to "pay" it in the sense that you'll have to write a check to your insurance company (which makes sense since it is called a Deductible and not a Pay-ible)—it is automatically subtracted from the Actual Cash Value, which simplifies things a tiny bit for homeowners. As a claim progresses and the insurance company and contractor meet to hammer out the final details of what work needs to be done and how much it should cost, a homeowner will typically receive revised estimates that reflect the adjustments made during negotiations. Usually these estimates are higher than the original and quite often there will be a check that represents payment of the new Net Actual Cash Value amount. On many occasions, homeowners who've received a revised estimate have called me, confused and a little irate that they've been charged their deductible twice. When a new, revised estimate is received, it may appear as though the deductible has been subtracted twice, when in reality it hasn't. All one has to do in this situation is look at the ACV and Net ACV amounts from both estimates:

First Estimate		Revised Estimate	
ACV:	$1000.00	ACV:	$1700.00
Deductible:	($ 500.00)	Deductible:	($ 500.00)
Net ACV:	$ 500.00	Net ACV:	$1200.00

First Payment: $500.00   Second Payment: $700.00

Revised Net ACV ($1200.00) minus the Original Net ACV

($500.00) = $700.00

In this case the homeowner received a first check for $500.00 with the first estimate and then another check for $700.00 for the revised estimate, while the deductible only applies once.

There's no getting around deductibles. As stated in the "Busting Myths" section earlier, deductibles always apply, even when it appears they don't. Let me explain: there are a few instances where the amount of damage for a particular type of coverage exceeds the amount of coverage. When this overage occurs, the amount of damage above the limit of coverage is subtracted from the deductible, reducing or eliminating the deductible altogether. Here's an example of wind damage with tree debris damage.

Structural Damage to House:	$1,000.00
Cost to lift tree off house and set on ground:	$2,000.00
Cost to cut up tree and haul away:	$2,000.00
TOTAL:	$5,000.00
LESS DEDUCTIBLE:	($ 500.00)
ACV/TOTAL AMOUNT OF CLAIM:	$4,500.00

However, there's one problem with the scenario above: the policy limit for cutting up and hauling away tree debris is only $500.00 for all trees, plus 5% of $500.00, or $25.00. (See **Section I – Coverages**, **Additional Coverages**, number 1, Debris Removal) This estimate has $2,000.00. This is what the actual estimate would look like:

Structural Damage to House:	$1000.00
Cost to lift tree off house and set on ground:	$2000.00
Policy limit to cut up tree and haul away:	$ 525.00
TOTAL:	$3525.00
LESS DEDUCTIBLE:	($ 0.00)
ACV/TOTAL AMOUNT OF CLAIM:	$3525.00

Since the cost to cut up and haul away the tree debris was $2000.00 and the policy limit is only $525.00, that means there's $1475.00 worth of damage that the insurance company won't pay for. What insurers do in this case is absorb the deductible, that is, reduce it by the amount over the policy limits. In this case, the entire amount of the deductible, $500.00. This means that there is still nearly $1000.00 that the insurance company won't pay for tree debris removal, regardless.

In the example above, the insurance company is still applying the deductible—it just happens that they've decided to reduce it to nothing since the damages went over the policy limits of tree debris removal. So, yes, the good news is that the deductible has been slashed to zero; the bad news, of course, is that there's still a substantial amount that the insurance company isn't going to pay.

Using the same example as above, let's say that the regular deductible is actually $2000.00.

Structural Damage to House:	$1,000.00
Cost to lift tree off house and set on ground:	$2,000.00
Policy limits, cut up tree and haul away:	$ 525.00
TOTAL:	$3,525.00
LESS "NEW" DEDUCTIBLE:	($ 525.00)
ACV/TOTAL AMOUNT OF CLAIM:	$3,000.00

What the heck? The actual cost to cut up and haul away the tree debris is $2000.00. The policy limit is $525.00. That means there's $1,475.00 ($2,000.00 - $525.00 = $1,475.00) worth of tree debris removal over the limit. This $1475.00 gets subtracted from the "normal" $2000.00 deductible, making the "new" deductible $525.00. In this case, only a part of the deductible is absorbed into the amount over the policy limit.

The Mortgage Company

When a homeowner gets a check from an insurance company, the name of their mortgage company or bank (if there is one) will often appear after the name of the insureds and will have to be endorsed by the homeowner and the lender. Mortgage company names should never appear on checks for personal property damage, only building damage.

Some of the most horrific stories I have heard about insurance claims have nothing to do with insurance companies, but with the mortgage company whose names appear on all structural damage checks issued to homeowners: checks getting lost in the mail, lenders who simply take the money, lenders who make homeowners take out temporary loans (complete with interest and fees) until the repairs are completed, lenders who dole out the money in bite-size chunks and collect interest on the principal. Luckily, not every insurance claim will entail frightening entanglements with a bank or a mortgage company and some lenders are less demanding. And not every claim will have the mortgage company listed as a co-payee.

Whether or not the name of a mortgage or bank (or an additional insured, more on them in a moment) differs with each insurance carrier and each mortgage holder: typically, if a claim is over a certain dollar figure (which varies greatly from insurer to insurer; sometimes it is when the total amount of the claim is over $3,000.00, $5,000.00 or $7,500.00 or a different amount) the name of the mortgage company must appear on any and all drafts issued to homeowners for building damage. However, there are some lenders who've made an agreement with the insurance companies that their names must be on all checks regardless of the total amount of damages.

The key words to keep in mind are "total amount of the claim": the check you get from the insurance company may be well under the threshold that triggers the mortgage company name being on the check, but if the total damages (the Replacement Cost Value), regardless of depreciation or the deductible, are over that amount, the name(s) will have to be on the draft. For example, if you have an insurer in which all claims over $7,500.00 are required to list mortgage holders on all checks for structural damage and the damages to your home from a wind storm totals $7,600.00 and you get a check for $5,100.00 ($2,000.00 for depreciation, $500.00 deductible) for the Actual Cash

Value payment, the name of the mortgage company/lender will have to have to appear on the check, even though the first payment is well below the benchmark $7,500.00 figure. Since the Replacement Cost Value is $7,600.00, this claim has crossed the mandated threshold.

The dumb answer as to why a mortgage holder's name must appear on checks is that it is part of the policy, what is called the "Mortgage Clause" (**Section I – Conditions**, number 10). Since the mortgage holders often have a substantial monetary investment in the damaged property and are as interested as the insurance company in seeing it repaired, they have made agreements with insurers that they be included in a claim on the property in which they have an interest.

If a property has multiple mortgages with different companies, all lenders that have an interest in a property will be listed on the check along with the name of the insureds and all will have to sign the check.

An adjuster is supposed to tell a homeowner if the name of the mortgage company needs to be included on the payment draft. If you are told this applies to you, it is imperative to ensure the insurance company has the right lender listed. A good adjuster will ask, "is your mortgage still with company X?" before they put the paperwork through and send an estimate with a check. But not every adjuster will do this and getting a check with the wrong mortgage company will cause unnecessary delays. If it happens that the wrong lender is listed, you are going to have to send documentation that verifies who the correct lender is. If you have recently paid off the mortgage and neither the mortgage holder nor you remembered to tell the insurance company, you are going to have to provide documentation that the loan has in fact been paid off, usually a satisfaction of mortgage notice. Sometimes mortgage companies take their sweet time doing this: a homeowner told me she had paid off her mortgage six months before the notice finally arrived.

If you are told that the lender's name will appear on the check with your name, *before* you get the check, before you start looking for a contractor, your first priority is to call the lender(s) and find out what their procedure is for getting the check endorsed, regardless if they are a local bank or on the other side of the country. Every institution has their own procedures, every lender does something a little different: some may simply sign the check and send you on your way, some may do what was mentioned above and hold part or all of it. Once the check arrives there are two important things to do: one, make sure *all* the names are listed on the check are correct (including your own) and two, ***don't sign the check.***

This cannot be stressed enough: make the lender sign the check first. Whoever signs the check last assumes control of the check and has the right to cash it. While it is rare, sometimes bank/mortgage companies will change their policies at the last second and decide that they, too want to hold onto the funds and not disclose this to a homeowner, (of course, a few weeks after you've sent them a signed check, a notice will arrive stating that the lender's procedure has recently changed) and sending an unsigned check will give you the advantage and put the onus on the lender to put into writing their procedures before they can take your money.

Since lenders can be located anywhere in the U.S. sometimes a check has to be mailed out of state or out of town. If you do have to mail a check, when you call to find out what your lender's procedure is, make sure to get the name of a specific person in a specific department to send it to before mailing it. It is essential to do this: if a check mysteriously disappears in the labyrinthine bowels of a mortgage company, this may be the only way to hold someone within the mortgage company accountable. Many, many times I've had homeowners tell me that they mailed their insurance check to their lender and the lender never sent it back without any record of receiving or sending it. Usually in these cases, the parcel was addressed only to the "Insurance Department," and not to a specific person, opening up the possibility of a check vanishing.

Along the lines of a mortgage company is what is called an additional insured. But unlike mortgage companies, additional insureds are *always* listed on insurance company claim check for structural damage, even though they are not actual policyholders. An additional insured is someone (quite often a family member) or something (a trust or estate) that holds a financial interest in the property: someone who lent the money to the homeowner to buy the property; the person selling a property on contract; the legal description or name of the trust or the estate. All names listed as additional insureds must endorse the check, whether they are living or deceased. Yes, deceased.

Deceased Policy Holders

It's just one of those things: a hurricane, tornado or some other devastating loss strikes and one of the homeowners listed on a policy has recently passed away—a name that will be listed on each and every insurance company check—putting even greater stress on the surviving spouse or family members. The good news is that whomever is deemed executor of the deceased person's estate can sign any and all drafts in their stead, often just by signing "The Estate of ____" after the executor has been established. The bad news is that without a will sometimes the legal hurdles for an executor to be named and granted that power can be a prolonged affair. The situation of those who suffer the loss of a loved one and damage to their property is never an easy one, but thankfully the solution is usually much less painful and stressful as one may first think.

Invisible Squirrels: What isn't in your Estimate

What are invisible squirrels? Squirrels that you can't see, of course.

Adjusters do not have x-ray eyes. Neither do contractors. Adjusters may be able to defy gravity to a certain extent, they may be able to see things that most others don't, but they definitely cannot see through walls or ceilings. Quite often, though, there will be damages that are not readily visible to the naked eye. For example, if a tree limb breaks a window and water pours onto a wood floor, it may be obvious that the hardwood floor is warped and damaged, but without ripping up the floor boards, there may be no way to know if the wood sub-floor is warped. Even the term "adjuster" implies that an adjuster's job is to adjust a claim to include previously unseen damage and to keep adjusting the claim until all damages, seen and unseen, are paid.

It is very ordinary to have a claim settled and then, later on, usually during the process of making repairs, additional damages are discovered and have to be added to the claim. What homeowners need to understand is that this is normal, that more often than not, once a contractor (or homeowner) start to make repairs, once they start ripping things out like drywall, carpeting, their hair, they discover hidden damages. The caveat of course is that in order to be included in the existing insurance claim the previously unseen damages must be caused by the original loss and not by an unrelated event; if they are not caused by the original loss, a different claim would be filed, assuming the newly discovered damages are covered. When additional repairs are needed due to hidden damages or because no one thought of or knew of the additional steps needed for repair, items that get added to a claim are called Supplements, and the payments for those are called oddly enough Supplemental Payments. Supplemental Payments are a normal part of the claims process and occur frequently.

As long as a claim is made for them, these previously unseen damages will always be included in the insurance claim, though not always right away. Sometimes these types of item are paid on an "as incurred" basis, which means when the work is actually performed and not a moment sooner.

There are some common-sense exceptions to the no-see rule: if water stains a top-story ceiling or an exterior wall, usually an estimate will include an allowance for insulation, though sometimes the type of insulation (batt or blown in or something else) is not always known at the initial inspection and adjustments may have to be made after the fact.

Once hidden or unknown damage is discovered, the first thing to do is to document it. Just about every contractor who isn't Amish carries a cell phone these days and most cell phones have cameras or video cameras. However it is documented, once the hidden damage is recorded, call the insurance company or have the contractor call the insurance company. Some insurers will take the word of a contractor that there are additional damages if the insurer has worked with the contractor before and the additional damages are relatively small, but other insurance companies will need to verify all claims for supplemental payments regardless of the size or extent of the additional damages; sometimes this is done with a follow-up inspection of the property or simply with the receipt of documentation showing the additional damages. At this point, the adjuster will issue another estimate with the additional items included and a check that covers the supplemental items.

The important thing to keep in mind is that any loss-related damages can be claimed at any time before the last coat of paint has been applied or the last nail has been hammered, even after a claim has been paid, even if numerous supplemental payments have been issued.

Chapter 8: Selecting Contractor(s): 10 Questions to Ask

As stated above, most insurers mail estimates to homeowners, which usually takes a week to several weeks, depending upon the adjuster (some *are* slower than others) and depending upon the claims review process. In the meantime, a homeowner's job is to get to work researching a contractor, if you don't already have one. Contractors can be great allies during the claims process; but the wrong contractor can be an even greater hindrance to getting your life back together than an insurance company. Everyone has heard stories of the contractor who didn't finish the job or was so utterly incompetent that it took two contractors to fix what the first one loused up, so on and so forth. But the question is, how do you avoid those awful contractors—for that matter, where does one *get* a good contractor? Friends, co-workers, neighbors, anyone you know who has remodeled their house or had any work done on their property similar to your type of claim are the best resources. Sometimes just getting a contractor recommended to you by someone you know (or by someone you know who knows someone) is a battle in itself. But once names have been secured, the arduous work of interviewing contractors begins. While there is no insurance-mandated quota of interviewing any particular number of contractors, the standard of three estimates/contractors is logical, giving homeowners a good rounded sense of the available options.

One mistake that many homeowners make is choosing the contractor whose estimate is closest to the insurance company estimate. More important than the amount of the estimate from a contractor—most contractor's estimates are going to be higher than the insurance company's estimate anyway—is how comfortable you feel working with that contractor, how trustworthy and reliable he is at the early stages of your dealings with him: if he tells you he'll have an estimate ready in a few days and two weeks later he finally sends you an estimate, this may be an indicator of what's ahead.

Your insurance company will work with whomever you choose. It's a little like getting to choose your own doctor in that respect. Insurers also want you to receive quality work. Insurance companies, whether they like it or not, really do want homeowners to select the company or person who best suits the homeowner's needs and who does quality work, which is yet another irony of insurers: they want you to get quality work done, they just don't want to *pay* for quality work.

Question 1: What Kind of Contractor is He?

Homeowners basically have two choices when it comes to hiring a contractor: a trade contractor or a general contractor (GC). Trade contractors, also called specialty contractors, usually have one specific trade: plumbing, electrical, roofing, drywall, carpentry, etc. General contractors, as mentioned in the previous chapter, are in charge of coordinating the efforts of numerous subcontractors/trade contractors. GCs typically build houses (or rebuild them), remodel homes, some build commercial structures and depending upon the contractor, may or may not have experience working with insurance companies. The question of whether or not to hire a GC usually depends upon the extent of the damages. If you have a windstorm that blows shingles off your roof and there is no other damage, you'll only need a roofer. If the damages are extensive and require coordination, a GC is usually your best option. The "three trades" guideline that insurance companies use to determine if overhead and profit should be paid on a claim are your best indicators as to the complexity of a job. Another indicator is how closely related the tasks are from one another. For example, if a wind storm blows a large patch of shingles off your roof, tears a small section of siding off your house and sends a neighbor's roof shingle through your window, you have three trades but three trades that are completely unrelated: fixing the siding is not contingent upon fixing the roof or the window and vice versa. However, if a wind storm blows a significant section of shingles off your roof and water leaks through the roof and damages the painted ceiling and walls of the rooms below, the trades (roofing, drywall, insulation, and painting) do require coordination: you'll have to fix the roof before you fix the drywall and paint the walls and ceilings in case it rains again and causes damage to what was just fixed. In the second scenario, while there isn't a *tremendous* amount of coordination involved, if you are a busy person, it may be worth your time to hire a GC to handle everything.

Some homeowners may be brave enough or have enough time to act as their own GC or project manager. Appointing yourself as GC means you get the wonderful opportunity to apply for all those building permits, coordinate city or county inspections at various stages of rebuilding or repair, research and interview the numerous trade contractors you'll need to do the work—then interview their references, draw up a construction schedule and finally, make sure everyone is doing their job on time and on budget. But unlike doing the work yourself, the insurance company won't pay you for your time to do all this coordinating even though you're saving them the money they would have to pay a GC for overhead and profit. (And it *does* take a lot of time—trust me, I acted as GC on the construction of my former home and it became a *full time job*.)

Another consideration to acting as your own GC is, of no small irony, the issue of liability should anything happen to a worker on your property while the repairs are being made. General contractors typically have of liability and/or worker's compensation insurance exceeding what homeowners typically carry (for homeowners, it's usually in the $300,000.00 range per incident) giving them a degree of protection most homeowners can't match. How ironic would it be that a worker who gets hurt while fixing your house winds up owning it?

Question 2: What Kind of Experience does He Have?

While it is important to know how long a contractor has been in business, it is just as important to ask what his range of experience is, what exactly has he done for exactly how long. Many contractors start out as one kind of contractor and evolve into a specialty or start in a specialty and broaden their scope and knowing the depth of experience of the specific areas of expertise is crucial. For example, if a contractor was a roofer for 19 ½ years and recently broadened into a general contractor who says he has 20 years experience, you'd want to keep in mind that his experience with coordinating subcontractors is relatively short and he may not be prepared for the numerous surprises that can crop up along the way.

But perhaps just as crucial as contracting experience is whether or not a contractor has experience working with insurance companies and how much experience he has. A contractor who has worked with insurance companies will be more prepared for all the surprises and hoops he'll have to jump through compared to a contractor who has never worked with an insurance company. Insurers demand more for less than typical customers and I've encountered a few isolated cases where a contractor has dropped a claim job before he began the repairs because the insurance company was too difficult to deal with.

Question 3: Do They Give Free Estimates?

Once you contact a contractor and tell them your situation, most contractors will offer free estimates as part of the incentive to choose them, a standard in the industry. In hurricane-devastated central Florida in 2004 however, after the third major hurricane hit the area a very, very strange thing happened: some contractors were so overwhelmed by the number of people calling for estimates that they eventually started telling homeowners they would not give them an estimate unless the homeowner signed a contract for their services. Most people I met who encountered this scenario refused to go along with signing a blank or blanket contract and while it's impossible to say whether or not those contractors were honest, upstanding contractors (and most have to be or they don't last long) and were simply overwhelmed by the demand for their services (entirely plausible in this extreme and rare situation), generally when this happens, it's time to move onto the next contractor.

As stated above, the test of the reliability of a contractor is whether or not he delivered his estimate when he said he would. If he told you it would be a few days before he had an estimate ready and it took two weeks, that may be the first indicator of what is ahead should you choose him.

Question 4: Are They Licensed and Bonded?

Every state issues contractor licenses and while not every state requires every contractor to be licensed—in some states, if you're caught practicing without a license, you could go to jail and pay a fine—it's a good bet that if a contractor *doesn't* have a license he is not legitimate. All legitimate contractors who are licensed can and should carry a card/license that fits nicely in a wallet or a pocket. Ask to see a contractor's pocket license. And it's a good idea to ask to see his driver's license to make sure that the name on the contractor's license and the name and photo on the driver's license actually match—it's a big no-no to use another contractor's license.

Some states require contractors who are licensed also to be bonded, which basically means the contractor posts cash or a bond with a surety company so that if the contractor violates state or local Business Codes a homeowner can collect compensation.

Question 5: Do They Have Insurance?

Another question to ask any prospective contractor is whether he has worker's compensation coverage and liability insurance coverage.

If you've had a claim then you know the unexpected can happen at any moment. Unfortunately, as alluded to above, if a contractor doesn't have worker's compensation coverage for his employees and an employee gets injured while working on your property, you may be held responsible. Likewise, a contractor needs to have liability insurance coverage just in case he accidentally damages your property while fixing it. For example, if he backs his vehicle into your previously undamaged garage door, you'll want to make sure that you don't have to pay for his mistake. It's always a good idea to get verification that a contractor who says he is insured is actually insured.

Question 6: What are the Terms of Payment?

When and how a contractor expects to be paid can also be an indicator of whether a contractor is legitimate or not. Most contractors will *not* expect full payment of work before the job is started. If a contractor requests full payment up front, this could be an indicator that he may not be financially stable or is a crook—if a contractor is not financially stable, a lien may be placed against your property if the contractor doesn't pay *his* supplier or workers. The majority of contractors I have come across usually request half of the estimated cost of repairs up front, and the rest due upon completion; some ask for 10% up front, some ask for 60%, some don't ask a cent. However the contractor expects to be paid, it's vital to find out before you sign a contract when and how you are expected to pay a contractor. Another important issue to iron out with a contractor before he begins is whether he expects to be paid per task/job or per hour. I strongly recommend homeowners insist on a contract that pays the contractor by the job and not by the hour and have this written into the contract.

Question 7: What is the Timetable for Repairs?

Let's say you get three estimates. The first two contractors tell you the repairs will take six to eight weeks to complete. The third contractor insists that once he gets in there it will only take two weeks. The old adage, "If it sounds too good to be true, it probably is" applies to contractors who give unrealistic or fantastical timetables for getting repairs made. Good, legitimate contractors will know approximately when they can start and when they will be done and bad contractors lie about the promptness with which they can start and when they will be done. Many factors influence when contractors are able to start and how long it takes to finish a job, including availability of materials or waste receptacles, the number of workers, the experience and skill level of the contractor, the complexity of the job, any building code or additional insurance company inspections that are necessary. Before choosing a contractor, sit down with him and discuss timetables and get firm dates on when he says he is available.

However, if you've never had work done on you property, you should be aware that even the best contractors with the best intentions often encounter unforeseen delays. Frankly, delays are inevitable and unless the job is a one trade task (replacing a roof, for example, which for composition roofing should only take a day or two, depending on the size of the roof) always add one to three days for each area/room being worked on from what a contractor tells you how long it will take him.

Question 8: What about Cleanliness?

Does the contractor clean up after himself/his crew every day, once a week, or wait until the job is done to clean up? Most homeowners don't think about this, but major repairs or renovations create a tremendous amount of debris and dust, especially when work is done on the interior of a home and there is sawdust and drywall involved (again, I speak from experience). It is important for homeowners to ask what steps a contractor will take to reduce or eliminate dust and debris and, if the homeowner plans to live in the house, what kind of barriers the contractor will put up to reduce particulate matter from drifting into the undamaged areas of the home. For one-trade contractors, roofers for example, they often won't clean up until after they are done, which is normal for a relatively short job. One question for roofers is if they use a metal detector when they're done to find the loose nails or staples that often fall into the yard.

Question 9: Does He Guarantee his Work?

Most legitimate contractors will offer a limited guarantee on the workmanship of their repairs. The duration of a guarantee can range from a month or two to a year or more. The main idea to keep in mind is that contractors will guarantee the *work* that he performed and not necessarily the materials used: quite often, the materials will have a separate warranty of their own and it is important to get in writing any guarantees for the materials used. I once encountered a lady who had some work done on her roof and was told by the contractor that the roofing shingles he used had a warranty against defects; however, when she called some months later to report defective shingles (which I told her about after she asked me nicely to look at her roof even though it had nothing to do with the claim) the contractor blew her off and denied that he'd ever said there was guarantee of anything.

If the contractor offers guarantees for his work, double check to make sure that the guarantees are written into the contract for the work and are not simply stated verbally.

Question 10: Does he have References?

Most people have enough sense to know that before a contractor is settled upon, the most important thing about a contractor is not his sales pitch or the cleanliness of his teeth or the kind of car he drives, but his references. References, references, references—they're the ABCs of finding a good, reliable contractor and good, reliable contractors are eager to give out references. If a contractor doesn't want to give you references or you discover all his references are also his relatives, that's a good sign of a bad contractor.

Here are some suggestions of things to ask a contractor's references:

• What work or repairs did the contractor do?

- Has the contractor worked with you (or your company) previously and if so, how long have you and the contractor been doing business together?
- Did the contractor do everything he said he was going to do?
- Did the contractor give a timetable for when the work would be completed? Did he stick to the timetable—and if not, did he notify you of delays?
- Was the property or area kept in order while the work was being done?
- Did he clean the area of all debris after work was completed?
- Did the quality of workmanship meet your expectations?
- If the contractor made mistakes, did he fix them promptly? Did he charge for these corrections?
- Was the contractor and his employees professional and courteous?
- Were there any disputes with the contractor? If so, how were they resolved?
- Are you related to the contractor?
- (And perhaps most importantly) Would you use this contractor again?

Chapter 9: Settling Your Claim: What Insurance Companies Don't Want You to Know

It was mentioned earlier (and on more than one occasion) the trap that many homeowners who have property damage claims fall into of thinking that an estimate from an insurer is what they will *allow* for damages makes insurers very happy. Really, who are they to make sure that homeowners understand that they are actually on equal footing with insurers when this misconception gives insurers an advantage? For each homeowner who believes this malarkey the more powerful insurers become. An estimate is not an *allowance*, the dollar amounts are not chiseled in stone.

One of the more interesting things about homeowners policies, if it's not a complete oxymoron to say that *any* part of an insurance policy is interesting, is that the wording of all policies fail to specifically indicate how much an insurance company can and will pay to repair or replace damaged property. On page 39 in the Conditions section, under Loss Settlement, number 3, item C., number 3, the sample policy states, "payments are restricted to what is actually and necessarily spent to repair or replace the damaged portion or portions of the buildings or other structures with the same construction for the equivalent use on the same premises." *What is actually and necessarily spent to repair or replace the damage*: in other words, an insurance company must pay the actual costs of repair or replacement for the same construction or the same item—not necessarily the amount *they* say it should cost. Insurance companies can't simply dictate prices (although they try to), they can't tell you how much something will cost to be repaired or replaced, all they can tell you is the price they don't want to pay. This the first key to understanding the settlement process, that every claim is, in essence, a *negotiation*. An insurance company can (and will) put forth how much they think it will cost to repair or replace damaged building items (personal property items are a slightly different story), but if you have replacement cost coverage, they are duty bound to pay the full replacement cost (up to the policy limits) of whatever was damaged, lost, stolen or destroyed, regardless of what those prices may be for equivalent construction and material. This is one of the policy provisions that insurance companies don't go out of their way to advertise and for good reason. Keep in mind, however, an insurance company is not going to pay $10,000.00 to replace a $500.00 section of fencing, they're not going to pay unreasonable amounts or amounts that aren't in line with local practices and standards.

In the same section of the policy (Section I – Conditions, number 9, Loss Payment), it also states that the insurance company and the homeowner must be in agreement before payment can be issued, which is insurance speak for "the insurance company must *approve* of the cost of the repairs before repairs begin." But it also means that you don't have to blindly accept what they put forth and that you have as much power as they do when it comes to loss settlement, that you have as much power as they do to decide whether to accept or decline a settlement offer. The policy is a contract between insurer and homeowner/policyholder and both sides must abide by it, putting homeowners on equal footing with insurers.

Who Should Settle Your Claim?

The first thing a homeowner needs to determine is *who* is the best person to settle a claim. Who should settle a claim depends on the type and complexity of a claim: the abilities and experience of the person settling the claim should match those of the person settling it. The four different people (or kinds of people) who most frequently settle claims with insurance companies are: the homeowner/policy holder; the contractor who will actually perform the restoration work; a public adjuster; or an attorney.

Homeowner/policy holder. Types of claims: personal property only claims; simple structural damage claims, like replacing a prefabricated utility shed that isn't wired for electricity or a fence-only claim.

If the damaged items are considered collectibles (artwork, rare books, stamp collections, items that actually appreciate in value over time), a homeowner can attempt to settle the claim himself but eventually most homeowners will want to hire a professional appraiser (the insurance company will hire their own appraiser who, if he wants their business in the future, will appraise the items a little on the low side) and settle the claim in arbitration/appraisal. For more on this see the section below on Personal Property Losses.

Claims for Additional Living Expenses (ALE), the additional cost of living away from a home when insurable damages render a property uninhabitable can and should be handled by homeowners themselves. For more on this see Chapter 22 in Part IV, Additional Living Expenses.

Contractor. Types of claims: moderate to total losses for structural property only. If there is damage from a hurricane, tornado, earthquake, flood, hail, fire, sewer and drain back up, typically a contractor should first be used to settle a claim.

For most types of real property damage, if the damages are covered by insurance and there is no dispute whether or not damages are covered, the firm doing the repairs will negotiate directly with the insurer, sometimes line item by line item. The upside of having a contractor negotiate directly with an insurer is that it doesn't cost a homeowner anything and will also save time and undue stress over having to act as an intermediary between a contractor and insurer.

If the primary issue of a claim is whether or not items are covered, insurers will want to see an opinion from a contractor stating what they consider to be to the cause of loss. From there, attorneys may have to be involved.

Public Adjuster. Types of claims: severe to catastrophic loss to personal property and structural damage. A good rule of thumb is if you are able to live in the home after the damages, a public adjuster should not be used.

Like contractors, Public Adjusters should only be used if a claim is covered under your insurance policy and there is no dispute about coverage. PAs, as they are called, are more prevalent in the Eastern U.S. than anywhere else and in some places (namely Philadelphia, Pennsylvania) they have a reputation for being unnecessarily aggressive. Public Adjusters do not perform repairs, they only estimate what repairs should cost—which, coincidentally, is the same function as a contractor—and negotiate with insurers over the initial settlement amount, billing homeowners a percentage of the Replacement Cost Value. THESE FEES ARE NOT COVERED BY YOUR INSURANCE. This is money you will have to pay out of pocket, or out of the settlement check if you don't have a few extra hundred or a few thousand dollars sitting around. PAs will work with the insurance company adjuster to bulk up an estimate (and coincidentally, their fees) and push and squeeze and badger the insurance company representative until seemingly every penny has been wrung out of a claim, collect his check and say *sayonara*. Their commitment ends with the initial settlement.

While homeowners who use a PA may get more money up front and feel less like their insurer has given them the shaft, this sense of fulfilment is not only temporary, it is a complete illusion. Public Adjusters don't actually settle claims once and for all. Their entire focus is on the front end of a claim, the initial settlement amount. This brings about two problems. First, after a PA has settled a claim with an insurer, a homeowner still has to find a contractor who will perform the repairs/restoration for the price negotiated by the PA; if the contractor says it will cost even more than what the PA or the insurance company says it will, this will add unnecessary delays to the restoration of a property. The second problem is that when the extent of damages is sufficient to require a PA, it is inevitable that supplemental payments (those Invisible Squirrels, usually paid after repairs have begun) for unforeseen issues and additional damages discovered during the restoration process will be required even after the best Public Adjuster has settled a claim—like adjusters and contractors, PAs don't have X-ray eyes, they can't see behind walls and under floors for hidden damages. Keep in mind that an insurance company is duty bound to pay the actual cost of repairs and when the repairs are extensive and complex, more often than not the initial settlement amount is much less than the final/ actual cost of repairs, rendering the use of a Public Adjuster on large complex claims completely moot. You will have paid hundreds or even thousands of dollars for an incomplete service, an especially bad situation considering that the exact same service comes free with repairs when you use a contractor to settle a claim.

Personally, I admire PAs about as much as I do insurance companies. The one thing they have in common is that they are equally willing and eager to take advantage of unsuspecting homeowners who don't know the claims process. PAs are unnecessary in the claims process and should be avoided.

Attorney. Types of claims: moderate to catastrophic damage to a property or home in which the insurance company declares that the damages are not covered or when the insurer refuses to settle a covered claim for the actual cost of repair.

An attorney should only be used as a last resort, only when the insurance company leaves a homeowner no other alternative. Insurance companies don't like to be sued—they like it almost as much as they like paying claims—not because of the money they lose (they can always raise rates), but because of the bad publicity it inevitably brings. An insurance company will only force a homeowner to sue them when it is absolutely necessary, when caving in to a homeowner would set a precedent that would force them to start paying types of claims that they had heretofore decided not to cover.

There are two examples of this. First, in Wisconsin, in Scheidler v. American Family Insurance, a couple sued American Family after their sump pump suffered a mechanical failure which caused water to damage their basement. Not having a sewer or drain backup/sump pump overflow endorsement (which would have automatically provided coverage), American Family denied the claim. However, the Scheidlers sued American Family on the grounds that mechanical failure was covered under their policy and that damages resulting from mechanical failure are covered, despite sump pump overflow being specifically excluded. The Scheidlers won and ever since, in Wisconsin only, American Family has covered structural damages resulting from sump pump mechanical failure.

The second example came after Hurricane Katrina, when thousands of homeowners on the Gulf Coast were forced to sue their insurance company (most notably, State Farm) when the insurance companies, following State Farm's lead, said that the damages to buildings were not caused by wind (which would have been covered) but by flood/storm surge (which is not covered, even if the storm surge is caused by wind), without any evidence to back it up. Usually, insurers try to give homeowners the benefit of the doubt when the cause of the damage is unclear, but in the case of State Farm, one stingy claims manager called in engineering firm after engineering firm until one gave her a report that suited her and allowed her to justify denying the claims. This irresponsible manager essentially manufactured the evidence to deny claims and in the end State Farm got what it deserved—they lost the first case against them and after being forced to pay $223,292.00 in property damages and $2.5 million in punitive damages to Norman and Genevieve Broussard of Biloxi, Mississippi they decided to actually be fair and friendly ("Good Neighbors") and began to settle other cases out of court, based upon unbiased engineering reports that stated that the damages to the properties in question were caused in part by wind. In the case of the Gulf Coast after Katrina, the sheer numbers of potential plaintiffs combined with potential multimillion punitive damages combined with volumes of bad publicity forced the insurance companies to stop forcing homeowners to sue them, though at the time of publication for this book, there are still several on-going court cases that have yet to be resolved.

Settling Your Claim

Regardless who settles a claim, there are two keys to keep in mind: 1) your insurer MUST pay the actual cost of repairs; and 2) the more detailed your settlement proposal, the faster your claim will get settled. Insurance companies give estimates not only for their sake (to help control their costs), but also so homeowners know the approximate range of a bid that is reasonable and within community standards. With an estimate in hand, an insurance company will expect you to know when a contractor is trying to price gouge you and them, and they will do their best to not allow that to happen. As stated earlier, an insurance company estimate is not written in stone, it is not the final and only amount they can and will pay; they understand that the final costs may be higher than what they originally estimated. But insurance companies also want to know that a homeowner has made a reasonable attempt to find the fairest price for the repairs, even if they choose a contractor whose bid is the highest.

Homeowners and contractors alike put emphasis on the bottom line without taking stock of the fine print of an insurance company estimate. One of the problems (if you can call it a problem) is that insurance company estimates are *all* fine print—you always know exactly what work is being suggested and how much they want to pay for it, whereas some contractor's estimates are not as nearly detailed. I've seen numerous contractor estimates that read like the following roof replacement estimate: "Remove existing shingles, haul away. Replace with new 25 year shingles: $4500.00." Seems harmless enough, seems straightforward: he'll replace the roof for $4500.00. The problem with this estimate is that it doesn't say *how many* square feet of shingles are being removed or replaced and one can only infer that it includes accessories like vents or flashings. Unless this estimate is the same or below an insurer's estimate, most insurance companies will balk at making final payments based upon a contractor's simple estimate like this because insurance companies like to know what they're paying for, they like to know what they're getting for their money. In the roofing example above, they want to know how many square feet of shingles will be used; if a roof has 10 squares—1000 square feet—the insurance company will want to know if the contractor is billing them for 10 squares or 30 squares.

That being said, the first set of details that need to be agreed upon is the Scope of Repairs. As a reminder, the Scope of Repairs is the blueprint from which a written estimate is based, the listing of what needs to be repaired, where it is located, the quantities and quality of materials used to make the repairs. Once it is agreed upon what exactly needs to be done, what kinds of materials and how much of the materials will be needed then the two parties can begin to agree upon *how* to make the repairs. This is where the estimate comes into play. An estimate is essentially a recipe for the repairs to a damaged property and the trick is to get two chefs to agree on the exact recipe for repairs at the same price while shopping at two different supermarkets.

The more complex the repairs, the more likely there are going to be discrepancies in the method and quantities needed for repair. The first thing that needs to be ironed out is what is and isn't included in the differing estimates: often a contractor's estimate will have line items that are not in the insurance company estimate and vice versa. What often happens is that estimates are compared line item by line item and any differences are ironed out between the two. If the adjuster is not very experienced, there may be a large number of items not included in his estimate. Some items may not be in an insurance company's estimate simply because the insurer won't pay them unless the costs are actually incurred, such as the tearing off existing shingles for a roof replacement (some contractors will put a second or third layer of composition shingles over existing damaged shingles, which is never a good idea but is much less expensive than complete removal.) Some items won't be included without justification and a contractor may have to put into writing why an item may be needed. For example: a three-story house needs roof repairs and the roofing contractor submits an estimate to remove and reset 30 feet of fencing in the back yard. Why would a roofing contractor give an estimate to lift out a section of fencing for a roof repair? In this case, due to the landscape the only access to the roof is from the back side of the house and to get access with the proper equipment they would have to take out the fencing and then put it back when done.

Once all of the fine print is settled upon and the insurer and contractor have the same scope of repairs and the same line items in their estimates, then consideration should be given to the bottom line. If the bottom lines are close, less then a hundred dollars, for example, then no problem, a minor adjustment here and there (adding a bundle of shingles, a few more square feet of carpeting, etc.) and voilà, claim settled. If the difference is more than a few hundred dollars, or even a thousand or more, all is not lost. The prices insurance companies use are median prices, meaning some contractors will charge more for one thing and some contractors will charge less for the same thing. When a contractor's overall price is higher than the going rate, then his charging slightly more then the median has to be justified.

This is where creativity and a little touch of imagination come into play on the part of the adjuster and the contractor. They both want the claim settled, they're both, at this point, pretty sick and tired of going back and forth on the scope of repairs and the estimate and want to put this thing to bed. When the gap between bottom lines is just enough to freak out upper management to be settled then and there, a justification is going to have to be inserted into an estimate in the form of what I'll call "creative adjusting." In some cases there may be actual reasons like difficult access to the damaged area or line of sight issues that fall into a grey area, but often the justification has to be pulled out of thin air or be an embellishment of an actual circumstance. Sometimes this justification comes in the form of a single line item; sometimes it is several lines items peppered throughout an estimate. An example: for a carpet replacement for a house that has an octagonal sunroom that opens to a square living room: "Additional charge for unusual number of cuts and angles due to the irregular shape of the sun room: $500.00." Or with siding replacement: "Additional scaffolding necessary due to the steep hillside on rear side of house: $300.00"—even though the "steep hillside" is a gentle slope going away from the home. This may sound like a lot of BS and the reason it may sound like BS is because that is exactly what it is. If insurance companies always estimated for the highest going rate, they would go out of business—premiums would be unaffordable. If they estimated only the lowest rate, claims would never get settled. In cases where rock meets hard place, sometimes a little axel grease is required, sometimes a little BS justification on the part of the contractor and the adjuster is just what the doctor ordered. In the brief cases above, the insurance company representative and the contractor agrees that they have essentially invented a reason for the claims to be settled when nothing else worked.

Appraisal/Arbitration

If it happens that a claim can't be settled and come hell or high water neither homeowner or insurer can agree on a settlement amount, before the lawyers are brought in, it is strongly suggested that the claim be put through the process of appraisal or arbitration. Most insurers call it appraisal, some may call it arbitration or mediation.

Each insurance company does something slightly different when it comes to appraisal, but the general process is about the same. Regardless of who initiates appraisal, each party selects an impartial appraiser to assess the value of the claim. These appraisers then select an impartial umpire to resolve any monetary differences between appraisers. Each appraiser does a valuation of the claim and submit their findings to one another. While the chances of two appraisals matching exactly are roughly the same odds as getting hit by lightning while holding a winning lottery ticket, if they do agree on an amount, case closed. Otherwise, the appraisers will attempt to reconcile the differences; if they can't, the umpire will take a gander at both appraisals and decide which one to settle upon or else determine a settlement amount. Generally, each party pays for their own appraiser and split the costs of the umpire. There is a time limit (typically 20 to 30 days) for each party telling the other who they have selected as their appraiser, so ask your insurance company what that time limit is if it is not stated in the policy.

Arbitration is similar in format, just replace the word "appraiser" with arbitrator. Some insurers require that all Arbitration be handled through the American Arbitration Association; some require that arbitration be done in accordance with the guidelines of the AAA, unless a suitable equivalent can be found and agreed to by both parties. Some insurers' guidelines state that both parties must agree upon an impartial arbiter in advance and have procedures set in place in case both parties can't even agree upon an impartial juror. Some insurers require that the party requesting the arbitration pay all arbitration expenses, while others will split the cost evenly with the homeowner.

With all the variations in the arbitration process, it is recommended that if a homeowner is considering initiating it that he does his homework with regards to his insurer's specific requirements and processes and the process of arbitration in general. In addition, it is recommended that, unless a homeowner is an experienced attorney or has ample experience in arbitration, that he acquire all the assistance he can avail himself to, be it an attorney with arbitration experience, a contractor who can speak with authority about repair techniques and pricing or other appropriate experts such as engineers.

For more information on arbitration, please go to www.Claim-GameBook.com and click on Resources.

Personal Property

As stated above, personal property (Coverage B) in some cases is handled slightly differently than Coverage A, building property. Generally speaking, if a piece of personal property loses value over time, you should get the full replacement cost value (assuming you have replacement cost coverage) when it is replaced. This applies to most Coverage B items: furniture, electronic equipment, power tools. However, if an item gains in value over time like fine art, antiques, collectible items (stamps, buttons/pins), then the insurance company is going to pay the Actual Cash Value, which means what the insurer deems to be the fair market value. This latter provision also applies for property that is not useful for its original or intended purpose; for example, a railroad car used as a storage shed or garage or an elevator car used as a closet. In these cases, if the items had been damaged and declared a total loss, the homeowners would get either the scrap metal value or the current value of a junked railroad car or a useless elevator car.

For depreciable/replaceable personal property items settlement is usually simple and quick: often you know how much you paid for ordinary things or have receipts for them. But keep in mind that if an item can be repaired, the insurance company will pay to have it repaired.

Typically if an item is destroyed an adjuster will first ask if you have the original receipt for the damaged item; if not, an estimated replacement price is either negotiated between the homeowner and the adjuster (for smaller dollar items like birdhouses and flower pots) or the price of an item is researched by the adjuster or the insurance company's pricing specialists. This is a typical settlement: if a tree falls on your five year-old gas grill and demolishes it but you don't have the original receipt, once the price of a grill of similar size, features and BTUs has been researched (a trip to Home Depot or similar store will do), you will get paid the Actual Cash Value until the grill is actually replaced. If want to buy a bigger, fancier grill, naturally you'll have to pay for the upgrade yourself.

For items damaged by power surge or lightning strike—electronics, appliances, microwaves, etc.—they need to be taken to or looked at by a repair technician to determine the cause of loss, whether or not it was damaged by an insurable loss like lightning and power surge or if it just stopped working, and also to determine if it is repairable or not. Make sure to get the analysis in writing from the repair technician. If an item can be repaired for less than what it cost to replace it, the insurance company will pay to have it repaired, otherwise they will pay to replace it. As with building items, depreciation is never taken for the repair of items, only when they are replaced.

Appraisal

Appraisal occurs most often for personal property items that gain in value as they age such as fine art, collectibles, or items that cannot be replace with new articles. The process for personal property items is the same as above.

To initiate the Appraisal process, inform the insurance company that an appraisal is necessary. Once that is done, if you haven't already, obtain an appraiser; the insurance company will obtain their own. There is a time limit (typically 20 to 30 days) for each party telling the other who they have selected as their appraiser, so ask your insurance company what that time limit is if it is not stated in the policy. The appraisers then get together and attempt to agree on a value; if they do, that's the amount of the settlement. If they can't agree, the two appraisers then select an umpire and whichever figure the umpire agrees with, that becomes the amount of settlement. If an umpire is necessary, generally the cost for him is split between homeowner and insurance company.

Salvage and "Buy Back"

There's an old saying, "you break it, you buy it." With insurance companies, that expression becomes "Mother Nature breaks it, we own it." In Section I – Conditions, number 8, Our Option, the policy declares that property they pay for or replace becomes their property. This is what the industry calls Salvage; anything that mother nature (or any other type of covered loss—a drunk driver parking in your living room) damages or destroys is now owned by the insurance company once they pay for it, and theoretically this applies to anything that is damaged, though typically Salvage usually refers only to personal property items, provided the damaged item still has some actual value left in it. Homeowners have no choice in this matter, unless they wish to give the money back and not claim the damaged item. A common example would be cloth seated patio chairs that gets nicked by hail, the seats now slightly (and only cosmetically) damaged: the items have been altered by a covered loss (hail) and the homeowners want to claim them and they want new chairs. Once the homeowners are paid to replace the chairs, at their option, the insurance company may hire a company to pick up these items and have them sold at auction to someone who doesn't mind patio furniture with a few nicks in the cloth. However, insurance companies typically don't like to do this:

it takes a lot of time, coordination and manpower, all of which costs them money. What they prefer is for homeowners to "Buy Back" the damaged items.

Using the example above, cloth covered patio furniture, if a homeowner decides to claim the damaged furniture but tells the insurance company that their just-out-of-college son wants to use the slightly damaged set, then the insurance company will offer to sell it back to them, which means that the homeowner gets a partial or discounted settlement for the furniture. If a brand-new set cost $1000.00 and the damaged set was two years old and this type of furniture depreciates at 10% a year, the Actual Cash Value, due homeowners at the time of settlement, would be $800.00 ($1,000.00 − 20%/$200 = $800) until they bought a new set, at which time they would get a total of $1000.00. The adjuster offers to sell the furniture back to the homeowners so they get a total settlement of $400.00 cash, plus they get to keep the furniture. Let's say the homeowners request $600.00. For the sake of argument, let's say both parties agree split the difference and the homeowner gets a check for $500.00—and they still get to keep a set of slightly nicked patio furniture. This is one of the rare instances when both the insurance company and the homeowner benefit: instead of paying $1000.00 to replace a new set and then recouping maybe two or three hundred dollars (after the salvage company and auction company take their cut), the insurance company only has to pay $500.00; and the homeowners get $500.00 in addition to the furniture—and if they want to, they can sell it to someone else and buy a new set. I think I read this example in a SAT test once.

There is no pre-set amount or percentage that insurance companies will subtract/discount from a settlement in order to sell an item back to a homeowner: this is purely a negotiation, as fluid and up to interpretation as a building estimate. Keep in mind that you don't *have* to buy back damaged property—but don't forget that the insurance company would *really* like it if you did, which you can always use to your advantage.

The Buy Back provision of settlement is frequently offered to a homeowner when one item of a pair or set is damaged and the insurance company doesn't want to pay to replace the entire set (which is how the policy is written—it's their option to replace part or all of a set, and guess which they would prefer to do). But they don't have to offer Buy Back, either. In a situation in which part of a pair or set is damaged, the insurance company may offer one of three things: pay the Replacement Cost of the lone damaged article, returning the pair or set to how much it was worth before damaged occurred (for the example above, if only one patio chair in a set of four was damaged, they might pay to replace that one patio chair, at a cost of $250.00); offer to sell back the lone damaged item (assuming it is still usable and not completely obliterated or blown away as in the case of a tornado or hurricane); or pay the difference between what the pair or set was worth before and after the loss: using the patio furniture example above, if one patio chair out of four was damaged, the insurance company would offer the ACV of the full set—$800—minus the value of the set now (three chairs)—$600.00—in this case, $200.00. Ask your adjuster about all your options.

Chapter 10: Destination: Restoration

O h, the fun part! The sawdust, gypsum dust, nails scattered everywhere, the giant dumpster in the driveway. At least there's light at the end of the funnel cloud at this point. Naturally, as insurance companies are wont to do, there are also restrictions and limitations placed on this aspect of a claim. For instance, homeowners must notify the insurance company of their intention to make the repairs/replacement within 60 days (this varies from insurer to insurer) after the ACV payment has been issued. Why? Well, it's not because they want to throw you a home repair party. They want to know what's happening to their money, whether or not you've put that money toward the insured property or a nice trip to the Bahamas. Oddly enough, though, in all my years as an adjuster, only once have I received letter from a homeowner stating his intentions to make the repairs; everyone else just gets the repairs done.

Time is Not on Your Side: Limitations on Collecting Payments

While it varies from insurer to insurer, one thing is the same regardless of the insurance company: homeowners have a limited amount of time to collect payment for Replacement Cost Benefits. Some insurers give homeowners six months, some one year, some give them two years.

The time limit to collect payments begins from the Date of Loss, *not* from the date you receive your first payment. If your adjuster does not tell you the time limit for collecting payment (though he should), it can be found in **Section I – Conditions**, Loss Settlement.

However, this time limit does not necessarily mean that you actually have to complete every last repair to collect Replacement Cost Benefits: with some insurers, once they receive a signed and dated contract between a policyholder and a contractor, they will release the Replacement Cost Benefits. The same time limitations apply to personal property: if you have replacement cost coverage and don't actually replace the damaged items within the time limit, you forfeit the remaining replacement cost funds owed you.

The reason for a time limitation (as the kids say these days) is *so* insurance company: they don't want to have to pay you unless they *have* to and if you don't play by their rules, if you don't follow the policy and their time limits, they won't have to pay you. More money for them, woo-hoo! Another executive gets that Porsche he's been eyeing!

But what if you're not working with a contractor, what if you decide to do the work yourself? If you're like most Americans, you feed on a steady diet of procrastination (if you filed your taxes at 11:59pm on April 15, this is probably you) and if you are fairly certain that you are not going to make the six month to two year deadline (now, come on, *two years*, what's wrong with you, man?!) you'll need to call your insurance company and request an extension. With some insurers, however, you'll also have to put it in writing as well—just think of it as a really exciting opportunity to put off doing something *else*!

The same goes for homeowners who aren't going to make the repairs themselves. If you or your contractor need more time than the stated limit, call your insurer and let them know you'll need more time and request an extension.

###

Living Allowance: ALE

Ah, yes, another form of insurance, another time limit, typically 12 months from the date of loss in the case of ALE (Additional Living Expenses). ALE is for when a loss makes a house or property unlivable, forcing you to temporarily move out, covering the expenses to live elsewhere while the house is being inspected for damages and repaired. Sometimes, though, there are situations when the damages to your property may not be enough to cause you to move out, but the *repairs* from those damages do force you to temporarily move out.

Insurance companies are very picky about who gets ALE and what situations warrant it. Typically they don't like to pay ALE during the repair phase of a claim unless they absolutely have to. ALE during repairs can become a very subjective area and if you want it, you're going to have to fight for it. In some cases, living in a house during repairs or construction can be *inconvenient* but not *impossible*. If living in a home is not possible, such as when there is no bathroom or if there is nowhere to sleep, an insurer will be compelled to pay ALE. If it is reasonable that you are able to live with the inconvenience of the repairs—piles of furniture crammed into one room, the pounding of hammers on the roof at seven in the morning, gypsum dust swirling about the air—the insurance company will want you to live there, and if you want to stay in a hotel, it's on your dime. However, there are always exceptions to mere inconvenience: if there is a pregnant woman living in the house and her doctor advises that inhaling paint fumes and gypsum dust and insulation should be avoided, the insurance company should grant ALE. If there is an infant or frail elderly person in the home, consideration for ALE should be given. If there is no kitchen, at the very least, *partial* ALE should be given, to cover food expenses. In the latter case ALE would only cover the expenses *above and beyond* what you normally spend for food, including what is typically spent on dining out.

For more details and a wonderfully in-depth look at ALE, please see Chapter 22.

Making upgrades

So a tornado passed through and sucked a sliding patio door completely out, leaving a gaping hole in the rear of the house. When nature gives you lemons, make lemonade, right? Instead of just replacing the sliding patio door (which would be covered by insurance), why not take advantage of the situation and build an addition onto the house (which would *not* be covered by insurance)—heck, the tornado just did ¾ of the demolition work a contractor would have to do to create an opening to an addition, so why not?

It *should* go without saying, but if you plan to make upgrades or improvements to your property, the insurance company is not going to pay for them—they're only going to pay the full replacement cost (if the policy is a replacement cost policy) of the original materials and construction of the loss. But, hey, sometimes you've just had enough of that garish orange shag carpet from 1976 and want to put in wood floors. Sometimes you want to upgrade from 25-year asphalt roof shingles to 30-year shingles. Good for you.

Here's how you do it.

1) Get an estimate from your contractor for the repairs covered by your homeowners insurance.

2) Get another estimate from the same contractor for all of the work, including upgrades. Set it aside.

3) Show the first estimate to your insurer.

4) Have your contractor negotiate a settlement as if he was going to do only the repairs covered by your insurance. Once a settlement is agreed upon, have the work done.

5) When the work is completed, give your insurer the final bill (with the upgrades on it) and tell them that you made some upgrades (warning: upgrades may increase the value of your home and therefore your premiums) and that you understand that this additional work isn't covered, but you'd like any Replacement Cost benefits that are pending. The insurer will then pay the negotiated Replacement Cost benefits. With the claim paid, the homeowner gets all that was owed him and

nothing more.

The objective is simply to get all that is owed you, to maximize your settlement without ripping anybody off. Sometimes getting an estimate and/or paying the final bill for repair in these situations can get a little complicated unless you have a simple system like the one above to separate who did what work when for how much and who's paying for it. Good contractors will have no problem giving *two* estimates should you decide to throw a little more work their way; you just want to make sure you and the insurance company understand and are clear about who is paying for what and for how much: sorting out a quagmire of paperwork and receipts can delay final or supplemental payments and delays can cost you if your contractor isn't paid on time.

Supplemental Payments

Supplemental payments, as mentioned earlier, are payments issued for items or repairs that are above and beyond the original, settled upon scope of repairs. Supplemental payments can include such things as hidden damages, intricacies in repairs not discovered until well into the repair process—finding asbestos below a layers of plaster would be an example—additional amounts of materials needed for a project, or simply when something wasn't noticed or taken into consideration by contractor and adjuster alike. Supplemental payments are common and expected for most large complicated insurance claims. As with any part of a claim, any request for additional payment has to be for damages that were directly or indirectly caused by the original loss or the result of the original loss.

Unless a homeowner is doing the work himself, typically a contractor will handle all supplemental claims, contacting the adjuster or claim representative directly and letting him know what needs to be included. Normally, the supplemental claim payment is based upon the contractor's request or needs (basically, they submit a bill or proposal) and sometimes the contractor is paid directly, other times the additional funds are issued to the homeowner, depending upon the procedure of the insurer. Contractors who work frequently with insurance companies know the procedure for supplemental claims and also know that, in some cases, an adjuster may need to come out and take additional photos, like when hidden damages are discovered. Experienced contractors will take photos (camera phones are wonderfully handy for this sort of thing) before any work is done or have the homeowner take photos to document the hidden damages. Contractors who don't often work with insurance companies may not know the procedure of filing and receiving payment for supplemental claims. If you are working with a contractor who hasn't dealt with many insurance companies in the past, you may have to handle the supplemental payment requests yourself.

Luckily, all this entails is a phone call to the insurance company and having the contractor amend his estimate to include the additional necessary work or items. If the work needs documentation and needs to be done *right away*, the insurance company will want you to take a photo if an adjuster isn't available to view the additional damages himself. Naturally, if you're planning to do the work yourself, the onus is on you to make sure all supplemental claims are reported and documented.

Lien Releases

Let's say you have a claim, it gets settled for a fair amount in a timely manner and the contractor you hired is reputable and does the work to your satisfaction and everything is fine—until three weeks later you receive a notice that a lien has been placed on your house by the company that supplied the construction materials to your contractor. It turns out the contractor you hired had a little girl who got cancer and instead of paying his materials supplier with the money you paid him, he used the money to pay off the astronomical medical bills that weren't covered by his own stingy insurance company. Since you didn't sign an Unconditional Lien Release with your contractor—and didn't know you were supposed to since he didn't tell you—the supplier *he* failed to pay is coming after *you* for payment on the materials used to repair your house. And if you don't pay up—that is, pay the same bill a second time—the supplier is going to end up owning *your* house.

El cheapo health insurance providers aside, this is a very real and very scary situation for all homeowners who have an insurance claim and hire a contractor to do the work. (Or who have a contractor doing *any* kind of work for them.) Without signing an *Unconditional* Lien Release, a homeowner could lose his home if the contractor doesn't pay his bills or his workers. Before any money is paid to a contractor, before one nail is hammered or one brick laid, be sure that you get your contractor to sign and date an Unconditional Lien Release, otherwise, you may be liable for a contractor's failure to pay. If the name of your mortgage company is listed on the draft payments to you, they may require your contractor, and sometimes his material suppliers, sign Unconditional Lien Releases before they endorse the check and disburse any funds. While this may sound like a pain in the you-know-what, this is one bureaucratic hurdle that is worth it, one where the return on the time and effort could turn out to be a lifesaver.

Doing the Work Yourself

For those of you who know which end of a hammer is used to drive a nail, you may feel tempted to make the final repairs to your property after a loss. The irony of making repairs yourself is that, in most cases, the actual work will often be more difficult and complicated than collecting any additional funds (i.e., Replacement Cost Benefits). But for those brave souls who feel compelled to tempt the construction gods there are a few things, aside from fielding questions about your sanity, that you need to know.

First of all, you'll need to know if your Mortgage Holder will *let* you make the repairs yourself. Some lenders may see nothing wrong with a homeowner fixing his own property, others may *require* you to hire a professional. Regardless, it is absolutely essential that you find out what flies with them and make sure you are playing by their rules. Secondly, there are the time limits mentioned earlier: limits on completing the repairs. Thirdly, like temporary repairs and securing the safety of the premises, all time spent by you and your family to make the repairs is subject to compensation up to the amount of the settlement, less the deductible. That means keeping a meticulous log of the time spent making repairs: time, date, person who did the work and what they did. It also means keeping all receipts for materials purchased and making copies. If it happens that, once all the repairs are made, the expenses for your time and the materials exceeds the initial payout (ACV payment), tell your adjuster (or whoever is handling your claim; at this point it may be someone other than the original adjuster) that you have completed the repairs and that it has exceeded the ACV payment and that you request the Replacement Cost Benefits owed to you and send him *copies* of all your receipts and Work Logs. Check to soon follow.

However, this does not mean you will automatically get the full amount of Replacement Cost Benefits that have been held back by the insurer. For example, if your estimated Replacement Costs are $5,000.00 and the depreciation taken is $2,000.00 with a $500.00 deductible (ACV payment of $2,500.00) and the cost of the materials is $2,000.00 and using their homeowner labor prices, the insurer determines your labor total was $1,000.00, instead of getting the full $2,000.00 in Replacement Cost Benefits, you would get $500.00. Since the actual cost of repairs were $3,000.00 and you were already paid $2,500, you get what's remaining of the actual cost of repairs.

Once again, the more detailed and specific your time log, the better. Also, rounding up to the nearest 15-minute increment makes you look good to the insurer, rather than rounding up to the next hour. Here's the sample work log for temporary repairs and tree debris removal from Chapter 4:

	5-11-09	5-12-09	5-13-09	5-14-09	Total
John, brace & cut oak tree off house:	4.5hrs.	3hrs.	2.5hrs.	0	10 hours
John, cut up oak tree & haul away:	0	0	0	8	8 hours
John, patch roof where oak hit:	2	0	0	0	2 hours
Bill, cut pine trees off fence:	1.25	3.75	0	0	5 hours
John, cut up pine tree & haul away:	0	2	0	0	2 hours
Bill, reset fence:	0	0	3	0	3 hours

TOTAL: 30 hrs.

However, unlike using a contractor, your insurance company won't guarantee the repairs to your property, that is to say, if you mess it up, it's your mess to keep and they won't pay to correct your ineptitude—to them, if you don't fix it right the first time, it is simple negligence on your part and that isn't covered. If you accidentally start a fire while making repairs, that *would* be covered. For a free work log go Forms at the end of this book or to www.ClaimGameBook.com/RedTape-Lounge.

Chapter 11: Denials

Booo! Hissss! No one likes the denial of a claim, not even insurance companies: it breeds bad blood and tends to cost them valuable customers. While denials are fairly common, most frequently for flood, which is only covered by the NFIP (National Flood Insurance Program), they are never ordinary. Denials are taken very seriously by insurance companies and are often given close scrutiny to make sure they are absolutely necessary and valid.

A claim can be denied for several reasons: if the cause of the loss is specifically not covered by the insurance policy, if a policyholder breaches the policy (example: if a large number of shingles are blown off your roof and you don't make temporary repairs and it rains three days later and causes of interior damage, the interior damage could be denied). One thing many homeowners may not know about denials is that an insurance company may deny *part* of a claim *or* all of a claim. A *partial* denial means the insurer pays one part of a claim while refusing to pay another: for example, if a hurricane blows shingles off a roof, causes a leak to appear on the ceiling and walls below the missing shingles *and* water seeps up from below the foundation in another part of a house and gets the carpet wet, the insurance company will cover the roof and damaged walls and ceilings but deny payment for the carpet as it would be considered groundwater, which is not covered. While every claim is different and has it own idiosyncrasies and distinctive qualities, what insurance companies look for when determining if a claim should be paid or denied is the context of a loss, the *what* and *how* of a claim: what damages occurred and how they were caused. Sometimes, though, this can appear to be subjective or up to interpretation. This is where most of the conflicts concerning denials come from, a difference of opinion and perspective: an adjuster, using his experience, may see something one way while the homeowner may see it another. Let's say a second story wooden deck collapses suddenly; the *context* of the collapse becomes very important: collapse *is* covered under the homeowner's policy if what caused the collapse is covered— but it's not covered if the cause of the collapse was something that is excluded, such as visible dry rot, improper maintenance, earth movement or poor construction. The question becomes, how and why did the deck collapse? If what caused the collapse is covered—wind, lightning, fire, accidental overloading—then the deck would be covered. If it fell in on itself because the timbers were old and rotted (or any other non-covered proximate cause), it wouldn't be covered. If an adjuster sees that some of the support posts are clearly rotted and the homeowner insists that the wind pulled the deck down, the adjuster would (or should) look for *collateral* (or corresponding) damage: downed tree limbs, shingles missing from the roof, reports from NOAA (www.spc. NOAA.gov) of high winds. For the sake of example, let's say there is no other evidence of powerful winds; the adjuster in this case is more than likely going to deny the claim due to rot. The homeowner may not agree with this assessment. What can a homeowner do if he doesn't agree with the adjuster's analysis?

When there is a difference of opinion, a homeowner has several options, within and outside of the insurance company. The least expensive option is to call your adjuster's supervisor and request a reinspection by another adjuster. Sometimes a different pair of eyes helps to see thing from a different perspective, sometimes one adjuster can catch something another adjuster missed—I've been on both ends of this, so I know that no one is perfect and even the best adjuster will miss something now and again. Having another adjuster reinspect a property is a relatively common occurrence, though it doesn't always yield what a homeowner might feel is desirable results.

If this doesn't work, the next step, a somewhat costly one, is to hire an expert: a structural engineer, an architect, or licensed general/ restoration contractor (hired as a consultant/damage investigator) to give you an opinion on the cause of the loss. Often an insurance company will offer to send a structural engineer out, on their dime, and a homeowner has to decide if he wants an engineer who is being paid by the insurance company (which does not mean the engineer will give a biased report) or hire his own. For your own protection, I recommend hiring your own experts. In the case of the collapsed deck, if an engineer gives a homeowner a report that, in his opinion, wind caused the deck to collapse, the homeowner should then forward this to the insurance company. If *this* doesn't work and the insurance company sticks to its denial, it's time to put on your climbing shoes.

Climbing the Ladder: Going up the Chain of Command

It's not an exaggeration to say that a claim is never really denied, until the President of the insurance company says it is. But before you shoot off a letter to Mr. President, and before you sue them, there are a few options at your disposal, a few rungs to climb in the chain of command before you reach that shining office on a hill. And one word of advice: don't mention the "L-word" (LAWSUIT!). Threats only stiffen resistance. You are dealing with professionals who have no personal vested interest in the outcome, so eliciting empathy always works better than breeding conflict.

The first step is to contact your adjuster's supervisor, often called a Team Manager or Group Manager. Team Managers work with field adjusters on a daily basis and are familiar with the level of expertise of the adjuster(s) who have scoped the loss and have come to depend upon their field adjuster's good judgment and are often inclined to stand by their man (or woman). To put it another way, they're not inclined to overrule people they helped to train. On the other hand, Team Managers have more experience than their adjusters and aren't afraid to use it. If the Team Manager concurs with the denial, the next rung on the ladder is his boss, often called a Regional, District or Branch Manager. At this level of management you will find professionals who have handled tens of thousands of claims, who know just about all there is to know about claims and adjusting losses. They trust the judgment of their Team leaders, but of course have the authority to heed the opinion of your hired expert and make his own decision.

The Ladder

❺ Company President

❹ Vice President of Claims

❸ Regional/District/Branch Manager

❷ Team Manager/Group Manager

❶ Adjuster

Next up is Corporate, the VP (Vice Presidents) of Claims. These are the guys who drive Porsches and Mercedes and build fancy McMansions and know piles about homeowners claims but who didn't get where they are by being radicals and railing against the system. These guys *are* the system, they are the establishment, the guys who built and maintain the status quo. But some of them also have ambition and want to separate themselves from the pack and won't turn down an opportunity for advancement by making a bold, gutsy decision. After the VPs (and there may be more than one) is the President of the insurance company. The Presidents are the disturbingly overpaid multi-multi millionaires who drive Bentleys and eat peanut butter and caviar sandwiches (just kidding) and who've reached the top and pay close attention to every penny that comes in and goes out of the company. The

President is beholden to stock holders and investors and is in a long term relationship with his company's bottom line and not only tows the line, but wears it like a suit. You'll be lucky if he takes your call.

But if you can get no satisfaction with Mr. President (is it just me or do you imagine that these guys sit around and listen to "Hail to the Chief" while no one else is around and pretend they're *the* President?) don't lose hope, there's still more avenues to explore.

The Insurance Commissioner

The Commish (yeah, don't call them that, by the way) or the head of the Department of Insurance as it is called in many states, are the governmental pit bulls that monitor the insurance industry and claims of every type—auto, home, life, health, etc.—and can launch an investigation into the doings of an insurance company should their doings be suspicious or illegal. The Insurance Commissioner's office knows the laws governing the insurance industry in their state (laws which, more and more, are being written *by* the insurance companies) and may be able to help you if their investigation determines that your insurance company hasn't been playing fair or hasn't been playing by the rules. Every state has their own laws, which vary *widely*, each Insurance Commissioner has their own level of authority and each state has it's own way of filing a complaint against insurance carriers. Every state now has a website for its Insurance Commissioner or Department of Insurance and, of course, varying levels of accessibility; some let you fill out complaint forms on-line, some require you to call or write. As each state's laws procedure for complaints, actions and authority vary, contact your state's Department of Insurance or Commissioner. For a list of state Departments of Insurance, please see the Resources section at the end of this book or www.ClaimGameBook.com/Resources.

The Last Resort: Suing Your Insurance Company

As stated earlier, an insurance company will only force a homeowner to sue them when it is absolutely necessary, when backing down from a denial would set a precedent that would force a veritable landslide of similar decisions like Scheidler v. American Family Insurance or the thousands of homeowners on the Gulf Coast who sued their insurer. When a claim is denied due to what they perceive to be a legitimate coverage issue, insurers will fight tooth and nail and spend millions of dollars not to pay for a claim that could be settled out of court for a few thousand dollars. Rarely is one lawsuit just about that one lawsuit, but about the future, about which claims an insurer is going to be forced to pay in the years to come, such as the Scheidler case. As the saying goes, you can't un-ring a bell. If coverage isn't the issue, if you're suing your insurer out of principle and not because you believe that something that clearly isn't covered should be covered, keep in mind that insurers don't really care about your principles. They care about money a whole lot more than they care about your sensibilities and your delicate sense of right and wrong. Once all other options for settlement have been exhausted, including appraisal or arbitration, then and only then should a homeowner consider litigation. By far it is the most costly and time consuming action one can take—and you had better make sure you're in the right. It goes without saying, but if you do sue your insurer you'll want to find an attorney who has successfully sued and won against a judgment against an insurance company.

There are two keys to suing your insurer. First, most homeowners policies say that suing is the last option (see **Section I – Conditions**, number 7, Lawsuit Against Us): "All legal action against us must commence within one year from the date of the loss and can only be brought after all policy conditions have been met." A homeowners policy is a contract between homeowner and insurer and it is expected that both parties follow the contract. If you've followed the instructions in this book—if you've secured the safety of the premises, done any and all necessary temporary repairs, kept a phone log of contact with your insurance company (most people can't remember exactly who they spoke to four years, three months and 22 days ago, which is what you'll be required to do in a lawsuit), if you've documented every little aspect of your claim—you will have followed the contract and have put yourself in a much more favorable position to win a lawsuit than if you haven't.

The most important part of the policy for homeowners to follow is **Section I – Conditions.** When a lawsuit occurs, the opposing side is going to nit pick every single detail of a homeowner's actions, what you did, how you did it, when you did it, what you didn't do, why you didn't do it, so on and so forth. The thing to keep in mind is that insurance companies require their adjusters and managers to document every little thing that happens in a claim, every conversation—who they talked to, the date and time—every letter, every estimate, engineering reports, every single item related to the claim. This meticulous record keeping is also going to document what you did and when you did it and also if you failed to act, if you failed to follow the exact letter of the policy conditions; if you did, they will not hesitate to use it against you.

The second key is that, as with every other aspect of a claim, there is a time limit placed upon homeowners to bring suit against them, usually one year. These time limits vary with insurers. Typically this isn't a problem except in unusual circumstances, such as Hurricane Katrina (nothing got done by anyone for a long time due to the lack of electricity, telephone lines, highways, etc. on the Gulf Coast), or in the case of a massive, wide-spread earthquake in which there just isn't any infrastructure left or enough personnel to go around and make coverage determinations and decisions.

Even though most insurance companies have armies of attorneys at their disposal, they don't like being sued. It's not so much the protracted bloodletting or expense that comes with a lengthy lawsuit but the adverse publicity that is generated by litigation. Insurers want to be your good neighbors, they want to put you in good hands and the more often they get sued, the more difficult it is to maintain an image of a good neighbor or sheltering hands—which, of course, isn't going to change the fact that they're going to do everything to win.

Part 4:

Common Losses and

Common Issues

Chapter 12: Hail

Hail can do strange things. I've been in towns where one street will have baseball size hail and will smash siding, rip window screens, chip paint off decking, while a block over there will be nothing—not a pea, not a marble, nothing.

Hail is formed when a cold front and a warm front collide and drops of rain freeze while falling and repeatedly get lifted or pushed back up into the clouds by warm updrafts of air, collecting and freezing more droplets of water and dust, cycling through this roller coaster until the hail becomes too heavy for the updraft; the warmer and stronger the updraft, the larger the hail will be. Most people have an image of hail as perfectly spherical, icy golf balls, while in actuality, most hail is irregular in shape, often with jagged and angular contours. If you look at a larger piece of hail close up you can usually see the different nubs and layers of ice that have collected on it. Hail is often found on the leading edges of a tornado and a strong indicator that a tornado may be on its way.

The extent of damage and whether or not there is property damage depends upon three factors: size, hardness and the amount of hail that falls. Most experts agree that hail golf ball size (about an inch and three quarters in diameter) and bigger is most likely to damage asphalt composition shingles if it is very hard and enough hail falls; anything smaller usually won't do much damage (penny size hail will dent aluminum roof vents and sometimes dent light gauge aluminum gutters), unless there is a tremendous amount of it driven by very high winds. Some hail can be the size of tennis balls but be very soft, breaking apart when it hits roofing or siding, causing no damage. The bigger and harder the hail is, the more likely there is to be *some* damage; how much hail falls determines how much damage there is. Most hail will fall for a few minutes or a dozen minutes or more. In 2003 in Liberal, Kansas, they had dense golf ball size hail for 45 minutes with wind gusts up to 80 miles per hour (hurricane force) and in the part of town that had the worst damage, most of the leaves were stripped from the trees (which gave the town an eerie, desolate feeling) and the houses looked as though the Marines had been using them for target practice. Dense golf ball size hail for that duration is very unusual.

Aside from dimpling the hood of your car, hail can cause numerous types of damage to property, some of which is obvious, some not so obvious. Among the obvious are siding: it dents aluminum, mars wood and cracks and chips vinyl siding (vinyl becomes brittle and more susceptible to damage after four or five years); metal awnings, metal roof vents, aluminum gutters, punctured window screens. When you see signs of the above damages, it is time to call your insurer.

Some items that are often overlooked:

- Air conditioner condenser fins (the soft, usually black fin-like sides). Hail will often push in the fins, which will need to be combed out, though sometimes the damage is so severe, the entire unit has to be replaced. If a service technician tells you it is beyond repair, have him put that in writing and submit it to the insurance company.
- Window screens: they don't have to be punctured to be damaged. If you look at a screen from an acute angle, you can see dimples and troughs in metal screens and sometimes small tears in nylon screens.
- Metal items: aluminum-clad windows—hail can actually dent

the frames; fascia, dryer vents, garage overhead doors and other doors, mailboxes.

- Plastic items: poly shutters, vinyl dryer vents; these items will crack like vinyl siding.
- Deck flooring and hand railing. Usually hail will chip the stain off, sometimes it gouges the wood, too.
- Paint: on wood siding or trims, concrete foundation walls, wrought iron hand railings.
- Exterior lights and lampposts, which are often dented on top where no one can see.
- Canvas awnings: hail will fray and sometimes puncture awnings.
- TV antennas and large analog satellite dishes (once in a while a small dish will get damaged, but rarely).
- Patio furniture, gas grills, (sometimes the paint gets chipped off the top and breaks the slats) gas grill covers, birdhouses.

One thing homeowners often notice after a hailstorm is that their double pane windows become cloudy. This is an indication that the window seal has been broken and most homeowners are disturbed to find out that most insurance companies won't pay to replace the windows when the seals are broken. There are two reasons for this: 1) window manufacturers guarantee window seals for the life of the window and homeowners should contact the window manufacturers to collect on the warranty; and 2) seals deteriorate over time and eventually all double pane windows will become cloudy and hail only speeds up a naturally occurring process. I'm not a window expert and I'm not sure if I completely believe either of the statements above, but in my experience I've never had a case when an insurer has paid to replace a window because of broken seals.

When it comes to hail, roof damage is always the number one concern for homeowners and insurance companies alike. As mentioned above, golf ball size and larger hail will damage asphalt roofing shingles, though sometimes you have to be an expert (i.e. a property adjuster or engineer) to detect the damage. Other factors of whether hail damages asphalt roofing include the age and condition of the shingles (the older roofing is, the more likely it is to be damaged, and the smaller the hail has to be), the number of layers of shingles (the more layers of shingles, the more likely roofing will be damaged), the color of the shingles (black and darker shingles have a shorter life span than lighter colored shingles), thickness of shingles, and the steepness of the roof (hail is less likely to damage a steep roof, 7/12 pitch or greater.)

In order for an insurance company to consider replacing asphalt composition roofing (the most common type), the functionality (the water shedding capabilities) of a shingle must be compromised or the lifespan be severely diminished. What this means is that hail must physically break or bruise asphalt shingles so that the layer of asphalt is exposed or the underlayment is actually fractured. When hail breaks a shingle, it dislodges the granules, sometimes creating a craggy-looking mini crater; a look at the underside of the shingles will reveal a thorough penetration of the underlayment and fracture lines. In the case of bruising, hail will dislodge granules but not necessarily fracture the shingle, but expose the asphalt. In both cases, the functional utility of the roof has been altered and the shingle(s) damaged need to be replaced or in time the areas where the hail impacted the shingles will deteriorate faster than the rest of the roof.

Often I've heard homeowners tell me that they've lost a lot of "grit" from their shingles but upon inspection of the roof there are no breaks or bruises on the shingles. Granular loss is a natural part of the weathering process of shingles: each time a roof is exposed to hard rain, high winds, ice or other harsh environmental factors, a roof will lose grains and granular loss is not in and of itself not considered damage by structural engineer roofing experts or insurance companies, nor does it effect the long-term lifespan of roofing.. For 25 year shingles that weigh 225 per 100 square feet, there are about 70 to 80 pound of granules.

Most insurance companies require their adjusters to survey a roof slope by slope, surveying each slope (each directional side) with what is called a "Test Square," a 100 square foot area (10' x 10' area typically) to determine the extent of the damage on that slope. Each company has its own requirements as to what constitutes enough damage to replace that slope, the "hits per square": one company may say if there are five hail hits in a square, that is enough to warrant replacement of that slope. Another company may say seven hits per square. Others have formulas that factor in the age and condition of the roof and attach a sliding scale for the number of hits required.

Hail is usually consistent over a slope of a roof and is typically driven from one direction by wind or comes straight down. Larger hail, baseball size for example, will often come straight down, too big to be pushed by the wind. If there is damage in one test square on a slope, there should be equal damage across the entire slope—hail, if anything is typically consistent across an entire slope, though that doesn't mean it is going to be consistent across the entire roof. Hail that comes straight down will likely damage every slope of a roof but directional hail will usually only damage one or two slopes. It varies from insurer to insurer, but some companies will pay to replace only the damaged slopes of a roof. If it is a simple gable roof (two slopes) and only one slope is damaged, they will pay only to replace that slope; if a roof is a hip and has four sides and only two are damaged, they will pay for those two slopes. Typically, though, if there is damage to 75% or more of the roof, they should replace the entire roof, although some insurers will replace an entire roof if there is damage to half of a roof or more and some will replace the entire roof if there is *any* damage to the shingles, regardless upon which slope the damage is found. Insurers only paying to replace part of a roof has always been a major complaint with homeowners, so be advised to check with your adjuster or insurer.

Years ago, I inspected the wood roof of a very nice house in a Midwestern city for hail damage. The hail had been very bad in that neighborhood, golf ball sized over a long duration and the wood shakes were severely gouged, shredded, really, but none were actually cracked or split by the hail, which is what engineers and insurers consider to be damage. As I inspected the roof, the homeowner's roofing contractor joined me on the roof and was astonished that I didn't find damage that would warrant replacement of the roof. Well, I did find damage to portions of some copper roofing, but I explained the guidelines for what is considered damage to the wood shakes and that there wasn't any insurance company defined wood shake damage. Gouging and marring of shakes by hail are considered superficial wounds to wood roofing and over time, the scarring will actually disappear through weathering, the natural exposure to rain, snow, ice, heat from the sun and even wind that wears away the surface until it is smooth again. In order for hail to damage a wood shake it must completely split the shake, a split that will run from the butt or bottom of the shingle to the top where the shingle gets attached to the roof.

Age, condition and thickness of wood shakes (they come in light, medium and heavy, a.k.a. small, medium and large) are factors in whether or not a shingle is likely to become damaged—and in the case of that particular roof, the shakes were actually in very good condition, except for the terrible beating they took from the hail. If there had been splits from hail, the standards for replacement are significantly more stringent for wood roofing than composition roofing. Depending on the insurer and the thickness of shakes, there needs to be 17 to 30 splits per square/test area per directional slope to replace that slope. Remember, the more expensive the cost to replace a building component, the less an insurer is going to want to pay to replace it and since wood roofing costs more than twice as much as composition roofing, the requirements for replacement are going to be proportionally equal to the cost of replacement.

The homeowner of that nice house with the wood roof was upset at my not finding "damage" but was very nice to me and was very understanding about the guidelines that I had been given and like the classy gentleman that he was, didn't take his frustrations out on me even while he told me he was going to sue the insurance company.

While hail rarely damages clay and cement tile roofs, it's been known to happen and like wood shakes hail needs to crack or spilt these as well, and also like wood shingles, there has to be a lot of damage on a slope or across a roof to warrant replacement of an entire slope.

If you're not sure if you have hail damage on your roof and you want to try and diagnose it yourself, before you risk life and limb, first look at other items that are damaged—siding, screens, gutters (it's easier to see damage to gutters from below)—and if there is a lot of large dents in the siding or gutters or the wood on a deck (or on wood siding) is gouged, there may be roof damage. If your roof is asphalt sometimes black "spots" may appear (unless the roof is black or dark colored), but often these are very difficult to detect unless you are trained to do so and if your roof is particularly steep, I'd strongly recommend you let the professionals handle it.

Chapter 13: Tornado and Straight-Line Winds

If you ask people who have survived both hurricanes and tornados which is more frightening, the response is always the same: a tornado is the scariest thing they have ever experienced. With winds that are up to three times more powerful than hurricanes, it's no wonder. Not to mention there are hundreds of tornados every year and, typically, only a few hurricanes that make land fall each season. We've all seen the pictures of towns flattened or torn asunder by tornados and while scientists still don't have a handle on exactly how or why tornados form, the devastation they render leave no questions about their fury and strength.

Like hail, damage from high winds and tornados is often easy to detect, even when a house or town isn't flattened: a large tree leaning against a house, rows of siding peeled off, sheets of shingles stripped away. Sometimes you can see that a house just isn't set squarely on the foundation or that it's leaning in one direction when it previously hadn't. But sometimes it's what you *can't* see that can be most troublesome. A tornado doesn't have to directly strike a house to cause damage; sometimes just being near a tornado, a few blocks or a few hundred yards away, is close enough for the wind pressure to wreak havoc on a house. Tornadic winds and intense atmospheric pressures can wrench a house, essentially throwing it out of alignment, causing unseen structural damage, minute and seemingly undetectable alterations to the basic construction of a house. A slight shift in the framing of a house can cause anything from collapse to constant and continuous roofs leaks, doors not opening and closing properly, or substantial and expensive heat loss. Often there are subtle signs that a house has shifted after a tornado has passed near. One time I encountered roof decking that poked up, an indication that the trusses had shifted after a tornado had passed by a few hundred yards away. Once I was at a house where the roof leaked repeatedly but their roofer had no idea how the water was entering; a few blocks away, a tornado had torn through the neighborhood. An examination of attic/roof framing sometimes reveals obvious signs of damage such as detached rafters/trusses or loose nails. In situations like these, a structural engineer is needed. Your insurance company will provide a structural engineer; however if you feel their assessment misses the mark or if you are dissatisfied with their evaluation, it may be necessary to obtain your own engineer, at your own expense. If your engineer and the insurance company's engineer fail to agree on what is damaged and what needs to be done, you may need to enter arbitration.

Of course, not every house that is hit with high winds needs a structural engineer. Nor is every leaky roof sign that your house has tornado damage. Some things to check when a tornado passes over or if powerful straight line winds batter your property are TV antennas or satellite dishes that are out of alignment (interrupting satellite service) or mangled, windows that are shifted, whole house air conditioners knocked off their foundations, decks thrown out of alignment, especially if they service the second story, and dryer vents that are pulled from a house from the change in air pressure.

A toothpick at 300 miles per hour can pass through a 2" x 4" like a bullet; a circular saw blade thrown by the wind at 300 MPH—well, you don't want to know what that can do. Flying debris comes in all shapes and sizes and is a big problem with tornados (and hurricanes), one that often gets overlooked, especially when the debris is small. A close inspection of the exterior or your house and any outbuildings is absolutely necessary after a tornado or high speed straight line winds: ripped screens, holes in aluminum or vinyl siding, scuffs on brick or stucco, dents on doors are common. Many times I've seen a tornado or high winds blow shingles, guttering and various roofing accessories off one house and cause damage to their neighbor's house. Note: if this happens to you, your neighbor is not liable for damage to your property, it's covered under your insurance. The key is simply to take a close look at the exterior and make sure your adjuster sees them, too, though this usually isn't a problem.

When you have to collect debris from your yard, whether it is from your house or someone else's, you can claim your time spent to pick up debris (assuming there is enough damage to your property to exceed your deductible) and with the exception of tree debris removal, there are no hard limits to non-tree debris removal except the total coverage limits of your property, though insurers will only pay the "reasonable" expenses for debris removal.

Chapter 14: Hurricane

There is a scene in the film *Forrest Gump* where Lieutenant Dan (played by Gary Sinise) sits atop the mast of Forrest Gump's shrimp trawler *Jenny* during hurricane Camille shaking his fists at God, laughing like a maniac and generally behaving like an ass. Broadly speaking this is not a good idea. Hurricanes are the largest and most destructive forces on earth: they can be a large as 1000 miles in diameter like hurricane Katrina became once it reached land and unfurled across the Ohio and Mississippi River valleys. Easily larger than any other type of weather event and able to generate winds that are 200 MPH and faster, a hurricane is an enormous high pressure weather system that can also spawn tornados and smaller, microburst storms on its outer bands that can be as forceful and destructive as the winds swirling around the hurricane's eye. And unlike tornados or straight line wind storms, which tend to come and go in minutes (or hours, like blizzards), hurricanes are the Energizer Bunny of weather systems: they keep going and going and going until you think all the rain and wind in the world must be hitting you.

The primary concerns with hurricanes are wind and water. Hurricanes can knock buildings over like they were made of Lincoln Logs, uproot trees like weeds and dump several feet of water in mere hours. If wind doesn't directly damage the outside of a home the combination of relentless rains and high winds set the stage for water infiltration around windows, doors, dryer vents, skylights, roof vents and roof valleys. Most of the time wind damage is obvious: shutters blown off the house, siding peeled back, downed fencing, missing shingles, window screens blown out. Sometimes the high pressure of a hurricane—and as you get nearer the eye, the pressure increases—can cause unseen structural damage, especially in the walls and roof trusses or rafters of wood frame houses (concrete walls are less prone to structural damage). As with tornado, if you suspect structural damage, whether it is from damages that you can see or damages you can't see but can detect in doors or windows no longer being plumb, request an inspection from a structural engineer if the problem isn't readily apparent.

As I can attest to from first hand experience, water stains on walls and ceilings can literally vanish before your eyes. One minute the wind from a hurricane is driving water against the outside walls like a pressure washer and a little leak develops around a window and a light water stain appears on the drywall and the next day, the light stain is gone, dried up. For this reason, it is imperative that a homeowner photograph a water stain, especially smaller stains, before they disappear, not only to document it for insurance purposes, but when it comes time to repair the area, you'll know exactly where it is and fix the right spot. In many cases, water damage to drywall or plaster is substantial enough that it isn't going to disappear in the blink of an eye, especially in hurricanes, when the water damage can be severe enough to cause part or all of a ceiling to collapse. But just because a water stain is gone, doesn't mean the moisture is, especially if you live in an area with high humidity. Even if there is a light stain and even if the stain disappears, it is essential that that section of drywall or plaster be cut out (even if it is only a 1' by 1' section) and repaired. Fiberglass or cellulose insulation behind walls can retain water and contribute to the growth of mold.

With hurricanes occasionally striking during the warmer summer months (September averages the most hurricanes) and the amount of water infiltration occurring with them, mold is a considerable concern when it comes to hurricanes. As with any other kind of damage, it is a homeowner's duty and responsibility to make sure that no more damage occurs to a property after a loss, this includes mold, which can spread faster than gossip. Some might find this a ridiculous proposition—"how do you *stop* mold?"—and while you can never fully stop mold, there are a lot of things a homeowner can do to keep it in check. As stated above, mold like hot moist places; it doesn't do well in air-conditioned, dry places and running the A/C will actually help to slow the growth of mold.

The most significant thing a homeowner can do to put the reigns on mold is simply to kill it when you see it. And killing mold is easier than some may think (the big problem, of course, is when you *can't* see mold, when it's behind the walls): you can buy germicide at home improvement stores. Some brand names for germicide/fungicide are Moldex, Jomax, Concrobium and Mold Armor. When sprayed on an area with mold, the mold dies. If you don't want to use germicide, a 5:1 solution of water and good old fashioned bleach also does the trick. Bleach, however, is generally not recommended as it is highly caustic and should not be used if there are small children in the home. The earlier you kill mold the better and a good spraying of germicide will show that pesky little life form who's boss. For more on mold, see the next chapter.

As far as insurance companies are concerned, there are two types of debris: tree debris and all other kinds of debris. When it comes to non-tree debris that may land in your yard or inside your house—roof shingles, insulation, chunks of drywall, etc.—including parts or all of your own property, there are no pre-set limits on coverage (except the policy limits), though most policies state that the insurance company will pay "the reasonable expenses" to remove debris. Like any other task you may do yourself, if you pick up debris from your yard after a hurricane, you can claim your time to pick up debris.

If a hurricane (or tornado) destroys an entire home, and if there is any debris left, the full replacement cost of the property *includes* the expenses to remove any debris, including tree debris. For a house with a replacement cost of $100,000.00 that is a total loss, the expense for debris removal will have to be come out of the $100,000.00 spent to rebuild the property. Sounds terrible, right? Luckily, there's an additional 5% of the policy limit ($5,000 in this case) available for situations like this. For more on this, see Chapter 27, General Debris Removal.

Tree debris is a whole other animal, a complicated and contentious animal. The first thing a homeowner needs to know is that in order for the removal of a tree or trees to be paid by the insurance company, the tree(s) or limbs must hit and damage structural property covered by your insurance: house, garage, fence, shed, carport, etc. If a tree or limb falls out in the middle of the yard and only roughs up the grass or the flower bed, there is no coverage; if it barely scrapes the paint on the fence, it is covered. If it falls on your freestanding gas grill, there is no coverage for tree debris removal; if the only damage from a fallen tree or limbs is personal property items, there is no coverage to remove tree debris.

When a tree or limbs fall and damage structural property the insurance company will pay "any reasonable expense" to remove the tree from the covered structural property. "Remove the tree from covered structural property" is interpreted by insurers as lifting or cutting the tree or limbs from the house (or whatever structure has been damaged) and placing the tree or limbs on the ground. "Any reasonable expense" means within local standards. If a tree contractor attempts to charge a ridiculous amount, your insurer may not pay it or else deal with the tree debris contractor directly. Once the tree or trees are on the ground, there is a $500.00 limit to cut up and haul that debris from the ground/land/yard. That's $500.00 *total*, for all trees or limbs, not $500.00 per tree or limb. Should the cost to remove the trees from the ground exceed $500.00, there is an additional 5% of the $500.00 tree debris policy limit available, a whopping extra $25.00. Should the cost to remove the trees that damaged the covered property from the ground exceed $525.00, your deductible can (and really should) be reduced by the amount that exceeds $525.00. (For more on how this works, please see Chapter 23, Tree Debris Removal.) These limits apply even if a homeowner does all of the work himself. Some states have laws concerning tree debris removal that may be slightly different than what is mentioned above, but these are the basics; if a tree does damage your property, ask your adjuster or insurance company representative if there are any laws or policies that differ from the above.

Hurricanes being what they are, they often force people out of their homes before, during and after they strike, which means our old friend ALE, Additional Living Expenses. The nitty gritty details of ALE are covered in depth in Chapter 22. In some cases, homeowners may be eligible for ALE *before* a hurricane hits, to cover the expenses of evacuation and hotel expenses. The industry standard is that your county or area must be put under a Mandatory Evacuation Order *and* your property must actually sustain damage above and beyond your deductible. In other words, if your state or local authorities declare a mandatory evacuation for the area you live but the hurricane makes a last minute turn (which happens) and misses your area completely, you would not be able to claim any evacuation expenses. If you leave voluntarily and your house is damaged, ALE usually won't be paid except under unusual circumstances, such as a person being on a respirator or other life threatening health concerns. If this is the case, notify your insurer. Also, these conditions will have to be documented. Every insurer has its own specific guidelines for paying ALE following a mandatory evacuation, your insurer may have different guidelines then what is mentioned above.

Once the hurricane hits, in order to be eligible for ALE, there has to be enough damage to make the house or property unlivable. If you lose your electricity for a few days, or if there are one or two small leaks, typically this is not enough. If living in the damaged property is merely *inconvenient* and not impossible, then it's more than likely the insurer won't cover it except under unusual circumstances like the ones mentioned above. Each insurer has its own parameters for what qualifies as "unlivable" and they often determine eligibility on a case-by-case basis. The health of vulnerable residents like the elderly, small infants, pregnant women, children or adults with severe allergies may be taken into consideration. A good rule of thumb is if there is no bathroom available for an extended period of time, several weeks or months, that ALE should probably be paid; this does not guarantee that it will be paid, however. As mentioned in Chapter 10, Restoration, once the claim has been settled and paid and construction begins, the extent of the repairs may be such that living inside the house becomes impossible—even if the damages weren't enough to force you out of your home initially. Conditions for being granted ALE during the construction phase usually come down to whether or not it is possible to live in the house or not and this, like all other requests for ALE, is often done on a case-by-case basis.

It has become standard operating procedure that if a hurricane is approaching an area, the homeowners snatch up every last bit of plywood at hardware and home improvement stores and begin to board up their windows and glass patio doors. This begs the question: will an insurance company reimburse homeowners for their time and expenses to protect their home from hurricane damage? The simple answer is that it depends on the insurance carrier. There are some insurers who see the boarding up of windows as a homeowner's duty to protect their home. Since most policies say nothing about the duties of a homeowner *before* a loss (only after, such as protecting the property from further damage, etc.), there is no hesitation on the part of insurers to do what the policy states: which is to say, nothing. Other insurers may say that they will pay for the homeowners' time and material expenses to board up windows only if the hurricane hits and actually does damage to the home above and beyond the deductible. Obviously, whether or not an insurer will compensate a homeowner is a very important question to ask *before* protective measures are taken. In the process of boarding up windows and doors, homeowners occasionally damage the windows, doors or exterior of the house unintentionally. Provided that there is damage to the home above and beyond the amount of the hurricane deductible, the expenses for accidental damages to a property in the process of protecting it are usually covered, as long as the damages are *unintentional.*

As mentioned in Chapter 6 ("The Dreaded Deductible") if you live in a Hurricane Zone—the Atlantic coastal plains, all of Florida, and the Gulf Coast—then the deductible for hurricanes is higher than the usual deductible for losses, either 2% or 5% of the property's insured value: for a $200,000 home with a 5% deductible, that a $10,000 deductible *per hurricane*.

Chapter 15: Mold

Mold has become a hot topic and a scary word for many homeowners. Stories circulate of people becoming deathly sick from toxic mold. It is true that people can and do get sick from some specific types of mold and it is also true that some people are much more sensitive to molds in general—about 25 million Americans are actually allergic to mold, but it is also true that, 1) every house has some mold somewhere; and 2) most molds are not toxic and in small doses are not going to harm people who are not allergic to them, though it should be noted that any type of mold in large quantities can cause illness (or temporary dizziness, as I can attest to) in healthy people. Mold in high levels can cause respiratory problems, headaches, nausea, lightheadedness, fatigue and a host of other symptoms. Sometimes it is very difficult to diagnose mold-caused illness as it can mimic various other aliments. Worse, and perhaps the most sinister aspect of mold, sometimes homeowners don't even know they have it: mold can grow behind walls and above ceilings, causing children and adults to get sick for no apparent reason.

Most people know mold when they see it. Mold is a fungus that is found in the air and in the ground and needs three things to grow: food, moisture and a cozy temperature, 45 to 145 degrees Fahrenheit. Once it finds a place with these three things, mold can begin to grow within 48 hours. Mold feeds on organic materials: wood, cardboard, paper, dust, leather, drywall (the paper covering) and grows best on organic items, but mold can grow, in small amounts, on non-organic items like glass, steel, concrete, ceramics, plastic, fiberglass and plaster provided there is enough organic food (dandruff and such) on its surface as well as heat and moisture. Generally, though, mold does not flourish on non-organic surfaces. Normal levels of mold inside a house are when the mold count is lower than the mold count outdoors. It is also normal to find the same species of mold inside a house as outside of it. Mold comes in a vide variety of colors: green, black, white, brown, even red. The telltale sign of mold, aside from its color is the smell, a dank musty odor. Sometimes the only way to know you have mold hidden behind the walls or under the floor is by the smell that permeates an area. As an aside, mildew is not mold and vice versa.

One "trick" that mold specialist have discovered in detecting mold growing behind walls and in other hidden places is to use a device that detects moisture levels. Like a stud finder, a water monitor that measures the moisture content behind walls (a good indicator of mold), allows experienced mold remediators to discern areas that may have hidden mold growing. If it is recommended by a mold specialist that "destructive testing" be done to determine if there actually is mold growing in an area, your insurer should comply. Destructive testing is just what it sounds like: knocking a hole in the drywall, lifting up floorboards, etc., in order to discover additional damages, in this case, to see if there is hidden mold. Ordinarily, deliberate damage done to a property is not covered, but if it is done in service of a payable claim it should be covered.

The bad news for most homeowners concerning mold is that it is specifically excluded under the homeowners policy. The good news is that mold *is* covered when it is caused directly or indirectly by an insured type of loss, although as of the writing of this book, only two states, Texas and Florida, require mold to be covered when mold results from a loss covered by the homeowners policy.

The key to coverage is *mold that results from a loss covered by the homeowners policy.* If the proximate cause of the mold is a covered type of loss, then the mold is covered. If wind tears shingles off a roof and allows water to enter a house, a water pipe bursts, or a washing machine or dishwasher accidentally discharges water, the resulting mold would be covered. If mold just appears one day without being directly caused by a covered type of damage, it is not covered, period, including in Texas and Florida. Naturally, mold caused by losses not covered—groundwater, flood, seepage into a basement or foundation from below—would not be covered either. As with any other claim, the cause of the damage—or in this case, the mold—is the most important factor when it comes to determining coverage.

When mold is caused by an insured loss occurs, the process of isolating and killing it is called remediation. Remediation can be as simple as applying germicide to a small patch of mold; germicide comes in spray or foam and is sold at hardware and home improvement stores. Some brand names include Moldex, Jomax, Concrobium and Mold Armor. Remediation can involve gutting an entire house, the drywall and any wood paneling/molding, cleaning the duct work of the heating and air conditioner system, including the air handler, replacing insulation, scraping and scrubbing wood framing (scraping wood framing is required in Florida), the hand cleaning of any and all books and papers that were in the same area as mold with a HEPA vacuum, HEPA vacuuming of every inch of the house, and dousing it all with copious amounts of germicide. In other words, your house could be turned into Elliot's house in the movie *E.T.* when E.T. is discovered to have been living there by certain unnamed departments of the government. Remediation can be a very, very expensive and very stressful process. Remediation is typically done by professional companies like Service Master or ServPro who have specific training in mold remediation. If there is a large amount of mold inside a home or property, it is *strongly* recommended that a homeowner not attempt to do this himself unless he is trained as a remediation technician.

Insurers have begun to cap the limits of coverage for mold remediation. In some states, insurers have experimented with $1,000.00 and $5,000.00 limits, the maximum amount they will pay per loss, without exception, regardless of the cause. At the next policy renewal, check with your agent to see if there have been limits placed on mold losses.

Also, for coverages that already have a specified limit, any mold remediation comes out of the limit for that coverage. For example, if a homeowner has an endorsement that covers Sewer Backup/Sump Pump Overflow, there is usually a coverage limit. Any mold remediation will be included in the policy limit for Sewer Backup/Sump Pump Overflow. If you have a $10,000.00, this means any mold remediation would have to be included in the $10,000.00 limit.

Chapter 16: Snow and Ice Buildup

Ice storms, aside from being a traffic and power outage nuisance, can also cause damage to property. Primarily damage will be caused to the roof, specifically asphalt shingle roofing. When snow and ice fall, it can collect in valleys and on eaves and sometimes in other places on a roof and the weight of snow and ice can cause bruising to shingles and create openings that cause leaks in interior rooms. Typically, a leaky roof is the first sign there is damage from snow and ice build up: once the snow and ice start to melt, it works its way into the house, forming stains on the walls or ceilings. Ice, specifically, will cause more damage when it builds up with snow than snow alone: ice is more dense than snow and the same volume of ice weighs more than snow (fill a bucket with powdery snow and then fill the bucket with solid ice and you'll see what I mean, though enough snow on a flat roof will make it buckle), but typically what happens is varying layers of both snow and ice deposit on a roof system and cause damage.

The weight of snow and ice can also cause minor structural damage. Wood rafters or trusses can crack or split under the pressure of weight, as can wood decking. Often this damage can be seen: the roof will bow or dip where the ice collected and crunch when walked upon—it goes without saying but you'll want to wait until the ice melts before you attempt to walk on it. Usually a structural engineer is not required in these cases: a peek in the attic will usually reveal damages, as ice damage tends to be isolated in pockets rather than across the entire roof system.

While valleys and eaves are the most likely areas to find ice damage, they are not the only areas that ice can collect: alongside or behind chimneys, where a roof joins one section of a house with another (where the roofing is flush with the siding/house exterior), on flat roofs or anywhere ice can wall up. If there is an ice storm in your area and you see large mounds of snow and ice but your roof does not leak after the ice and snow melt, you may still have roof damage. Bruising of roof shingles will shorten their lifespan and in valleys and areas where the shingle abut with another section of roofing or the house exterior and can increase the risk for leaking in these areas later on. Insurance adjusters are trained to determine if roof shingles are bruised; if you suspect that ice may have damaged the roofing, call your insurer. Also, if there is a large heap or mound of ice that is pressing down on a section of the roof and you suspect damage, if you're able to, take a picture before it melts.

As stated above, usually ice damage will occur in a small area on one or more sections of roofing. Rarely does ice damage an entire roof system. For most roofs, this means a repair is recommended—in other words, the roof will be patched with new shingles and possibly new tar paper (assuming there is tar paper under the shingles as there is supposed to be). Understandably, some homeowners don't want a "patched" roof, with mismatched shingles blended in with the older, weathered shingles. Unfortunately, the policy is actually on the side of insurers with this particular issue. Most policies owe for "equivalent construction," i.e. the same quality and type of material in the same place and as long as the insurer pays for the same type and quality of shingles and the contractor uses the same type and quality of shingle, they are actually following the policy. Insurers will argue that it is not reasonable to replace an entire roof or an entire slope of a roof because a small section needs to be repaired. The good thing about ordinary asphalt composition shingles is that they are easily replaceable: you can take a few out and put a few back in their place with ease.

Chapter 17: Earthquake

Earthquakes don't just happen in California. Far from it. While there are over 10,000 earthquakes a year in southern California alone (according to the NGS, National Geological Survey), Alaska actually has more. And in December 1811, a powerful earthquake along the New Madrid fault in Missouri caused the Mississippi River to temporarily flow north (or so the legend goes) and made church bells ring in Boston, Massachusetts. A destructive earthquake hit the Seattle area in 2001. In fact, more U.S. states have earthquakes than don't: in the last 30 years, only a handful of states *haven't* had earthquakes, including Iowa, North Dakota, Wisconsin and Florida. But dollar-wise, California is king when it comes to earthquake property damage.

Earthquakes are only covered under the standard homeowners policy if the specific endorsement that covers earthquakes is purchased. If your property is in California, you can purchase the earthquake endorsement (if your insurance company offers it, which 2/3 of residential insurers don't) or buy it from an insurance company that is a member of the CEA, the California Earthquake Authority, a state governmental body has partnered with private insurers to issue earthquake insurance through private insurance companies. Private insurers provide the financial backing, while the state administers the program, with private insurers adjusting losses for a fee.

If you have the earthquake endorsement or CEA insurance, the deductible is a percentage of the property's insured value, 5%, 10% or 15%: for a $200,000 home with a 5% deductible, that's a $10,000 deductible *per earthquake* (aftershocks within 72 hours are considered one event), though the base CEA deductible is 15% of a home's insured value (yeah, you do the math on a million dollar home—and then thank God you don't live in California). A lower CEA deductible can be "bought," however.

Major earthquakes cause major damage. Earthquakes can level buildings, rip apart highways, split the earth wide open and if the fluctuations are just right, toss a salad perfectly. Damage to a property depends upon the intensity of the earthquake, the vertical location of an earthquake within the earth and a property's location in relation to the epicenter. The greater the magnitude of an earthquake, the closer it is to the earth's surface (most damaging earthquakes occur within 50 miles of the earth's surface) and the closer you are to its point of origin (which increases the intensity of the shock waves), the greater the chance for destructive or catastrophic damage.

Most damage to a home and personal property items from an earthquake is readily apparent. But often the most significant damage from an earthquake will be hidden, either totally or partially: the foundation of a house. The foundation is the most important part of a house or building—without it, nothing above it matters much. A cracked foundation is an invitation to a variety of other problems including structural instability to the rest of the house, moisture penetration, and even insects. From the adjuster's and insurance company's point of view, the foundation is the center of attention after an earthquake. Whether a foundation has cracked or has shifted so that one section is higher than the other can make an enormous difference in the method and cost of repair. Whether or not a foundation is repairable or if it is more cost effective to tear down a house and start over again are also factors to consider.

Since most homeowners aren't experts in foundations and concrete, they must rely on the experts, structural engineers. As part of their training, adjusters who work earthquakes in California are required to take a course that teaches them to identify when a structural engineer is required (in other words, adjusters are trained to know their own limitations when it comes to foundations) and depending upon the amount and type of damage, a structural engineer may be required before repairs can begin.

The primary focus is often how the integrity of a foundation effects the remaining property, whether or not it can support walls and the roofing system or how it has effected the efficacy of the walls and roof. Usually if the foundation is cracked or shifted, there will be visible damage such as cracked or shifted walls or even the roof system; however, cracks in the drywall or plaster doesn't necessarily mean the foundation has been compromised: drywall and plaster are not nearly as strong as concrete and will crack and split more easily. That being said, if substantial cracks appear in the walls or exterior of the home it may be an indicator of problems with the foundation. Not only is a foundation the single most important part of a house, repairing it can also be an expensive and time consuming proposition, underscoring the importance for both homeowners and insurance companies to pay close attention to it.

While the primary focus for earthquake damage is on the foundation, some less obvious items may get overlooked in the process. Things to look for when it comes to earthquake damage include:

- broken water and gas lines
- cracked swimming pools
- windows that won't open or close
- doors that are no longer flush with their jambs and don't open and close properly
- gaps between walls and cabinetry, showers and baths
- misalignment of porch and deck floors or supports
- ductwork segments that may have become detached or loosened
- loose wall and ceiling lighting fixtures
- bent or warped garage overhead doors

- misaligned or bent roof vents, which may cause leaks if not corrected
- air conditioners or furnaces shifted off their bases
- uneven shelving
- detached or damaged TV antennas or satellite dishes

With regards to repairing foundations, cracks wider than 1/8" and cracks with a plane offset of more than 1/16" may require a structural repair. Cracks larger than 1/8" with no offset may only need an epoxy injection, patch or elastometric sealant. Epoxy injections can be used for cracks up to 1/4" wide. If there is an offset of more than 1/16", the offset can usually be repaired with leveling compound. Grinding and leveling vertical offsets of greater than 1/16" may be necessary.

There are obvious situations when an earthquake strikes that a homeowner can and should be granted ALE (Additional Living Expenses) by their insurer: if the city or county inspector says a property is no longer structurally sound and therefore unsafe to inhabit; if there is little or anything left; if it is not practical (that is, if it is impossible and not merely inconvenient) to live there. As mentioned in previous chapters, insurers will only want to grant ALE if it is absolutely necessary and often the decision to grant ALE is taken on a case-by-case basis, with consideration given to the health and safety of the homeowners and other factors.

The settlement process of a homeowners claim with an earthquake endorsement is the same as any other type of claim.

CEA: Earthquakes in California

The policy for the CEA is a little different from the standard homeowners policy. In order to *get* an earthquake policy from the CEA, you first must have a "regular" homeowners insurance policy through a traditional insurer, what the CEA calls a companion policy, and then buy the CEA-backed earthquake policy through that same insurer. If there's ever a loss, that insurance company will adjust the loss, paying for the damages from the CEA fund.

Here are the basics of the CEA policy:

- It is a Replacement Cost policy.
- Base deductible is 15% of the policy limit. Homeowners can "buy" a 10% deductible. A $1,000,000 home would have a $150,000 base deductible at 15%.
- The home, any appurtenant structures and personal property have one combined limit equal to the amount the home is insured for under the companion policy. Example: if the companion policy limit for the home is $200,000.00 and the personal property limit is $120,000.00, then the total limit for home, personal property and any additional structures under a CEA policy is $200,000.00.
- Detached structures such as garages, sheds, guesthouses are covered provided they share a foundation with the home, have a foundation adjacent to the home's or share a roof line with the home. The total policy limit applies to damages to these structures; unlike the regular homeowners policy, there is not a separate limit for these structures.
- Base personal property coverage is $5000.00. Policyholders can buy up to $100,000.00 in coverage. Any amounts of damage to personal property above the policy limits can be applied to the deductible, reducing the deductible. Personal property coverage is limited and excludes: animals, motorized vehicles (including lawn mowers, but motorized wheelchairs and motorized conveyances for the elderly are covered), artwork, glassware, crystal, china, trees, shrubs or plants, swimming pools, hot tubs, spas, antennas or satellite dishes, valuable papers and trailers.
- Base ALE (Additional Living Expenses) coverage is $1,500.00. Policyholders can buy up to $15,000.00 in coverage. These amounts can also be used to permanently move to another residence if the policy holder(s) decide not to rebuild.
- *Only structural damages apply to the deductible.* The CEA won't pay for ANY personal property damage until structural damage meets or exceeds the percentage deductible. For example: a

$200,000.00 home with a 15% deductible ($30,000.00) must have at least $30,000.00 in building/structure damage in order to receive payment for any type of damage. However, the CEA will pay for ALE whether or not the structural damages meet or exceed the deductible.

- There is a $5000.00 limit on chimneys, excluding the hearth and any mantels. If the damage to a chimney is over $5,000.00, the amount over $5,000.00 can be used to reduce the deductible by the same amount. For example: if two chimneys are damaged and it costs $8,000.00 to rebuild both of them, then the $3,000.00 over the policy limits can be used to reduce the deductible by $3,000.00.

- Decks, walkways, driveways, sidewalks are only covered if they provide essential pedestrian access to and from the home.

- Bulkheads, piers, retaining walls or other stabilizing structures are covered if they are essential to stabilizing the property.

- There is a $10,000.00 limit to rebuild or stabilize land that is essential to supporting the dwelling. The limit includes any engineering costs.

- There is 5% of the policy limits available for emergency repairs. For example: a $100,000.00 policy would have $5,000.00 available for emergency repairs such as temporarily shoring up the piers of a house built on a hillside to prevent it from sliding down the hill.

- For debris removal, there is an additional of 5% of the policy limits available. This amount is only available once the cost to rebuild a property has gone over the policy limits and the additional 5% of the policy limits is needed and is actually used. This is an extra amount of insurance.

- There is up to $10,000.00. available for building code upgrades. This is an extra amount of insurance.

- Destructive testing may be performed in order to determine the extent of damage or the cause of loss. If the extent of the known damages are over the deductible, the CEA will pay for any additional repairs needed due to the damage caused during testing. If, however, the known damages are under the deductible and the policyholder requests that destructive testing be done, the homeowner/property owner must bear the costs of any repairs due to destructive testing. If the results of the destructive testing reveal additional earthquake damages (or reveals that the damages were caused by earthquake) and the damages discovered during the destructive testing make the claim to go over the deductible, the costs to test and make repairs to the area tested would then be covered.

- All earthquakes that occur within 360 hours (15 days) are considered one event with one deductible.
- After a large earthquake, there may be a policy surcharge of up to 20% at the next policy renewal date.

Coverage and Settlement Disputes

CEA claims are adjusted just like regular homeowners claims, estimated just like regular homeowners claims, though when it comes to payment, no depreciation is ever taken. There are a few important differences when it comes to coverage and settlement disputes. With a CEA policy, the insurance company adjusting the loss doesn't have the authority to make coverage decisions when there is a question as to whether or not coverage applies. Coverage questions and disputes are put before the Claims Coverage Committee and a response as to whether or not there is coverage in a specific instance should be provided within 30 days. The insurer adjusting the loss will submit a Coverage Review Form to the Committee with the story of the loss with all the notes, diagrams, estimates, photos and any other applicable file material and wait for a decision.

Unfortunately, this process excludes homeowners/property owners and it is wholly contingent upon the insurance company adjusting the loss to initiate the proceedings and provide all file materials and documentation to the Committee without input from the homeowner or property owner and then communicate the results of the decision to the policyholder. On the upside, because the CEA is quasi-governmental and because of the very strict protections set forth in the California Fair Claims Practices laws, it is extremely difficult to wholly exclude property owners and to get away with any monkey business.

In some cases the financial settlement process is also slightly different. If the insurer and the homeowner can't agree on the amount of settlement, the homeowner can request mediation through the CDI (California Department of Insurance). If no progress has been made during the typical settlement negotiations a homeowner should request mediation. Every adjuster should have a copy of or access to CDI Mediation form 526 EQMED 12/99 to initiate the mediation process. Over the years, the CDI mediation program has proven to be a fair and highly successful way to expedite the resolution of a claim. CEA claims, more so than regular Homeowner Policy claims, lean upon mediation as a quick and decisive method of resolution.

CPR: Claim Payment Ratio

In case of "the Big One"—the earthquake to end all earthquakes, the kind of epic seismic event that has every Chicken Little declaring that the sky is falling—when the number of claims and the dollars estimated to pay those claims exceed the ability of the CEA to pay them, the CEA may decide to pay a percentage of every claim in place of the 100% replacement cost that the CEA policy states.

How do they get away with this? For one thing, the CEA is funded by a coalition of participating private insurers and well, it just wouldn't be fair to ask them to do what they said they would do, even if they signed a contract to do it. For another, the California Legislature lets them. For this reason, the CEA has declared that there is no guaranteed replacement coverage for their policy.

In the event of a large high magnitude or a series of aftershocks in combination with this, the CEA will estimate the amount of claim payments it expects to have to pay out and compare that to its ability to pay. If their ability to pay is less than what they expect to pay out in claims, they will then reduce across the board all payments to all Policyholders, a democratic but painful way of spreading the wealth/

agony.

Fair Claims Practices

The California Legislature, despite the CPR mentioned above, has been very pro-active in ensuring that policyholders are well protected and informed about every aspect of their claim. Fair claims practices don't just apply to earthquake claims, but to all property damage claims in California and are an important part of every homeowner property damage claim. Insurers *must* follow these guidelines or they will find themselves open to lawsuits and penalties from the Department of Insurance.

Here is a summary of the timelines for Fair Claims Practices according to California Statues:

- **Within 15 calendar days:** insurers must acknowledge receipt of a claim or pay the claim; they must provide all necessary forms, instructions and assistance; they must begin investigation of the claim.
- **Within 15 calendar days:** insurers must respond to a piece of correspondence from a policyholder or entity making claim.
- **Within 21 calendar days:** respond in writing to a complaint filed at the Department of Insurance.
- **Within 30 calendar days:** after acceptance of a claim, make a full or partial payment of all items which are not disputed.
- **Within 40 calendar days:** an insurer must accept or deny a claim after Proof of Loss is given/taken; if more time is needed, the insurer must state in writing every 30 days why the claim has not been accepted or denied.
- **Within 60 calendar days:** an insurer must notify the policyholder/claimant that statutes of limitations or contract limits are going to expire.

Chapter 18: Sewer and Drain Backup/Sump Pump Overflow

If you have a finished basement, partially or fully finished, you need to have a Sewer and Drain Backup/Sump Pump Overflow endorsement. This endorsement protects homeowners from water that enters a house or property from the outside through the sewer or water system or when a sump pump can't keep up and accidentally overflows, which is ordinarily excluded under the policy. Having this endorsement is the only way to cover property damage resulting from this type of loss. This does not mean that flood will be covered by this endorsement, or that water that seeps in from beneath a foundation or through foundation walls will be covered. That being said, unless there is a clear, obvious path from where the water entered the house, it is usually impossible to tell how water actually entered a basement and it is for this reason that homeowners are more often than not given the benefit of the doubt.

Like hurricane and earthquake, the deductible for Sewer and Backup losses is often different from the normal deductible. For Sewer and Drain Backup losses, there is a $1000.00 deductible with many insurers. With some insurers, this means is the highest deductible may apply. For example: if the regular deductible is $1500.00, then the regular $1500.00 deductible would apply; if the regular deductible is

$500.00, the deductible for Sewer and Drain Backup would then be $1000.00. With some insurers, Sewer and Drain Backup losses always have $1000.00 deductible, even if the normal deductible is higher.

Unlike hurricane and earthquake, there is usually a much smaller limit on coverage (the limit for earthquakes and hurricanes is the total policy limits, the amount the house is insured for), which, with most companies is typically $5000.00 or $20,000.00, though some insurers allow you purchase more coverage. Some insurers, in some states, allow homeowners to purchase this coverage without a restrictive limit, which means coverage is the amount for which the buildings are insured. If you have Sewer and Drain Backup coverage, the limit should be listed on the Declarations page.

Water from a backed up sewer, drain or sump pump will basically flood a basement (but we can't call it "flood"! that would be wrong). The most common types of damages from Sewer and Drain Backup or Sump Pump Overflow are, naturally, to the low-lying materials: flooring (if there is carpet or other floor coverings), baseboards, lower sections of walls (drywall or paneling), cabinetry and furniture. Depending on how high the water gets, there may also be damage to items like water heaters, furnaces, refrigerators and freezers. If you have a foot of water in your basement and your gas water heater isn't on a raised platform, the igniter may have gotten wet and may rust over time so that one day it simply doesn't light. It is very important to remove any personal property items that can be removed from the basement or area where the Back-up occurred and allow it to thoroughly dry; anything a homeowner can do to mitigate further damage to property is not just a good idea, it's required under the policy. While many of the structural items that get wet like flooring and cabinetry will more than likely have to be thrown out, it is important to keep a sample of these items until the insurance company can conduct an inspection; place these already-ruined items outside or in a garage (it's not like they're going to get *more* ruined). Insurers need to know the quality, materials and dimensions of all items that are damaged and covered by insurance. If drywall gets wet, take a photo of the height of the water and cut or have someone cut the wet drywall out; it's also a good idea to cut more than what just got wet: for example, if the water was one foot deep, it is a good idea to cut away the bottom two feet of drywall.

It is essential that any areas that get wet be dried out with fans and dehumidifiers. This is usually where a remediation company (or restoration service company) comes in, professionals who have experience drying out areas that have been infiltrated by water or sewage. Some insurance companies will call a remediation or restoration company for you, others leave it to you. Once an area has been dried, for any and every item that can handle it, it is recommended that it be doused with germicide or fungicide such as Moldex, Jomax, Concrobium or Mold Armor to prevent mold from growing. If a remediation company or restoration company is called in, they will often automatically do this—and if they don't, you should insist that they do. The overarching goal is simply to remove any and all moisture from the effected area to stall the growth of mold. Keep in mind that the expense of expert remediation will come out of the policy limits, leaving less money for repairs.

If, however, more than just water enters your house—that is, raw sewage—homeowners need to be aware that while policies cover the removal of raw sewage, most policies do *NOT* cover any additional expenses to remove toxic or hazardous pollutants like oil, gas, or industrial wastes that just happen to wind up in the sewer system. This can become a very complicated issue and in cases like these, while rare, pollution experts may be necessary to determine the correct course of action.

When it comes to personal property damaged by a Sewer and Drain Backup/Sump Pump overflow claim, some insurers are very picky about what they will and will not cover, often forcing homeowners to take out extra coverage for additional personal property protection. A Sewer and Drain Backup endorsement with what is called Listed Coverage B items only covers specific items, usually appliances like clothes washers and dryers, refrigerators and freezers, ranges and ovens, dishwashers and dehumidifiers. It is extremely important to check and double check what kind of coverage you have and to make sure you have all the coverage you feel appropriate before it is too late. Not having the coverage you need can be a costly mistake.

Chapter 19: Lightning and Power Outage or Surge

L ightning is a powerful and mysterious thing. One time I inspected a property where lightning hit a tree, split it apart and then traveled a good 50 yards across a pond to strike the nearby house, damaging electronic equipment inside. Lightning can also start fires, kill trees and of, course, cause the power to go out. A power surge can be destructive to electronics and appliances and a long-term power outage can be quite expensive.

Like everything else with an insurance claim, there are procedures when lightning or power surge damage electronics or appliances— DVD players, TVs, computers, stereo tuners, refrigerators, etc. If you tell your insurance company that several items were damaged by a lightning strike or a power surge and are no longer working, damaged items may need to be taken to an appropriate repair shop or facility to have an expert examine it, although with refrigerators and larger appliances, a service call to your house may be more appropriate. If it is determined that the item is no longer working due to lightning or power surge, the expert must put that in writing and the homeowner must submit the written report to the insurance company. Be aware that some companies have a $1000.00 limit on each separate item that is damaged by lightning or power surge.

Good news: when lightning strikes a tree, shrub or plant (a lawn is considered one plant and yes, I've seen lightning damage a lawn), it's covered! Bad news: insurers will only pay $500.00 per tree, plant, or shrub to replace it, *including* any costs to remove any and all of the dead or damaged tree and stump. Like electronics and appliances, an insurance company will want to see some proof that lightning actually damaged a tree, though you won't have to call an arborist: trees hit by lightning will usually leave tell-tale burn marks or scar a tree so the bark is removed in a discernable pattern. Absence of burn marks or other indicators means that without an eye witness who actually saw lightning strike a tree and signs an affidavit to that effect, that more than likely an insurer is not going to cover the loss of a tree.

As stated earlier, food loss that results from a power outage is also covered. Documentation of food loss—lists of food lost, photos of refrigerators and/or freezers if the food loss is substantial—is just as important with food loss as any other type of loss. While many insurers don't have specific limits on this type of coverage, some do: American Family, for example, has a per unit limit for food loss due to power interruption—of course, the upside is, with American Family the deductible doesn't apply to this type of loss.

Food loss lists don't always have to be extraordinarily specific. Generally, it is acceptable to group most items: vegetables, $25.00; condiments, $35.00; cheeses and lunchmeat $45.00, etc. However, if there are specific items that are more costly, they should be itemized. For example: if you have a freezer packed with four whole heritage breed turkeys ($80.00 each), 40 pounds ground beef, 20 pounds of beef roast, eight whole chickens, half a side of venison, three whole ducks, and one whole geese you'll want to make a specific list. The more expensive the loss, the more details the insurer will need.

In the case of venison or other wild game, a per pound price may have to be researched with a call to a specialty meat shop or else the price can be negotiated with your insurer. If you've hunted and dressed these items yourself, I recommend that you negotiate the price, adding a nominal fee to the per pound/per item price that one might pay at a specialty shop for your time to hunt, kill, dress and freeze these items.

If you lose electricity and think it may be out more than a week and you decide to buy a generator, guess what—your insurer is not going to pay for it. Some insurers may pay the cost to rent a generator for an equal amount of time, but they will not pay for the generator.

However, if you buy a generator or already own one, you can claim the gasoline used, provided you used the generator to stop food loss and not to power your margarita machine/blender.

If you buy dry ice in an attempt to preserve food spoilage (which is not that uncommon) you should be reimbursed for the expense to buy the dry ice.

Chapter 20: Fire

It was December, 1985, I had just turned 13 and my mother was in Colorado, having driven my oldest brother to the Olympic Training Center in Colorado Springs (he was a bicyclist and a few years later would race and defeat Lance Armstrong in their only contest together) when a winter storm hit our small Wisconsin town, knocking out the power. My older brother woke to cold darkness and lit a candle to dress by before heading out on his paper route. Not only did a fire start from that candle, but I was caught literally with my pants down, the kindly old house sitter interrupting my morning shower to frantically shout through steam and soapy glass doors that the house was on fire. Dressing faster than I had ever in my life, I dashed past my brother's smoky smoldering room and down the stairs and out the front door where moments later I was ushered into the back of a police cruiser while the fire department did their best to water the furniture of my brother's room. Returning to the house, shivering and in shock, my frozen spiky hair making me totally Punk Rock, we discovered that my brother's room was nicely toasted and the entire upstairs of the house smoked more than a slab of bacon, not to mention the firefighters broke the window in my brother's room while tossing the smoldering mattress onto the snow. With all the bedrooms and the only full bathroom upstairs, the house was deemed temporarily unlivable and my brother and I were separated and sent to stay with friends. Like any responsible parent, when my mother learned of the fire and my brother's and my sudden homelessness, not to mention our shock and utter bewilderment, she decided the best thing for her to do was to stay in Colorado and hit the slopes, raid the bars and crash every party from Vail to Steamboat Springs. Skiing, drinking and partying while her traumatized children were shuffled from one house to another after a disaster—hey, it was the '80s, that's what parents did, it was the days of *Miami Vice* and *Risky Business* and fighting for the right to party. Ah, yes, the good old days. After a long, slow recovery, with three of the four bedrooms damaged either by smoke or fire and in need of repair, the four of us crammed into one bedroom (in two sets of bunk beds), listening to the Beatles on vinyl, and generally loving and hating each other's guts and close proximity from one moment to the next. It took several months, but eventually our house was back to normal. The three of us who had substantial smoke damage to our rooms swapped bedrooms and after the upstairs was returned to normal we decided to remodel the downstairs. As was typical with our family, a few months after we finished the remodel and got the house exactly as we wanted it, we moved a thousand miles away.

Obviously fire can be devastating; even items like plaster, which are supposed to be fire resistant, don't hold up to the intensity of flames. Fire itself can do plenty of damage but when a house or portion of a house isn't destroyed by fire, the smoke produced and the water used to put out the flames can be just as devastating. Which I can attest to.

Smoke gets *everywhere*. Smoke gets in heat ducts, on lamp shades, in the carpet, on the walls, on the furniture, in the furniture, on picture frames, on window glass and drapery, in the cracks of TV remote controls, on the covers and edges of books, in blankets and bed sheets, in the slats of smoke detectors, in your nose and up your hair, I mean in your hair…never mind. After even a small fire, the smoke damage can end up costing more than the damage from the flames. Every single item that comes in contact with smoke will be "damaged" by it, meaning that if the smoke doesn't render the item completely useless that that item will need to be cleaned. It is inevitable after a small fire that homeowners will discover areas of smoke penetration weeks or even months after the fire and that these areas can and should be included in a claim, even if the homeowner does the cleaning himself. That being said, when getting an estimate from an insurer, special attention should be paid to areas of smoke damage. Fire is one of the few listed losses in which coverage is extended to trees, plants and shrubs: if you have houseplants and they are destroyed by fire or inundated with smoke, there should be payment to either replace the plants or wipe them clean. Seriously, you can claim cleaning plants. Cleaning tip: Q-tips work well on cactus plants.

The water used to put out fires can also wreak havoc in a room or area that catches on fire and it's not unusual for the water to find its way to other areas. Like smoke, water will works its way into places you couldn't possibly think it would: between floor boards, behind cabinets, onto ceilings of rooms below, behind the walls. And like smoke, special attention needs to be paid to the areas where water may penetrate and cause damage. In some cases, destructive testing may need to be done to determine whether or not water has damaged an area or to determine the extent to which water has damaged an area.

With our house fire, we were not given ALE (Additional Living Expenses) because it was still possible to live in the house. It was a little cramped, a little inconvenient but not impossible: we still had a bathroom, kitchen and one bedroom, not to mention the whole downstairs if we wanted to go to our separate corners. As with any other type of loss, ALE is typically determined on a case-by-case basis and given when it is necessary, when living in the home is more than difficult, more than unpleasant, but impossible.

The final word about fire damage has to do with the repairs, or in our case, the cleanup from smoke and water damage. It is strongly recommended that professionals handle the preponderance of the clean up efforts. One reason is that your policy covers it and that's what it's there for, but the main reason is that there is occasionally toxic elements in smoke, depending upon what was burned and how much of it was burned, and letting professionals who have the proper equipment handle the task of cleaning up is the best way to ensure that exposure to potentially toxic substances is limited.

Chapter 21: Mutiple Losses: Multiple Deductibles?

Let's say a straight-line windstorm strips all of the shingles off the front slope of a roof. Temporary repairs are made in the form of a tarp on the roof. The claim is settled to repair the roof, no other damage was done. Before permanent repairs can be made, another storm with high winds and torrential downpours blow the temporary repairs off and hundreds of gallons of water pour into the house from the exposed roof, causing several ceilings to collapse and numerous walls to become stained. There is no other damage to the property. Is this one claim or two?

One claim means one deductible, multiple claims mean multiple deductibles. Whether two separate occurrences/losses are covered under one claim depends upon whether the losses are related or not. If a loss occurs and subsequent damages are a continuation of the original damages or exacerbates the original damages, then it is one claim. If the second event causes damage completely unrelated to the first and do not worsen the damages from the first event and occur in a different area or location on the property, then, unless you have an extraordinarily generous insurer, the two losses will be considered two separate claims with two separate deductibles.

The example above of a second storm that blows the tarp off

and causes additional damages would be considered one claim, and therefore be subject to one deductible, as the second storm caused damage that was a *continuation* of the first storm: water caused the ceilings to collapse because the first storm stripped the shingles off the roof, therefore the proximate cause was the original wind storm and not the second thunderstorm. In this example, the relationship between the first windstorm and the second is readily apparent.

If, however, using the same example as above, a second storm not only causes a large amount of rain to collapse the ceilings but also causes a large oak tree to fall on a new sun porch on the back side of the house—would this be one claim or two? The first storm blew singles off the front slope of the roof. The second storm caused damage to the back side of the home. In this scenario there would be two separate claims: the water that damaged the ceilings and walls would be included in the first windstorm loss and would be paid under that loss (and that deductible); the tree that damaged the sun porch in a different area/location of the house would be another claim and would fall under another deductible.

Whether or not two losses will be paid under one claim and one deductible isn't always so cut and dry, especially when it comes to earthquakes: aftershocks can occur days or even weeks after the first quake and can be just as powerful. Let's say an earthquake causes damage to the entire slab foundation of a property, which weakens the support of all the walls and roof trusses above it, but only damages one part of the house. For this example, let's say our house is a simple ranch, 30 feet deep by 50 feet wide that runs, length-wise, east to west and the west side has collapsed, destroying two bedrooms but the east side has sustained no damage at all, not even cracks in the walls. However, there is a crack in the foundation that runs the length of the house. If another earthquake occurs three weeks after the first, before any repairs can be made, and the previously undamaged east side of the house then collapses, bringing down the rest of the house with it, would this be considered one loss or two?

In this particular case, since the foundation was compromised along its entire length after the first earthquake, the structural integrity of the rest of the house was also compromised and therefore any damages that occurred to the remaining portions of the house would be covered under the claim for the first earthquake.

There are literally countless scenarios in which two or more losses could occur and raise the question of whether or not there is one claim or two, there are countless grey areas where it may come down to a judgment call of the adjuster, structural engineer or insurer to determine what is what and what happened when.

The keys to remember when applying to your own situation are the relationship between the multiple losses, whether or not the damage occurs in a different area or section of a house and whether or not the damages are exacerbated or are a continuation of the original damages.

Chapter 22: Additional Living Expenses (ALE) and Loss of Rents

ALE and Loss of Rents falls under Coverage C: Loss of Use. This is the coverage that applies when a homeowner is forced from his home due to an insured loss and suddenly faces living expenses above and beyond what they normally spend or when the owner of a rental property experiences a loss of rent due to an insured loss.

ALE

As noted in previous chapters in regards to ALE, there has to be enough damage from a covered loss to make the house or property unlivable. If the electricity is off for a few days, or if there are one or two small water leaks in the ceiling or walls, typically this is not enough for an insurer to grant ALE; if living in the damaged property is *inconvenient* but not impossible, this, too, is usually not enough. Each insurer has its own parameters for what qualifies as "unlivable" and they often determine eligibility on a case-by-case basis. The health of vulnerable residents like the elderly, small infants, children or adults with severe allergies and pregnant women may be taken into consideration. A good rule of thumb is if there is no bathroom available for an extended period of time or if there is no place to sleep for several weeks or months, that ALE should probably be paid. As mentioned in Chapter 10, once a claim has been settled and paid and construction begins, the extent of the repairs may be such that living inside the house becomes impossible, even if the damages weren't enough to force you out of your home initially.

Homeowners may also be eligible for ALE *before* a hurricane hits, to cover the expenses of evacuation and hotel expenses. In this case, the county or area you live in must be been under a mandatory evacuation order and once the hurricane passes through, your property actually has to have sustained damage above and beyond your deductible. If there is no mandatory evacuation and you leave voluntarily and your house is damaged, ALE usually won't be paid except under unusual circumstances, such as a person being on a respirator or other life threatening health concerns.

Okay, now that you know what ALE is, you're just dying to know how it works, right? As mentioned earlier, ALE will pay expenses *above and beyond* what is normally spent by a homeowner to cover the cost of living somewhere other than the insured property. Let's take the example of the Smith family, John, Joan and their kids Kate and Jimmy, who live in Smithville, USA. A windstorm causes a 300 year-old oak tree to fall on their simple four-bedroom ranch-style house, destroying half of it, making it uninhabitable. The claim to fix the house is settled and the contractor who is doing the work says it should take about six months to complete; translated into English from Contractor, that means it will probably be eight or nine months until the Smiths can return home. The mortgage on the Smith's house is $1000.00 a month, including payments for taxes and homeowners insurance; while they are living elsewhere, they will still have to pay their mortgage and any other normal bills—electricity (for the contractors), water, garbage pick-up, etc. At first they move into a hotel and have to eat out for breakfast and dinner; naturally, they keep all receipts for the hotel and dining out. The cost of the Hotel rooms, which do not have kitchens, is $600.00 a week and they spend another $500.00 a week for dining out. They live in the hotel for two weeks before finding a short-term lease condominium for $600.00 a month (water included), which they happen to begin renting at the beginning of a month. Once they move into the condo, they resume a fairly normal life: they cook at home and eat out the same amount as they did before the tree fell on the house, dining out twice a week, cooking at home the rest of the time, spending $120.00 a month to dine out and $150.00 a week for regular groceries. But there are also additional expenses: electricity, gas, phone, etc., that are not included in the rental price of the condo. Also, the condo is the same distance from where John and Jane work so their travel expenses are the same, but the condo does not have a clothes washer and dryer, so they must go to a laundromat.

Mr. Smith meets with their friendly neighborhood insurance adjuster a month after they have moved out to go over the ALE. This is what they come up with:

Expense	Amount Spent	Amount Normally Spent	Overage
Housing			
Hotel	$1,200	$ 0	$1,200
Rent	$ 600	$ 0	$ 600
Utilities			
Electricity	$ 220	$120	$ 100
Gas	$ 60	$ 35	$ 30
Water	$ 20	$ 20	$ 0
Telephone	$ 65	$ 35	$ 30
Food			
Dining Out	$1,000	$120	$ 880
Cooking	$ 300	$300	$ 0
Transportation			
Automobile	$ 350	$350	$ 0
Miscellaneous			
Dry Cleaning	$ 50	$ 50	$ 0
Laundry	$ 20	$ 5	$ 15
Garbage	$ 24	$ 12	$ 12
TOTAL			**$2,867**

The amount claimable for the first month of ALE is found by subtracting what is normally spent (for example, dining out, $120.00 a month) from was actually spent (in the case of dining out, $1,000.00): $1,000.00 - $120.00 = $880.00. The total ALE for the Smith's first month away from home is $2,867.00. Some of the Smith's living expenses remained the same: automobile (gas: $350.00), dry cleaning ($50.00), home cooking ($300.00) and water ($20.00); some were more, like laundry expenses ($15.00 more) and some were nearly double than what they normally spend: electricity, gas, water, and telephone, since they had to pay these expenses for the condo *and* for their regular home, which they continue to pay anyway. And in case you're wondering, no, insurance does not cover bank overdraft fees when your checks start bouncing because your expenses are suddenly double what they were before.

The most frequently overlooked ALE items are often the lesser ones: laundry, utilities, travel expenses. If the condo had been father from work than the Smith's home, they could have included the extra gas/mileage in the ALE claim.

The example of the Smiths underscores the importance of keeping good documentation of *all* insurance-related expenses, even if you're not sure whether or not it's covered.

Like everything else with insurance, there are limits to ALE. As far as dollar limits, most policies state that insurers will only pay the "necessary increase" of your expenses to maintain your standard of living while you are displaced. That is, they set no hard dollar limit, but whatever is considered necessary and reasonable. But most policies do place a time limit for ALE, though if necessary, a request can often be made in writing to extend this if there are extenuating or extraordinary circumstances, especially in cases of a total loss (some large houses take much longer than a year to build, for example) or in cases like catastrophic hurricanes (like Andrew, in which some homeowners weren't able to rebuild for *four* years or hurricane Charley) or earthquakes (Northridge in 1994, San Francisco in 1989) where the overwhelming need for contactors and builders can't be filled in time to make all the repairs to all the houses damaged.

For a handy dandy free downloadable ALE form to help you track your expenses, go to www.ClaimGameBook.com/RedTapeLounge.

Loss of Rents

For rental property owners, Coverage C, Loss of Rents, is a little different. In order to claim loss of rents, first, there actually has to be someone renting the property at the time of the loss. Secondly, the type of damage actually has to be covered and thirdly, there has to be enough damage to warrant the renters moving out, though in my experience the conditions for this to occur are usually left up to the renters to decide—an insurance company can't *force* a renter to stay in a damaged property. In this regard, Loss of Rents is very different from the conditions required for homeowners to get ALE: with ALE, the insurers decides whether or not to grant ALE; with Loss of Rents, the insurers have no say if the renters choose not to live in a substantially damaged property, though if the extent of damage is minimal (a few water stains on the ceilings, for example), the insurer will question a claim for Loss of Rents.

Once it has been determined that rent has been lost due to covered damages, the owners must present a signed copy of the lease with the tenants. Payments for loss of rent will be paid until the property is repaired or when the lease expires, whichever comes first. Sometimes property owners are also required to give a copy of their previous years' taxes, specifically the IRS form 1099-MISC, which lists income from Rents, to verify that a property owner did, in fact previously earn rent from the damaged property. Like ALE, there is a limit of one year for most insurers to collect Loss of Rents due to an insured loss; if you require an extension, you'll want to call the insurance company and ask if they will give you one (most insurers won't) before requesting it in writing.

Chapter 23: Tree Debris Removal

One of the most contentious and frustrating issues for home-owners is tree debris removal expenses. There are limits and exclusions galore with tree debris removal, there are seemingly arbitrary conditions and stipulations to when and how you can use this coverage and unlike many other types of coverage, you can't purchase more. The numerous exclusions and conditions of tree debris removal coverage have caused an equally numerous coalition of homeowners to leave their insurance company out of frustration over this single issue—but what those who quit their insurer out of frustration don't know is that all insurers have pretty much the same limits, conditions and exclusions to coverage and will incite the exact same frustrations should the same thing happen again.

As far as insurers are concerned, there are two types of tree debris removal coverage: 1) the removal of a tree (or limbs) from a structure covered by your insurance (house, garage, shed, fence, carport, etc.) and setting it on the ground; and 2) removal of this same tree (or limbs) from the premises, what insurers often refer to as the tree or limbs being "cut up and hauled away," which sometimes means putting what's left of the tree or limbs on the curb for the city to pick up and sometimes means hauling the cut up tree or limbs to a landfill or mulch processor. As far as insurers are concerned these two categories of tree debris removal are as distinct as night and day. From their perspective these two categories are, in a way, two separate and completely different types of coverage, each having its own limits, conditions and exclusions that have nothing to do with the other type of tree debris removal.

For the first type of tree debris removal, the most important thing to know is that for these expenses to be covered by an insurer, the tree (or trees or limbs) must hit (or land on) and damage a *structural* piece of property covered by your insurance such as the house, garage, fence, driveway, shed, carport, etc. This coverage does not apply to Coverage B items. If a tree falls on a 20-foot tall ornamental windmill in the back yard and doesn't damage anything else, there is no coverage to lift it off the windmill. If a tree falls in the middle of the yard and roughs up the grass or the flower bed but fails to damage to any Coverage A property, there is no coverage. If a tree slowly tips over and comes to rest on the side of your house but doesn't do any damage, there is not supposed to be coverage, although adjusters are always told that if this scenario happens, they are to *find* damage, even it means cleaning the sap off the side of the house. If a giant tree branch dangles by mere threads over your house, without touching the property or having damaged it yet, there is no coverage—that is, until it falls. Yes, that's right, kids, insurance companies would rather pay $20,000.00 to repair a house damaged by a fallen limb in order to avoid paying $2000.00 (or however much it cost) to remove a dangling limb that hasn't damaged anything yet.

Once a tree or limb has landed on and damaged covered structural property insurance companies are bound to pay any "reasonable" expense to remove the tree from the covered piece of structural property, interpreted by insurers as lifting or cutting the tree or limbs from the damaged property and setting the tree or limbs on the ground. In other words, there is no hard limit or cap on the amount for this type of tree debris removal expense and it can often cost thousands of dollars for a complex operation, especially when cranes are needed to lift a large tree off damaged property. Typically, insurers prefer homeowners get more than one estimate for the removal of an especially large tree (to prevent price gouging), but sometimes after a large storm event (a hurricane, for example) it can be difficult just to get a tree service company to come to your house and in situations like these, there may only be one choice. If a tree company attempts to price gouge, once you give the insurer the final bill for tree debris removal, it essentially becomes their problem and an insurer will take a tree debris removal company to court or report it to local authorities.

The second type of tree debris removal, cutting up the trees or limbs once they have been lifted or cut from the damaged structural property and hauling them away, is the one that often gets homeowners steaming mad. First of all, in order for insurers to pay for the second type of tree debris removal, the first type must first be paid. When a tree or limb lands on a covered structure, damages it and has been lifted or cut from the damaged property and is on the ground, there is a $500.00 limit to remove the remainder of the tree debris from the premises. That's $500.00 total, for all trees or limbs that are eligible for coverage, not per tree. Most homeowners, of course, aren't aware of this limit and aren't able to advise the tree service company doing the work that there are strict monetary limits to cutting up and hauling away tree debris and homeowners often find themselves paying hundreds or even thousands of dollars out of their own pocket because they simply didn't know to tell their tree service company how to structure a bill so that only $500.00 goes toward cutting up and hauling away the tree debris once it has been removed from a covered structure that was damaged. It's at this point during an inspection that homeowners give me the hairy eye and declare their intention to leave their insurer.

There is some good news on the stringent $500.00 limit to cut up and haul away tree debris. Should these costs exceed $500.00, there is an additional 5% of $500.00 available—a whopping extra $25.00! Okay, that's not *great* news, but there is better news: should the cost to cut up and haul away tree debris exceed $525.00, your deductible will be reduced by the amount that exceeds $525.00. For example, if you receive a bill for $888.00 to cut up and haul away covered tree debris, the policy limits take care of the first $525.00, leaving $363.00 that is over the policy limit. The $363.00 gets subtracted from your deductible and if you have a $500.00 deductible, this means your deductible would then be $137.00 ($500.00 - $363.00 = $137.00)). If you have a $1000.00 deductible, your deductible becomes $637.00. Of course, if your deductible is $250.00 your deductible become $0.00—however, this also means that there is $113.00 ($250.00 - $363.00 = - $113.00) that will not be covered at all and will have to be paid out of pocket.

Tree debris removal expenses are typically included within an estimate for building damage and become part of the overall claim, normally given its own section in an estimate separate from everything else. No depreciation should be taken for tree debris removal items. What this also means is that, more than likely, you will receive a bill for tree debris removal, pay it and then get reimbursed from your insurer. In order to reduce delays in getting reimbursed it is essential that homeowners who have a tree service company remove trees or limbs that damage their property request the tree service company divide or break down the bill into the two separate and distinct categories of tree debris removal expenses. Otherwise a tree service company that hasn't handled debris removal for an insurance claim will typically give a bill with one total sum, which will require further inquiry by the insurer as to how much each portion actually is, causing an unnecessary delay.

The conditions, exclusions and limits of both of the types of tree debris removal apply even if a homeowner does all of the work himself. For those with chainsaws and the time to hack away, documentation of a homeowner's time spent to do the work and the materials used — gasoline/fuel, dump truck rental, etc.—becomes essential. Here's the sample time log from earlier:

	5-11-09	5-12-09	5-13-09	5-14-09	Total
John, brace & cut oak tree off house:	4.5hrs.	3hrs.	2.5hrs.	0	10 hours
John, cut up oak tree & haul away:	0	0	0	8	8 hours
John, patch roof where oak tree hit:	2	0	0	0	2 hours
Bill, cut pine trees off fence:	1.25	3.75	0	0	5 hours
John, cut up pine tree & haul away:	0	2	0	0	2 hours
Bill, reset fence:	0	0	3	0	3 hours
				TOTAL:	30 hrs.

In this case, the homeowner doesn't need to do anything more than he has already done as far as separating the two types of tree debris removal: the adjuster would take the figures above and put them into the appropriate areas of his electronic estimate. In this case the first type of coverage, removing tree/limbs from a structure, adds up to 15 hours (the first line and fourth line) and the second type of tree debris removal, cutting up and hauling away of tree limbs, comes to 10 hours (second and fifth lines). Get a free work log at www.ClaimGameBook. com/RedTapeLounge.com or at the Forms section at the end of this book.

Some states have laws concerning tree debris removal that may be slightly different than what is mentioned above. But these are the limits and restrictions that are followed by every insurance company that issues a homeowners policy. That being said, if a tree does damage your property, ask your adjuster if there are any laws or policies that differ from the above limits and conditions *before* you pay anyone to remove tree debris.

Chapter 24: Siding

No matter what type of claim it is—wind, hail, fire, vandalism, even earthquake—when siding is involved, it instantly becomes an issue no matter what part of the country you live. Siding is an issue that frustrates homeowners and causes countless homeowners to vow to leave their insurance carriers. If you have a house with a wood, stone, brick or stucco exterior, count yourself as amongst the lucky, as far as insurance company claims are concerned. But for those with vinyl, aluminum, asbestos, masonite, hardboard and even steel siding, this chapter is for you.

There are two primary issues with siding: paying to match; and siding that is no longer made or is no longer available.

Replacing all of the siding on a house when just one portion, section or side is damaged is called paying to match and except in cases of total losses, siding is rarely damaged on every side of a home, which means insurers are not going to automatically replace all of the siding on a home if only one side is damaged. The fading of siding color (even white) is inevitable and if one panel or one section on one side of a house is damaged and that one piece is replaced with a new one, the new piece will stick out like a three-headed dog. Even if you replace an entire side (also called an elevation), the new siding will be slightly different than the old, possibly reducing the resale value of a home.

Some insurers will tell you they will not pay to match under any circumstances. They will pay to match but they just *say* they won't, they're deathly allergic to those three words. If you have replacement cost insurance, you are entitled to have your home returned to the way it was before the loss and most insurers interpret this differently than someone with common sense may. For example, if you have four year-old vinyl siding in the color "sky blue" on every side of your house and wind-driven debris damages half a dozen panels on the north side, your insurer (depending on the insurer) will either pay to "repair" those six panels (which means you get six new panels of sky blue vinyl siding) or replace the entire north elevation. From the insurer's point of view, you had sky blue colored vinyl siding on your house before and now you also have sky blue vinyl siding on your home. This is not what insurers consider paying to match, this is what insurers consider as their duty to provide replacement cost coverage. Needless to say, homeowners aren't often happy about this and countless homeowners have sued insurers countless times for this perceived violation of the policy. But to my knowledge, no homeowner has ever won this type of case.

Now let's say you have 14 year-old vinyl siding on all sides of your home, the color of which at one time was sky blue, though after 14 years it's more white than blue. Let's also say that this siding is of a very unusual profile, with an unique wood grain pattern and an unusual size, let's say 3 ¾" (this means individual laps or clapboards are that tall). If wind damages half a dozen panels on the north side, you are going to discover a wee bit of a problem: that color of siding, in that particular size and grain pattern are no longer made and can no longer be purchased. In this case, when a reasonable match of the size, color and texture/pattern of a particular kind of siding cannot be found, your insurer is going to have to pay to replace all of the siding on your home. This is what insurers call paying to match.

The caveat to this is that you must have replacement cost insurance for your insurer to pay to match. If you do not have replacement cost insurance, your insurer may pay to replace just the damaged panels or the elevation that was damaged, and nothing more.

If you have replacement cost insurance and there is not a reasonable match to the size, color or pattern/texture, then your insurer should replace all of the siding on your home, provided all the siding on your home is currently uniform. If you have two different styles or types of siding on your home and one kind is damaged, all of the siding will not be replaced regardless of the size, color or pattern.

Here's a crash course on the variables listed above, size, color and texture or pattern.

The size of siding refers to the height of the panels or in some cases the combined height of the panels. Most aluminum and steel siding comes in either single panels that are eight or 10 inches tall or double panels of smaller heights. Most vinyl siding comes in double or triple panels with heights that vary from three inches to six inches, with double four inch panels being the most common. If you don't know the size of your siding, get out a measuring tape and look at the vertical seams where the panels overlap. The height of one slat and the number of clapboards tells you your size. For example, siding that is comprised of two four inch clapboards is called double four inch; if there are three three inch panels, it is called triple three inch, and so fourth.

Panel size is important because if the height of the panels on your house cannot be matched with what is currently on the market, the old and new siding will not line up and at corners where the siding meets your siding will have an uneven staggered appearance. Unless you had siding that didn't match before a loss, the insurance company owes to return your property to the way it was before the loss, that is, with siding of the same size on every side of the house. If your siding comes in an odd size—around the Washington, D.C. area, there is a tremendous amount of double 3 ¾" aluminum siding whose sole manufacturer went out of business *long* ago—and every contractor you talk to tells you they can't find that size of siding, all of the siding on a house may have to be replaced.

Siding color varies from manufacturer to manufacturer and one company's "green" siding may not necessarily be the same green as another's. What insurers mean by "a reasonable color match" means that the exact color or a color that is virtually identical to the manufacturer's original be found. If the company that originally made the siding on your home went out of business, it may be impossible to find a reasonable color match. If a manufacturer produced a particular color as a special run and never produced it again, it may be impossible to find a reasonable match.

For homeowners who have previously painted their aluminum or steel siding (or had the siding painted by a previous owner) the issue of color is a little different. If the siding is damaged on one elevation only and the same size and grain pattern of aluminum or steel siding is still available, typically what insurers will pay for is to replace the damaged area(s) of siding with new siding and paint the new siding on the damaged elevation only. Some insurers will go a little farther and pay to repaint all sides of the house. Check with your adjuster to find out what the procedure is for painting part or all of a house. Of course, if the size or grain pattern/texture cannot be matched, then the insurer may have to pay to replace all of the siding, though they most likely wouldn't (and you probably wouldn't want them to) pay to repaint the new siding.

Aluminum, vinyl and steel siding typically come in two textures: smooth and faux wood grain. Once in a while you will see beaded aluminum siding or siding with vertical striations, but these are far less common than smooth and wood grain. Smooth eight inch steel siding is readily available in a handful of colors (made by Alcoa) and typically speaking it is easier to find a matching color of smooth siding, regardless of material, provided you can find siding of the same size. But siding with a grain pattern is different. Quite often you can find the same size and specific color of siding to match the damaged siding on your property but the grain pattern embossed into the vinyl, aluminum or steel siding isn't even close. Grain patterns change every few years and some grain patterns may become obsolete after just a few years. Like size and color, if the pattern of grain cannot be matched with the existing style, your insurance company should pay to replace all of the siding on your property if you have replacement cost coverage.

But matching grain patterns isn't a problem exclusive to vinyl, aluminum and steel siding. Older forms of siding with grain or other patterns, like asbestos, Masonite and the disappointing "hardboard" siding (which has, unfortunately, shown susceptibility to moisture penetration), also have grain pattern matching issues, primarily due to the fact that none of them are manufactured anymore, which doesn't automatically mean that an insurer is going to pay to replace all the siding on a property. With these types of siding, once in a while a matching size and pattern can be found (color is not an issue as these types of siding need to be painted) either in another more recent material—fiberboard cement siding for example (which, like vinyl steel and aluminum, can be molded into just about any pattern by a manufacturer, but unlike hardboard siding is resistant to moisture)— or, believe it or not, matched from existing stockpiles of asbestos or Masonite siding that's just laying around, waiting for homeowners to find them.

The current "lifespan" for particular styles of vinyl, aluminum and some steel siding seems to hover around eight to ten years. This means that after eight to ten years the siding can be very difficult, if not impossible, to find in the exact size, color, and pattern. Manufacturers follow home building trends and every few years, as should be expected, tastes change.

So your siding was damaged on one side, you file a claim and your adjuster tells you they're going to pay to replace all of the siding on the damaged elevation only. But then your contractor tells you that the damaged siding on your house is no longer available. What you then do is have your contractor put into writing that, to his knowledge, the siding on your house is no longer available and all the siding needs to be replaced for this reason.

That may be good enough for some insurers to replace all of the siding on your house, but not for others. When it is doubtful that siding can be matched (which means if it is 10 years or older or of an unusual size or profile) larger insurers have their adjusters cut a small siding sample from a damaged section (but not from a spare piece that happens to be lying around in the garage as it may not actually be the same siding on the house). An authority within the insurance company then analyzes the sample, or the sample is mailed to another branch of the insurance company for analysis where its size, color and grain pattern are studied. The "original" color can often be found on the backside of the sample, where it hasn't been exposed to sun and the elements, or on the lip edges that overlap one another. The contrast between the original color and the faded color can be startling. When a siding sample is taken and a reasonable size, color, and grain match is found, the insurance company will advise the homeowner where the siding can be purchased locally. If no match is found, they should pay to replace all of the siding.

Chapter 25: Roofing

There are many type of roofing and regardless the type of roofing you have—asphalt composition, wood shakes, clay tile, concrete, tar, built-up, slate or composite tile—a sound roof overhead is, next to a solid foundation, the most important element of a property. There are a plethora of issues concerning different kinds of damages to roofs and a variety of issues concerning each type of roofing. Some have simple solutions, some complex, and some have solutions that have nothing to do with insurance companies.

Asphalt Composition Roofing

There are three parts to modern asphalt shingles: from bottom to top: the mat, made either from organic materials or fiberglass; an asphalt coating; and lastly, granules. Asphalt composition shingles come in a variety of sizes and thicknesses and even a few different shapes. The most common type of shingle are three tab shingles, which means there are three tiles (or what many call shingles) for each shingle. In the U.S., three tab shingles are exactly three feet in horizontal length. The second most popular shingle are dimensional or architectural shingles, which have multiple layers (the mat, asphalt and granules) stacked atop one another. These shingles are growing in popularity and are also three feet in length. There are other types of asphalt composition shingles that are popular in some areas, such as the northern great plains: what are called T-lock shingles (which are no longer made), shingles that when installed, interlock with one another. There is a wide variety of asphalt shingles in various tab lengths and thicknesses, but they're all made and layered in pretty much the same way.

Perhaps the only issue that raises the ire of homeowners more than matching siding is matching roofing. Like siding, the sun and elemental wear and tear can change the color or tone of many types of roofing over time, most notably asphalt composition and wood shakes. Matching shingles only becomes an issue when a loss damages part of a roof and not the entire and the insurance company opts to pay to repair only the damaged part of the roof, which is standard operating procedure with most insurers. Some companies have percentage rules, meaning that if wind (or hail) damages a certain percentage of shingles (in relation to the total square footage of a roof) that they must replace it. With some insurers, replacement can come down to a judgment call, a judgment that may need to be disputed. If a total replacement is not called for or recommended, what homeowners are often left with after the repairs is an unmatched roof that has a patchy look, an aesthetic that many homeowners find unacceptable and one which incites repeated vows to leave their insurer for another (who, more than likely, would do the exact same thing should the same type of damage occur). However, most insurers insist that they are following the letter of the policy by replacing damaged items with like materials and construction. Which, unfortunately for homeowners, seems to be the prevailing legal opinion.

Unlike siding, there is an enormous amount of uniformity with shingle manufacturers when it comes to size and thickness of shingles, which is to say, the only differences between the shingle of one manufacturer and another is often the variation in color/granule pattern and in some cases, the way the shingles interlock with one another. While an experienced roofer can often determine which brand of shingles and sometimes which pattern a homeowner has on his roof, unless the roof is only a few years old, that exact color may no longer be available, though there is almost always something reasonably close to the original color. Insurers know that there is tremendous consistency and uniformity with the material and construction of asphalt shingles throughout the industry. If, for example, a windstorm tears off a patch of standard three tab 25 year "Spruce Green" asphalt shingles from one side of a roof, the insurance company will pay to repair that patch and only that patch with standard three tab 25-year shingles, knowing that any manufacturer's three tab 25- year shingle will conform to the length and thickness of the surrounding shingles and that there are so many shingle manufacturers making so many different shades and colors of shingles that a "reasonable" match can more often than not be found, fulfilling their obligations under the policy.

In most cases, however, there is little a homeowner can do about this except strap on his climbing gear and prepare for an ascent up the Chain of Command and failing that, write a letter requesting Arbitration. Some states, such as California, have "line of sight" laws that state that there must a uniform appearance in a given area, making "patching" a roof more challenging, although California is in the minority on this point.

Once in a while, however, matching size of asphalt shingles can be an issue that can lead to an entire roof being replaced because of a small patch of shingles. This is rare and doesn't happen often. Once upon a time there were a greater number shingle manufacturers than there are now (who sold exclusively to local markets) and some of the producers went out of business having made shingles that didn't conform to modern standards and when a small area of those shingles get damaged, there is no way to match the size or thickness of the existing shingles because they simply don't exist anymore. In some cases, major manufacturers have stopped making a particular type or style of shingle due to poor performance and obtaining these shingles can be difficult if not impossible. If a shingle is an unusual size or style or if that particular shingle is no longer available and cannot be found on the market, an insurer should replace the damaged slope regardless of the extent of the damage. If there is damage to all slopes, the entire roof should be replaced.

Of course, there are some shingles that give the *illusion* of not conforming to the U.S. standard of a three foot length and do not require an entire roof replacement in order to return a roof to its previous condition. Metric shingles, which are used primarily in Canada, have the same thickness and quality as U.S. composition shingles but are a slightly different length than U.S. shingles. Metric shingles are still widely available and more often than not a reasonable match can be found.

Broken Seals

Asphalt composition shingles are self-sealing, which means they don't need external adhesive to stay affixed to the roof. Comp shingles (as they are referred to in our name shortening-obsessed society) come with a sealing strip on the underside of each shingle that is supposed to "melt" when heated by the sun and make shingles adhere to the shingle below, which is why it is best to install new shingles in the spring or summer, to ensure that they seal properly.

The seal that shingles make are supposed to be permanent and last the life of the shingle. However, wind and other factors can change that. Sometimes shingles aren't nailed down properly and they never seal right; sometimes the shingle manufacturer doesn't put enough sealant on the shingles. Wind, of course, can blow shingles off of a roof. Wind can also not completely blow shingles off a roof but break the seals of the shingles. When this happens, shingles become loose and flap in the wind (a *very* annoying noise when you're inside a house), but are still attached. When shingle seals break it is a permanent condition. Broken seals is roof damage and should be payable under all insurance homeowners policies, however insurers don't see it that way.

The degree of damage from broken seals can vary from roof to roof. Sometimes you will find just one shingle (or one tab) that is loose; sometimes it is across the entire slope or, on rare occasions, across the entire roof.

The controversy when it comes to insurance claims and broken seals is that sometimes roof shingles *don't* seal down when they are installed, a condition which is not covered. This is considered a manufacturing defect and the shingle maker is liable. The question then becomes how to tell the difference between shingles that have had their seals broken by wind and shingles that just never sealed properly. This can be challenging, but sometimes a roof and its surroundings can offer clues. When seals have been broken by the wind, little bits and pieces of debris, pine needles, pieces of leaf or paper or even feathers, will often become embedded under at least some of the shingles. If the wind was strong enough to break the seals of the shingles, then it must have been strong enough to hurl light little pieces of debris and a shingle with a broken seal becomes like a hand in the air, standing straight up, trapping debris in its mitt. The key about finding debris under shingles that have had their seals broken is that is if it is recent damage and not a manufacturing problem, the debris will be *fresh* and isn't old and decaying as though it has been there for months and months. After a fierce windstorm, if a homeowner notices that many or most of the shingles are loose and flappy, if he is able to, peek under a few to see if there is any fresh debris. It has been my experience that it is inevitable that there is going to be fresh debris under newly loosened shingles. When broken seals are thought to be found, that is when an inspection for "collateral damage" is done: if there is other wind damage or evidence of high winds (a large number of tree limbs down for example) that is consistent with the kind of wind that would break shingle seals, it makes for a strong circumstantial case in the favor of broken seals. Conversely, if the shingles were already loose and there is no collateral damage and no fresh debris under the loose shingles or old debris or a mix of old and new debris, then logic dictates that if the wind was strong enough to break shingle seals then it should have been strong enough the tear the shingles completely from the roof.

Manufacturing Defects and Installation Errors

As mentioned above, there are three parts to modern asphalt shingles: the mat, made either from organic materials or fiberglass; an asphalt coating; and granules. Manufacturing defects can occur at any stage of manufacturing and are not covered by insurance policies, nor should they be. If shingles have manufacturing defects but are also damaged by a covered loss, then payment can and should be made for any and all covered damages. There are also several errors that can be made during the installation of shingles that will effect the lifespan and performance of composition shingles.

- **Shingle Seals.** As mentioned above, asphalt composition shingles are self-sealing, which means they don't need external adhesive to stay affixed to the roof. Shingles have a sealing strip on the underside of each shingle that is supposed to "melt" when heated by the sun and make shingles adhere to the surface below. When these seals don't function properly, the shingles never become permanently attached to the roof surface. This problem can occur in a section or across the entire roof.

- **Blisters.** These go by different names, depending on where you live—some call them heat blisters—but sometimes during the manufacturing process the moisture or volatile elements that accidentally get trapped within the asphalt form tiny "bubbles" (usually smaller than a pencil eraser in size) on the surface of the shingle once the shingles are heated by the sun. A roof with this defect will have an area or patches that look like it is afflicted with small pox or very bad very bubbly acne. Eventually, if these shingles are not replaced, these bubbles or blisters will burst, shedding the granules atop the blister, forming thousands of tiny little craters across the effected area. This problem is often only found in small patches, though sometimes they can be found across a broader area.

- **Granular Defects.** Heaped atop layers of asphalt are the granules of composition shingles. Aside from giving shingles their color, this thick bed of granules adds toughness and durability to roofing. Without a defect, a roof will lose granules uniformly across the entire surface over time. However, when granules are applied unevenly to shingles during the manufacturing process, the appearance of the shingle is compromised and their usefulness and lifespan are vastly reduced. Sometimes this defect is so bad that no granules get put on the shingles, ensuring that they will not last long. Look for black patches (where the asphalt shows through) or whitish grey patches with laminated shingles. Like heat blisters, this problem can be isolated and doesn't always present itself over the entire roof.

- **Delamination.** This is when the various layers of shingles literally separate from one another in a way that results in a greatly weakened shingle. A good analogy would be a wicker chair that has half the wicker strands removed from the seat, making it unable to hold any weight. A shingle that has delaminated will sometimes look like the surface granules have been worn away and the separated matting (usually fiberglass) underneath is exposed. In the case of fiberglass matting, the shingles will have the appearance of frayed silk strands. Sometimes the granules are intact and the layers beneath simply separate and only a close inspection will reveal this defect. Like the previous two defects, delamination is usually only found in patches.

- **Cupping and Clawing.** Cupping occurs when, over time, the top part of a shingle shrinks and the bottom doesn't, resulting in an upward curling at the shingle corners. This often gets mistaken for wind damage, making the shingles look "lifted." Clawing is the opposite, when the bottom shrinks and the top doesn't and the shingle curls downward, creating a dome-like appearance of part (usually the corners) or all of the shingle. Neither of these is caused by wind or hail. It is common that a large section of roofing or an entire slope or an entire roof will cup or claw.

- **Cracking/Crazing.** After many years, certain types of shingles will undergo shrinkage and become more brittle and what results is a network of craggy lines that appear across part or all of the roof surface. The manufacturing process of certain laminated composition shingles causes this.

- **Nail Pops.** This occurs when nails work their way out of the wood decking to which shingles are nailed and stick out, propping the shingle up tent-like, or in some cases, actually puncturing the shingle—rusty nail heads (if the nail's been exposed for a while) then appear randomly. There are two causes of nail pops: nails or staples that are under nailed when the roofing is installed; and the natural expansion and contraction of the wood decking due to variations in heat and cold, which causes the nails to thrust upward over time.
- **Unsealed Tabs.** Just like it sounds, this is when tabs never properly seal down. This can be caused by improper installation (misplacement of the nails) or by not enough sealant being put on the shingles at the factory. Refer to the previous section for ways to discern if shingles are unsealed because of wind damage or manufacturing or installation issues.

If you, your roofer or your insurance adjuster find manufacturing defects, a claim should be made—not with your insurer, but with the shingle manufacturer. If the shingle maker is not readily known, most roofers should be able to tell you what brand it is. Once the manufacturer is determined, contact them (or have your roofer do so) and tell them the approximate size of the area that is defective. Most companies will offer a settlement for the estimated square footage that is defective, though they won't admit any wrong doing or that it was their fault.

Wood Roofing

Wood roofs are a lovely pain in the ass. Few can resist the rustic appeal of a well-maintained wood shake roof. But maintenance is one of the drawbacks of wood roofing—unlike most other kinds of roofing they require yearly maintenance (which very few homeowners actually do) including a light cleaning and, if you want it to last, treatment. The most common material used today for wood roofing is cedar, which is naturally water and insect resistant.

With cedar shake shingles, there is uniformity with manufacturers concerning thickness (though, often, not horizontal width in heavier shakes, which is what gives some roofs an even more rustic look), but wood being wood, it comes in two basic colors: new and worn. Some new shake shingles often look "silvery" compared to older shingles when they are mixed in after a repair, which, unlike composition roofing, isn't as great of a concern as sun exposure and the elements will eventually cause the new shingles to blend in much better than patches of composition shingles. Insurers much prefer to pay to repair wood roofs than replace them. The maxim "The more expensive it is to replace something, the more likely an insurer is to repair it" applies doubly for wood roofs, which are more than twice as expensive as composition roofs. That being said, the level of damage needed for the total replacement of a wood roof is much greater than for most other building components. For hail, for example, while composition roofs require 5 to 9 hail hits in a test square (100 square foot area) to replace the slope, wood shingles require 15 to 32 per square, depending upon the thickness of the shake and the requirements of the insurer.

Age, sun exposure and harsh elements effect wood roofing just like any other component. Even the most well maintained wood roof will eventually go through a physical transformation over time. The most obvious change is in the color of shakes, turning a deep rich brown over time, a color that is part of the rustic appeal of wood roofing. But wood shakes also get thinner over time. Rain, snow, heat, hail and other elements slowly erode shingles, eating away the layers of wood, weakening them, and in the case of heat, making them more brittle over time.

Aside from the color change, the most obvious physical change wood shakes go through is cupping and warping. Cupping is when the shingles begin to curl, usually turning upward, making it look like the shingles are trying to form the letter U. After a strong windstorm, folks who don't normally spend time looking at their roof will take a close look at their wood shakes and notice that the shakes appear to be "lifted," which is cupping having sneaked up on a homeowner while he wasn't paying close attention. Cupping's cousin is warping, which is just what it sounds like, the random misshaping of wood shakes over time due to exposure to the elements and inconsistent shrinking of an individual shake. Cupping and warping are, to one degree or another, inevitable changes in wood shake roofing.

Chapter 26: General Debris Removal

Unless a property is a total loss, there is no hard limit on what insurers will pay to removal all non-tree debris from your property that results from a covered loss. Most policies state they will pay the reasonable costs to remove debris from the covered property (i.e., the structures: house, fence, shed, garage, etc.) and from the premises, the actual land. This is usually interpreted as whatever it cost to get the job done without being price gouged. Simple enough.

Structures that are a total loss are often a little more complicated, but if you understand ACV, RCV and depreciation, this should be a cakewalk. The first thing to know is that all general debris removal expenses are included in the total amount of a loss: if a house, for example, is insured for $100,000.00 and a tornado completely levels it, the expenses to removal all the building debris would come out of the $100,000.00 limit to rebuild the property. This sounds like a raw deal, but luckily, when it comes to non-tree debris removal there's an additional amount of money available for situations when the costs to remove the debris *and* rebuild exceed the policy limits. Homeowners are entitled to an additional 5% of the policy limits specifically for non-tree debris removal. In the case of a house with a replacement cost of $100,000.00, that's an extra $5000.00.

This extra amount also applies to all dwelling extensions/ appurtenant structures, such as detached garages, fences, sheds or barns, which have their own separate policy limits. Typically, unless these structures are scheduled separately (such as an extra large four car garage, for example), there will be one blanket coverage amount for all outbuildings/appurtenant structures. This limit can be found on the Declarations Page of your policy. When buildings are scheduled and there is a separate limit for each buildings the additional 5% for non-tree debris removal applies to each individual building and not in the aggregate for all the buildings. For example, if a garage has a limit of $10,000.00, there would be an additional 5% of $10,000.00 or $500.00 for debris removal should the garage be completely destroyed and the cost to rebuild it *and* remove all the debris go above $10,000.00. If a barn insured for $30,000.00 was also damaged but not leveled and the amount of repairs plus the removal of debris goes above the $30,000.00 limit, there is an additional 5%—or $1500.00—available. These additional amounts are only paid if they are actually needed or, with some insurers, if the ACV is over the policy limits.

If there are several buildings under one blanket coverage, then the 5% of policy limits for debris removal would be one amount for all buildings if all of the buildings were a total loss.

But as infomercials like to declare: but wait! There's more! Should the policy limit *and* the extra 5% for non-tree debris removal be exceeded, there is yet *another* amount that can be included for the expense of removal of general debris, the deductible. For the house insured for $100,000.00 with an additional 5% ($5000.00) for debris removal, if the deductible is $1000.00 and the debris removal expenses and the cost to rebuild the property is over $106,00.00, the deductible would be completely absorbed into the amount of the loss:

Amount of loss: $109,975.00
Policy limits: $100,000.00
5% Debris: $ 5,000.00
Deductible: $ 1,000.00
TOTAL ACV: $106,000.00

If, however, the total cost to rebuild and remove the debris came to $105,600.00, at that point the $1000.00 deductible would be reduced by $600.00, the amount over all policy limits, so that the new deductible would be $400.00.

Amount of Loss: $105,600.00

Policy Limits: $100,000.00
5% Debris: $ 5,000.00
TOTAL: $105,000.00

Amount not covered:
                   $105,600.00
               - $105,000.00
               $ 600.00

Subtract this amount
from the deductible: $1000.00
                       - $ 600.00
New Deductible: $ 400.00

                   $105,600.00
               - $ 400.00 deductible
Total payable: $105,200.00

If several buildings are scheduled and are destroyed, only one deductible applies. In other words, only one deductible can be absorbed, meaning any costs above the limits, the additional 5% and the one deductible will come out of your pocket.

Chapter 27: Buying or Selling a Damaged Property

Years ago in Indiana, I once encountered a situation where a few days before a couple were to sign the contract of sale for their home, a hailstorm caused damage to the home and the sale was put on hold until something could be worked out. I met with the homeowners/sellers to go over their options with them—withdraw their claim and reduce the amount of the sale by the amount of the estimate for damage; go through with the claim and make the repairs themselves; or go through with the claim and sign over all claim payments to the buyers so they could do the repairs. They decided to fix the property themselves and signed the contract for sale once this was done.

A few years later I encountered a homeowner who also happened to be a realtor and we started talking about selling a property just after an insurable loss had damaged it. She said that she'd gone through the same situation as above with a property she had bought for investment. Wind damaged a property just as she had begun trying to sell it. She'd decided that she would file the claim and then endorse all insurance payments over to the buyers, thinking that if *she* had been the buyer, she would have wanted to know who was going to do the repairs, so that she could choose her own contractor rather than having it chosen for her, in doing so, also choosing the level of quality of the repairs.

That made sense to me: would you want someone who no longer has a stake in your new home fix it or would you want to have it fixed yourself? The only downside to doing it this way is if the buyers select a contractor whose estimate for repair is so far above the amount of the insurance company offer that settlement becomes next to impossible. If this is the scenario that homeowners wish to pursue, it is recommended that the buyer's contractor agree with the insurance company's estimate, or work out any differences, before anything is signed.

The "rules" for which party can claim what when a property is damaged in the middle of a sale are cut and dry. If a property is damaged before a contract for sale is signed (assuming the sellers still have a policy in force) the claim is paid on the seller's insurance policy. If a contract for sale is signed at 3pm and at 6pm of the same day a tornado damages the home, the buyers are responsible for the loss. The key about which party assumes responsibility is the Date of Loss in relation to the time and date the contract for sale was signed. Years ago, a claims manager told me a nightmarish tale: unbeknownst to the sellers of a property, in the months before they sold a home, an insurable type of hidden damage was causing silent, unnoticed damage. The damage was discovered after the home was sold by the new buyers during a remodel and when they called their insurance company their insurer said the damage had begun before the policy went into force and therefore they couldn't cover it. The buyers then went to the sellers of the property and said they would have to file a claim with their insurance to claim the damage, which, in this case, would have been covered because it was still within the 60 day notification deadline, but the former sellers refused. (They probably thought their premiums would go up if they did.) You can imagine the mess that ensued. After threats of legal action, the sellers eventually did the right thing and filed a claim with their insurer, but the buyers agreed to pay the deductible.

If the sale of a home is done privately, without realtors, and damage is done to the home before the final sale, make sure that whatever agreements or deals are worked out between buyers and sellers is written and signed by both parties. To repeat an insurance mantra: if is isn't in writing, it doesn't exist.

Chapter 28: Re-inspection

R e-inspection" has kind of a sinister sound to it, like when a doctor tells you he needs to do additional testing—what kind of testing, testing for what, what could I have, Doc? Re-inspection in regards to insurance claims can be as simple as a routine exam or as difficult as pulling teeth. There are two types of Re-inspections: the follow-up and, for lack of a better term, a second first inspection. The follow-up inspection is fairly common and fairly routine, an inspection to discover further damage that was not visible upon an initial inspection like damage behind walls, under floors, beneath roof shingles, damages found during the course of repairs. Usually this entails an adjuster, sometime the original adjuster, sometimes a different adjuster, stopping by, taking a few pictures, a few notes, some measurements, simple and painless. At this point, a supplemental estimate and payment is issued, often based upon what the contractor submits to the adjuster for additional work necessary. Simple and painless.

A "second first" re-inspection can be a little more trying. First of all, what the heck does a "second first inspection" mean? What it means is that a second adjuster inspects the damaged property as though it has never been inspected by an adjuster before. It's the second inspection done as though it were the first and only inspection. Insurers don't typically willingly send adjusters out to do this type of re-inspection, except in the case of Quality Control Re-inspections that are done to make sure that the adjusters are doing what they're supposed to and don't miss things. A "second first" re-inspection is requested, sometimes demanded, by homeowners when they feel they haven't received the best or most thorough inspection possible, or if they disagree with the assessment of the first adjuster. Insurers are reticent to send out a different adjuster to do the same inspection because of time lost and money spent. Sometimes if an inspection was clearly botched by an inexperienced adjuster, it becomes necessary (I've re-inspected a few homes where the adjuster didn't do the best job; one time, the previous adjuster had photos in the claim file that didn't even belong to that house!) or missed enough damaged items to warrant a re-inspection. If a homeowner demands that a re-inspection be done because they disagree with the assessment of the adjuster, an insurer is going to be less willing to send another adjuster to "bid against" the first adjuster. It does happen, though, in order to preserve high levels of customer service. If a homeowner wants a re-inspection because of this, he is going to have to complain very loudly to the right people to get his way. It is not automatic that an insurer is going to agree to this type of re-inspection: chain-of-command ladders may have to be climbed, agents may have to be called, calls to upper management made. If a homeowner is insistent and persists that a re-inspection be made, an insurer will eventually meet his demand.

Chapter 29: Home Inventories: Why They Make Sense

Before a tornado, hurricane, fire or earthquake destroys all of your personal property, one thing homeowners can do is prepare a detailed home inventory. To be sure, home inventories are not a task for those who have mastered the art of procrastination.

A home inventory is just what it sounds like, a detailed accounting of every last one of your personal property items, and is a way of documenting a loss before a loss occurs. A home inventory could be a comprehensive written list or a list augmented with photos, videos and receipts. When prepared before a catastrophic loss, a home inventory can save a preposterous amount of time and effort it would otherwise take to attempt to remember every last dish, pen, DVD, book, tool, etc., after a total loss.

As with any other form of documentation, the more detailed a home inventory is, the better. The information needed for items in an inventory include its age, place of purchase and, if known, its replacement cost. When doing my inventory, it helped to go room by room, and then further categorize some items, like media (DVDs, CDs, etc.) within a room.

For appliances and big-ticket items, (like that new flat screen TV) aside from a clear photo, it is important to note not just the model number but also the serial number. A documented serial number will go a long way toward substantiating a claim for an item, especially if it specially scheduled like jewlry or high-dollar item like the aforementioned TV:

"Yeah, Mr. Adjuster, I bought a 60" LCD TV a few months ago. Cost six grand."

"Have any documentation to prove you had a giant TV?"

"Uh...no, why, do I need it?"

That's one less phone call or visit to a bank, credit card company or store to verify a purchase and provide proof of loss.

Storing a home inventory can be an interesting dilemma. Obviously you want to keep a home inventory outside your home, such as in a safety deposit box. Of course, for those who are digitally inclined, the internet has become a wonderful resource for just this sort of thing. The website www.KnowYourStuff.org from the Insurance Information Institute offers free on-line software that allows users to build a list of their personal property items. I've e-mailed my home inventory to myself and keep it on line. There are also a plethora of inventory services on-line, including www.InsuranceVault.net, where you can store a home inventory for free. There's even an iPhone application for home inventories called iInventory.

Glossary/Index

Accident
A sudden, unintended event or occurence that casuses loss or damaged to insured property. 33, 34, 35,37, 38, 39, 40, 45, 54, 57, 64, 65, 187,191, 204.

Actual Cash Value (ACV)
Replacement Cost Value minus depreciation (RCV – Depreciation = ACV); the present value of an item with regards to its age, condition and lifespan. Some items, such as collectibles, gain in value over time, increasing their ACV; some items decrease in value over time, lowering their value. 69, 107, 109, 114, 115, 118, 122, 123, 124, 242, 243

Adjuster
An individual who inspects and adjusts insurance claims. Also known as claim representatives, adjusters work for insurers to assess claims and negotiate settlement. Adjusters that work for homeowners are known as Public Adjusters. See Public Adjuster below. 15, 24, 68, 85, 87, 88, 90-101, 103, 106, 110, 120, 126, 128, 130, 131, 142-144, 148, 149, 151, 153-156, 159, 160, 162, 165-167, 170, 174-176, 181, 186, 194, 196, 197, 202, 215, 218, 222, 225, 229, 230, 239, 247, 248, 250

Additional Living Expenses (ALE)
The necessary living expenses paid to homeowners after an insurable loss renders their home unlivable. ALE can be paid after the damages occur or during the reconstruction or repairs. ALE are expenses above and beyond all normal living expenses incurred by living away from home, include rental/hotel, food, utilities, laundry, transportation, etc., when a loss is caused by a type of covered damage. See Chapter 22. 67, 68, 142, 157, 186, 187, 198, 199, 200, 216-220

Appraisal/Arbitration
The process of settling a claim in which an independent third party places a value or judgment upon the item(s) that are disputed. 43, 142,

149, 151, 152

Appreciation
The increase in value of an item over time. Most homes appreciate over time while their individual components may actually decrease in value over time.

Appurtenant Structures
Building items that are permanently affixed to the real estate but are not directly attached to the dwelling, such as detached garages, fences, sheds on a permanent (concrete) foundation, gazebos, docks, driveways. See also Dwelling Extensions. 199, 243

Buy Back
The process that allows homeowners to keep damaged personal property items for a discounted settlement amount that is below the full replacement cost. See Chapter 9, "Salvage and Buy Back." 152, 153, 154

Claimant
A person or entity that makes a claim on a loss. 203

Collateral Damage or Corresponding Damage
Damages that match other damages to a property after a loss. When there is a question whether or not damages were caused by a specific kind of loss, adjusters look for collateral damages or the absence of them to aid in determining cause of loss. 236

Conditions
The section of a policy that states what homeowners must do after a loss, the method of valuing a loss and the specific rights granted policyholders following a loss. 28, 41, 42, 43, 46, 55, 68, 69, 70, 71, 78, 100, 103, 105, 126, 141, 142, 152, 156, 169, 170, 222, 224, 225

Contents
Personal property items insured under a homeowner's or renter's insurance policy. Also known as Coverage B with some insurers. Contents can be scheduled, in which each item individually listed, or fall under a blanket policy limit. Types of damages/losses for contents are limited to what is specifically listed under Section I – Losses Insured. 33, 34, 35, 37, 41, 59, 62, 64

Coverage A
For most insurers, Coverage A is structural or building items that are connected to the realty, including a home, an attached or detached garage, shed on a permanent foundation, fences, docks, gazebos, in-ground swimming pools that are covered under a homeowners policy. Some policies list the residence as Coverage A and all appurtenant structures as Coverage B. 29, 30, 35, 38, 42, 44, 45, 46, 47, 48, 49, 52, 58, 59, 61, 66, 67, 119, 150, 222

Coverage B
Personal property items covered under a homeowners policy. Some policies list personal property as Coverage C or Coverage D. 29, 30, 34, 35, 36, 42, 44, 58, 60, 61, 66, 150, 206, 222

Coverage C
Coverage that provides for the loss of use (Additional Living Expenses and Loss of Rents) of a home or rental property or rented garage. Some insurers call this Coverage D. 29, 32, 58, 67, 217, 220

Deductible
The amount of a loss that a homeowner is responsible for paying. This amount is deducted from the final settlement amount. 21, 23, 34, 31, 33, 34, 35, 50, 61, 62, 68, 72, 83, 87, 88, 108, 113, 114, 117, 118, 121-125, 162, 181, 185-188, 196, 199, 200, 201, 204, 205, 208, 213, 214, 217, 223, 224, 243, 244, 246

Depreciation

The decrease in value of an item over time. While most homes appreciate over time many individual components may actually decrease in value over time. Deprecation is generally based upon the age and condition of the items in question versus its expected lifespan. Insurers use depreciation to determine the present value of a loss and pay that amount until the items stolen or damaged are replaced. 69, 107-109, 113-121, 151, 162, 201, 224, 243

Documentation

Any physical record of a loss, including photos, receipts, invoices, a log of communications with an insurer, a log of hours doing work for a claim. 19, 41, 42, 82, 84, 85, 86, 89, 90, 91, 96, 97, 126, 130, 160, 201, 208, 219, 224, 249, 250

Dwelling Extensions

Building items that are permanently affixed to the real estate but are not directly attached to the dwelling, such as detached garages, fences, sheds on a permanent (concrete) foundation, gazebos, docks, driveways. See also Appurtenant Structures. 30, 35, 42, 44, 45, 46, 47, 50, 55, 243

Endorsement(s)

Policy add-ons that may increase, limit or provide a specific type of coverage beyond what is stated in a standard policy. Some endorsements include Earthquake, business use of a dwelling, additional coverage for jewelry and furs, computers, sewer backup/sump pump overflow, and firearms. See also Rider. 52, 55, 56, 68, 71, 72, 73, 144, 192, 195, 196, 198, 204, 206

Estimate

When given by an insurer to a homeowner, it is the written approximation of the value of a claim, stating the total amount of the loss and any depreciation or deductibles that may apply. When given by a contractor to a homeowner, it is the approximation of how much money it may cost to replace or repair items damaged by a covered loss. 15, 42, 69, 83, 96, 102, 103, 105-119, 122, 123, 126, 128, 129, 130, 132, 134-136, 140, 143, 146-151, 153, 158, 159, 160, 170, 201, 212, 222, 224, 225, 246, 247

Exclusion(s)
The items listed in a policy for which there is no coverage. Some exclusions may be overridden when the proximate cause is a type of loss that is covered. XII, 28, 32, 38, 40, 50, 52-59, 62, 221, 220, 224

Flood Insurance
Insurance protection against the peril of flooding. Flood insurance is issued only by the NFIP, the National Flood Insurance Program, and is not covered under homeowners insurance. 68, 164

Indemnity
The financial security or protection against an insurable loss.

Indemnify
The compensation for an insurable loss.

Insurable Loss
A type of loss that is covered under a policy or is not specifically excluded. 67, 151, 245

Insured
The persons or entity that buys an insurance policy from an insurance company. 108, 125, 126, 127, 128, 155, 217

Lien Release
A document that waives a contractor's or material supplier's right to put a lien against a property in case the property owner does not pay the contractor or if the contractor does not pay the material supplier. 160, 161

Line Item

The individual items found in a written estimate from an insurer or contractor. Each line item should have a brief description, the quantity and may also have price per unit. 107, 108, 110, 111, 113, 114, 117, 142, 147, 148

Line of Sight

Laws stating that there must be uniform appearance for materials or items within a continuous line of sight. 104

Loss

The damage, misplacement or theft of a policyholder's property; or the physical injury of a claimant. 15, 23, 29, 30-52, 55-63, 66-70, 77-90, 95-100, 102, 103, 105, 108, 113, 115, 128-130, 140-143, 150-152, 154, 156, 157, 158, 159, 161, 164-167, 169, 184, 187, 188, 190-102, 196, 198, 201, 204, 205, 208, 209, 212-217, 220, 226, 228, 233, 237, 242-247, 250

Loss of Rents

When an insurable loss causes a rental property to become uninhabitable or otherwise forces the renters to vacate the premises, this is the amount of money paid to the property owner to compensate for the loss of the rental fees. 67, 68, 216, 220

Loss of Use

See Additional Living Expenses and Loss of Rents. 29, 32, 66, 67, 216

Mediation

Reconciliation of a dispute that uses an unbiased third party to decide the final settlement amount of a contested claim. 149, 202

Mitigation

The prevention or reduction of further damage/loss after an insurable loss. Mitigation of damages is a primary responsibility of a policyholder after a loss. 81

Mortgagee

The company or individual that loans money for another party to purchase an item, especially a home. 43, 44, 70

Open Peril

A type of insurance policy that provides coverage for all sudden accidental direct losses that may be sustained by a policyholder except for the types of losses that are specifically excluded. Some policies are open peril for building and personal property items, some only offer open peril coverage to structural items. 29, 45, 52, 59, 66

Peril

An event that causes damage or loss to property. Perils may be man-made (such as theft and vandalism) or natural events such as wind, hail, lightning, fire and water. 29, 34, 35, 37, 41, 45, 46, 48, 52, 59, 66, 67

Policy

The written contract between an insurer and policyholder for which the insurer promises to provide the coverage stated in the policy in exchange for payment for that coverage. XII, 14, 16, 21, 22, 24, 28, 29, 30, 32, 33, 34, 37, 39, 41-53, 55-57, 59-62, 64, 66-69, 71-73, 76, 77, 80-82, 85, 87, 89, 90, 95, 100, 101, 105, 106, 115, 123, 124, 126, 127, 128, 140-143, 145, 149, 152, 154, 156, 158, 164, 165, 169, 170, 184, 185, 187, 190-192, 194, 195, 198-206, 212, 223, 225, 227, 234, 242-244, 246

Policy Limit

The stated limit of financial liability of an insurer for a specific type of coverage. 34, 42, 45, 47-49, 51, 59-62, 69, 71-73, 89, 123, 124, 141, 184, 185, 192, 199, 200, 205, 206, 223, 242, 243, 244

Premium

The annual, semi-annual or monthly payment a policyholder makes to an insurer in exchange for insurance coverage. 76, 246

Proof of Loss
The written statement given to an insurer that declares a policyholder's loss due to an insurable loss and the facts pertaining to a loss. 41, 68, 85, 203, 250

Proximate Cause
The root cause of damages. When investigating losses, insurers look for the proximate cause to determine whether a loss is covered or not. 45, 46, 49, 50, 54-56, 59, 95, 165, 191, 214

Public Adjuster
An adjuster hired by a policyholder to determine the value of a claim in exchange for a percentage of the amount of the settlement. 142-144

Replacement Cost Value (RCV)
The financial value of item(s) in which the full replacement may be made. Homeowners policies that are replacement cost policies insure for the total replacement of items that are lost, stolen or damaged by a type of loss for which the items are insured. 107, 109, 113, 115, 242

Remediation
The reduction or elimination of damages from water or mold. Remediation contractors such as Serv-Pro and ServiceMaster rid properties of water and visible mold. 51, 191, 192, 206

Rider
Policy add-ons that may increase, limit or provide a specific type of coverage beyond what is stated in a standard policy. Some endorsements include Earthquake, business use of a dwelling, additional coverage for jewelry and furs, computers, sewer backup/sump pump overflow and firearms. See also Endorsement.

Risk
The property that is insured. With homeowners insurance, the Risk is the home and/or property being insured. 15

Salvage
Personal property items that are damaged but still have useful life which are hauled away by an insurer and then auctioned at a discounted price. See Chapter 9, under Salvage and Buy-Back. 33, 152, 153

Scheduled Items
An item that has its own specific policy limits and is listed separately in the declarations page. Scheduled items might include items that require additional insurance or limits like special pieces of jewelry, a valuable painting or artwork or even an extra-large garage that would require additional coverage above and beyond what is ordinarily provided. 71, 73, 243, 244, 250

Scope of Loss
The information collected by an insurance adjuster that tells the story of a loss: what happened, how it happened, where it happened, what was damaged, the age and condition of the items damaged, how much time, if any, a homeowner spent making temporary repairs, etc. Any record that documents the loss becomes part of the Scope of Loss. 96

Scope of Repairs
The methods, quantities and quality of materials to be used to make the repairs to a damaged property. The information collected in the Scope of Loss becomes the basis of the Scope of Repairs, which in turn becomes the estimate generated by the insurer and given to the homeowner. 96, 103, 104, 147, 148, 159

SIU or Special Investigative Unit
The division of an insurance company that investigates potential insurance fraud. Adjusters forward suspected cases of fraud to them.

Subrogation
The financial liability of a third party for a loss. An insurer may opt to pay a claim and then pursue legal action against a non-insured to collect their portion of a claim when it is the opinion of the insurer that

a third party is partially or wholly responsible for the loss. For example, if a thief breaks into a home and steals property and is then caught, the insurer may sue the thief for any property damage or loss of property that they have already paid. 44

Subsidence
Downward or upward movement of land that causes damage to a property, especially to the foundation or walls of a home. The settling of a house is one form of subsidence. 40, 56

Supplement/Supplemental Payment
An additional payment of a claim above and beyond the initial settlement amount that is not part of the deferred payment. Supplemental Payments are often for previously unknown/unseen damages that are discovered after the inspection of the property or are made for additional work that is required as the result of additional damages or additional steps needed for the repair of damaged property. 25, 129, 130, 143, 159, 160

Underwriting
The process of insuring items or the department in an insurance company that determines how much or if a property should be insured.

Valued Policy/Valued Policy State
In the case of a total loss, a valued policy automatically pays the policy limits, less ACV. Some states mandate this kind of loss assessment for all total losses. Some states limit types of losses, like Mississippi, which only applies to fire losses. Arkansas, Florida,Georgia, Kansas, Louisiana Minnesota, Mississippi, Missouri, Montana, Nebraska, New Hampshire, North Dakota, Ohio, South Carolina, South Dakota, Texas, West Virginia, and Wisconsin are all valued policy state. Check with an adjuster or an attorney from your state for any restrictions or limits.

Resources

Free forms available at www.ClaimGameBook.com

Homeowner advocates: www.UnitedPolicyholders.org

Insurance Information Institute: www.III.org; www.KnowYour Stuff.org.

Home Inventories:
www.InsuranceVault.net (free)
www.EProoft.com
www.KCHomeinventory.com

Consumer Action Website (basic information on homeowners insurance): www.consumer action.gov/caw_insurance_homeowner_renter.shtml

Federal Citizen Information Center (publications on insurance; listed under "housing"): www.pueblo.gsa.gov

American Arbitration Association: www.ADR.org.

Haag Engineering: www.Haag Engineering.com

National Weather Service Storm Prediction Center: www.SPC.NOAA.gov

State Departments of Insurance:

Alabama
Alabama Department of Insurance
P.O. Box 303351
Montgomery, AL 36130-3351
Phone: 334-269-3550
FAX: 334-241-4192
Web: www.ALDOI.org
E-mail: insdept@insurance.alabama.gov

Alaska
Alaska Division of Insurance
Juneau:
9th Floor Office Bldg.
333 Willoughby Avenue
Juneau, AK 99801
Anchorage:
Robert B Atwood Building
550 W 7th Ave, Suite 1560
Anchorage, AK 99501
Phone: 907-465-2515
Web: www.dced.state.ak.us/insurance
E-mail: insurance@commerce.state.ak.us

Arizona
AZ-DOI
2910 N. 44th St. Suite 210
Phoenix, AZ 85018-7256
Phone: 800-325-2548
Web: www.id.state.az.us

Arkansas
Arkansas Insurance Department
1200 West Third Street
Little Rock, AR 72201
Phone: 800-282-9134
Web: www.state.ar.us/insurance

California
Phone: (in state) 800-927-4357
Phone: (out of state) 213-897-8921
Web: www.insurance.ca.gov

Colorado
Division of Insurance
1560 Broadway, Suite 850
Denver, CO 80202
Phone: 800-930-3745
Web: www.dora.state.co.us/insurance
E-mail: insurance@dora.state.co.us

Connecticut
State of Connecticut Insurance Department
153 Market Street
Hartford, CT 06103

Phone: (CT only) 800-203-3447
Web: www.ct.gov/cid/site/default.asp

Delaware
Delaware Insurance Department
841 Silver Lake Blvd.
Dover, DE 19904
Phone: (DE only) 800-282-8611
Web: www.state.de.us/inscom

Florida
Office of Insurance Consumer Advocate
200 East Gaines St.
Tallahassee, FL 32399-0308
Phone: 800-342-2762
Web: www.fldfs.com

Georgia
Insurance and Safety Fire Commissioner's Office
2 Martin Luther King, Jr. Drive
West Tower, Suite 704
Atlanta, GA 30334
Phone: 404-656-2070
Phone: 800-656-2298
FAX: 404-657-8542
Web: www.gainsurance.org

Hawaii
Insurance Division
P.O. Box 3614
Honolulu, HI 96811
Phone: 808-586-2790

FAX: 808-586-2806
Web: www.hawaii.gov/dcca/
areas/ins/main
E-mail: insurance@dcca.hawaii.
gov

Idaho
Department of Insurance
700 West State Street
P.O. Box 83720
Boise, ID 83720-0043
Phone: 208-334-4250
FAX: 208-334-4398
Web: www.doi.state.id.us

Illinois
Springfield:
Division of Insurance
320 W. Washington Street
Springfield, IL 62767-0001
Phone: 217-782-4515
FAX: 217-782-5020

Chicago:
Division of Insurance
James R. Thompson Center
100 W. Randolph Street, Suite
9-301
Chicago, IL 60601-3395
Phone: 312-814-2420
FAX: 312-814-5416

Web: www.idfpr.com/doi/main
E-mail: Director@ins.state.il.us

Indiana
Indiana Department of Insurance
311 West Washington Street,
Suite 300
Indianapolis, IN 46204-2787
Phone: 317-232-2385
FAX: 317-232-5251
Web: www.ai.org/idoi/index
E-mail: doi@state.in.us

Iowa
Iowa Insurance Division
330 Maple Street
Des Moines, IA 50319-0065
Phone: 515-281-6348
Toll free: 877-955-1212
FAX: 515-281-3059
Web: www.IID.state.ia.us

Kansas
Kansas Insurance Department
420 SW 9th Street
Topeka, KS 66612-1678
Phone: 785-296-3071
Toll free (Kansas only): 800-432-2484
FAX: 785-296-2283
E-mail: webcomplain@
Ksinsurance.org
Web: www.ksinsurance.org

Kentucky
U.S. Postal Mail:
Kentucky Office of Insurance
P.O. Box 517

Frankfort, KY 40602

Other delivery services:
215 West Main Street
Frankfort, KY 40601

Phone: 800-595-6053
TTY: 800-462-2801
Web: www.doi.ky.gov/kentucky

Louisiana
Louisiana Department of
Insurance
P.O. Box 94214
Baton Rouge, LA 70802
Phone: 225-342-5900
Toll free (Louisiana only): 800-
259-530
Web: www.ldi.state.la.us

Maine
Bureau of Insurance
124 Northern Avenue
Gardiner, ME 04345
Phone: 207-624-8475
Toll free (Maine only): 800-300-
5000
FAX: 207-624-8599
Web: www.state.me.us/pfr/ins

Maryland
Maryland Insurance
Administration
525 St. Paul Place
Baltimore, MD 21202-2272

Phone: 410-468-2000
Toll free: 800-492-6116
TTY: 800-735-2258
Web: www.mdinsurance.state.
md.us

Massachusetts
Division of Insurance
1 South Station, 5th Floor
Boston, MA 02110
Phone: 617-521-7777
Toll free (MA only): 888-283-
3757
FAX: 617-973-8798
E-mail: consumer@state.ma.us
Web: www.mass.gov.doi

Michigan
Office of Financial and Insurance
Services
P.O. Box 30220
Lansing, MI 48909-7720
Phone: 517-373-9273
FAX: 517-335-4978
E-mail: ofis-fin-info@michicgan.
gov
Web: www.michigan.gov

Minnesota
Minnesota Department of
Commerce
85 7th Place East, Suite 500
St. Paul, MN 55101
Phone: 800-657-3602 (MN
only)

Phone: 651-296-2488
FAX: 651-296-4328
Web: www.state.mn.us

Mississippi
Mississippi Department of
Insurance
P.O. Box 79
Jackson, MS 39205
Phone: 601-359-3569
Toll free (MS only): 800-562-
2957
Web: www.doi.state.ms.us

Missouri
Missouri Department of
Insurance
P.O. Box 690
Jefferson City, MO 65102-0690
Phone: 573-751-4126
FAX: 573-751-1165
Web: www.insurance.state.mo.us

Montana
State Auditor's Office
840 Helena Avenue
Helena, MT 59601
Phone: 800-332-6148
TDD: 406-444-3246
Web: www.state.mt.us/sao

Nebraska
Nebraska Department of
Insurance
Terminal Building

941 "O" Street, Suite 400
Lincoln, NE 68508-3639
Phone: 402-471-2201
Toll free: 877-564-7323
TDD: 800-833-7352
Web: www.doi.ne.gov

Nevada
Nevada Division of Insurance
Carson City:
788 Fairview Drive, Suite 300
Carson City, NV 89701
Phone: 775-687-4270
FAX: 775-687-3937

Las Vegas:
2501 East Sahara Avenue, Suite
302
Las Vegas, NV 89104
Phone: 702-486-4009
FAX: 702-486-4007

E-mail: insinfo@doi.state.nv.us
Web: www.doi.state.nv.us

New Hampshire
New Hampshire Insurance
Department
21 South Fruit Street, Suite 14
Concord, NH 03301
Phone: 800-852-3416
FAX: 603-271-0248
Web: www.state.nh.us/insurance

New Jersey
New Jersey Division of Insurance
P.O. Box 325
Trenton, NJ 08625
Phone: 609-292-5360
E-mail: commissioner@dobi.
state.nj.us
Web: www.state.nj.us/dobi

New Mexico
New Mexico Insurance Division
P.E.R.A. Building
120 Paseo de Peralta
P.O. Box 1269
Santa Fe, NM 87504-1269
Phone: 505-827-4601
FAX: 505-827-4734
Web: www.nmprc.state.nm.us/
insurance

New York
Phone: 800-342-3736
Phone: 212-602-0429

Albany:
Insurance Department
One Commerce Plaza
Albany, NY 12257

New York City:
Insurance Department
25 Beaver Street
New York, NY 10004

Buffalo:

Insurance Department
Walter Mahoney Office Bldg
65 Court Street
Buffalo, NY 14202

Syracuse:
Insurance Department
620 Erie Blvd West
Suite 105
Syracuse, NY 13204

Web: www.ins.state.ny.us

North Carolina
North Carolina Department of
Insurance
1201 Mail Service Center
Raleigh, NC 27699-1201
Phone (NC only): 800-546-5664
Phone (outside NC): 919-733-
2032
E-mail: consumer@ncdoi.net
Web: www.ncdoi.com

North Dakota
North Dakota Insurance
Department
State Capitol, Fifth Floor
600 East Boulevard Avenue
Bismarck, ND 58505-0320
Phone: 701-328-2440
Toll free: 800-247-0560
FAX: 701-328-4880
Web: www.state.nd.us/ndins

Ohio
Ohio Department of Insurance
2100 Stella Court
Columbus, OH 43215-1067
Phone: 614-644-2658
FAX: 614-728-1280
E-mail: property.casualty@ins.
state.oh.us
Web: www.ins.state.oh.us

Oklahoma
Oklahoma Insurance
Department

Oklahoma City:
2401 N.W. 23rd, Suite 28
Shepherd Mall
P.O. Box 53408
Oklahoma City, OK 73152-
3408
Phone: 405-521-2828
Phone: 800-522-0071

Tulsa Office:
3105 E. Skelly Drive, Suite 305
Tulsa, OK 74105
Phone: 918-747-7700
Phone: 800-728-2906

E-mail: feedback@insurance.
state.ok.us
Web: www.oid.state.ok.us

Oregon
Oregon Insurance Division

P.O. Box 14480
Salem, OR 97309-0405
Phone: 503-947-7980
FAX: 503-378-4351
Web: www.cbs.state.or.us/ins

Pennsylvania
Insurance Department

Harrisburg:
Room 1321 Strawberry Square
Harristown State Office Bldg. #1
Harrisburg, PA 17120
Phone: 717-787-2317
FAX: 717-787-8585

Philadelphia:
Room 1701 State Office Bldg.
1400 Spring Garden Street
Philadelphia, PA 19130
Phone: 215-560-2630
FAX: 215-560-2648

Pittsburg:
Room 304 State Office Bldg.
300 Liberty Avenue
Pittsburgh, PA 15222
Phone: 412-565-5020
FAX: 412-565-7648

Web: www.insurance.state.pa.us

Puerto Rico
Oficina del Comisionado de
Seguros

Edif. Cobian's Plaza Piso LM
Ave. Ponce de León #1607
Parada 23
Santurce, PR 00909
Tel.: 787-722-8686
FAX: 787-722-4400
Web: www.ocs.gobierno.pr

Rhode Island
Department of Business
Regulation
Insurance Division
233 Richmond Street, Suite 233
Providence, RI 02903-4233
Phone: 401-222-2223
FAX: 401-222-5475
TDD: 401-222-2999
Web: www.dbr.ri.gov

South Carolina
Department of Insurance
P.O. Box 100105
Columbia, SC 29202-3105
Phone: 803-737-6180
Toll free: (SC only) 800-768-
3467
Web: www.doi.state.sc.us
E-mail:cnsmMail@doi.state.sc.us

Tennessee
Department of Commerce and
Insurance
500 James Robertson Parkway
Davy Crockett Tower
Nashville, TN 37243-0565

Phone: 615-741-2241
Web: www.state.tn.us/commerce

Texas
Texas Department of Insurance
333 Guadalupe
Austin, TX 78701
Phone: 512-463-6169
Toll free: 800-252-3439
Web: www.tdi.state.tx.us

Utah
Utah Department of Insurance
3110 State Office Building
Salt Lake City, UT 84114-6901
Phone: 801-538-3800
Toll free: 800-439-3805
FAX: 801-538-3829
Web: www.insurance.state.ut.us

Vermont
Banking, Insurance, Securities &
Health Care Administration
89 Main St.
Drawer 20
Montpelier, VT 05620-3101
Phone: 802-828-3301
FAX: 802-828-3306
Web: www.BISHCA.state.vt.us

Virginia
Bureau of Insurance
P.O. Box 1157
Richmond, VA 23218
Phone: 804-371-9741

Toll free: 877-310-6560
TDD: 804-371-9206
Web: www.scc.virginia.gov/
division/boi
E-mail: bureauofinsurance@scc.
virginia.gov

Washington
Office of the Insurance
Commissioner
Phone: 360-725-7080
Toll free: 800-562-6900
TDD: 360-586-0241
FAX: 360-586-2018
E-Mail:CAD@oic.wa.gov
Web: www.insurance.wa.gov/oic

West Virginia
Phone: 304-558-3386
Toll free: 888-879-9842
Web: www.WVinsurance.gov

Wisconsin
Office of the Commissioner of
Insurance
125 South Webster Street
Madison, WI 53702
Phone, Madison: 608-266-3585
Toll free: 800-236-8517
TDD: 711 (ask for 608-266-3586)
FAX: 608-266-9935
Web: www.oci.WI.gov/oci

Wyoming
Wyoming Insurance Department
Herschler Bldg. 3rd Floor East
122 West 25th Street
Cheyenne, WY 82002
Phone: 307-777-7401
Toll free: (Wyoming Only) 800-438-5768
FAX: 307-777-5895
Web: www.insurance.state.WY.us
E-mail: wyinsdept@state.wy.us

Appendix

Depreciation Tables

Structural items:

Item	Life Expectancy (in years)	Yearly Depreciation (by %)
Appliances – Built-in		
Dishwasher	10	10 %
Garbage Disposal	10	10
Range Hood	20	5
Trash Compactor	10	10
Awnings and Patio Covers		
Metal	30	3.33
Canvas	5	20
Cabinetry		
Wood cabinetry	20	5
Concrete and Asphalt		
Concrete wall	200	.50
Concrete slabs	30	3.33
Asphalt	10	10
Doors		
Interior	35	2.86
Exterior	50	2
Drywall		
All	50	2
Flooring		
Carpet	10	10
Ceramic Tile	100	1
Vinyl	25	4

Wood	100	1
Laminate	20	5

Fencing

Wood	12	8.33
Vinyl	35	2.86

Finish Carpentry Trim Work

All	75	1.33

Finish Hardware

All	20	5

Fireplaces

Masonry	100	1

Framing Lumber

All	100	1

Decks

Wood	15	6.67
Composite	30	3.33

Glass

All	100	1

Insulation

All	100	1

Masonry

All	100	1

Ornamental Iron

All	75	1.33

Plaster

All	50	2

Paint

Interior	15	6.67
Exterior	10	10

Roofing

Composition – 20 year	20	5
Composition – 25 year	25	4
Composition – 30 year	30	3.33
Composition – 40 year	40	2.50
Composition – 50 year	50	2
Built-up	30	3.33
Metal	35	2.86
Rubber	10	10
Slate	75	1.33
Tile clay/concrete/ composite	50	2
Wood shakes	35	2.86

Sheds

Metal/vinyl	25	4

Siding, Soffit, Fascia, Guttering

Wood	50	2
Metal	30	3.33
Vinyl	30	3.33

Windows

Aluminum	20	5
Vinyl	30	3.33
Wood	40	2.5
Window Screens	15	6.67

Personal Property Items

Item	Life Expectancy (in years)	Yearly Depreciation (by %)
Appliances		
Freezer	15	6.67 %
Microwave	10	10
Range/Oven	15	6.67
Refrigerator	15	6.67
Others	10	10
Cameras		
Cameras/Camcorders	15	6.67
Accessories	10	10
Clothing and Luggage		
Shoes	3	33
Undergarments and		
Socks	3	33
All Other Clothing	4	25
Luggage	20	5
Computers and Peripherals		
All	7	15
Electronics		
Cellular Phones	5	20
All Others	10	10
Firearms		
All	20	5
Furniture		
Indoor Upholstered	10	10
Outdoor	15	6.67
Solid Wood	50	2

Housewares
Curtains/Drapes	10	10
Mirrors	20	5
Clocks	20	5

Infant Products
All	5	20

Lawn and Garden
Electric Powered Tools	20	5
Grills	10	10
Gas Powered Tools	7	15
Hand Tools	20	5
Toys/Play sets	5	20
Yard Decorations	10	10

Linens
Blankets	10	10
Kitchen Linens	5	20
Pillow Cases	5	20
Sheets	5	20
Quilts	20	5
All Other Bedding	5	20

Office Supplies
Safes and Vaults	50	2
All Other Items	10	10

Pet Supplies
All	10	10

Sporting Goods
All	10	10

Tools

Electric	20	5
Gas	10	10
Manual	20	5

Toys

Electronic	5	20
Non-electronic	10	10
Outdoor	5	20

Watches

All	10	10

Roofing

When removing roofing, the actual square footage is used. When Replacing roofing, waste is added to the quantity; how much waste depends on the shape of the roof. Roofing is quantified in squares. There is 100 square feet in one square. To calculate number of squares, divide square footage by 100. Example: 1,000 SF ÷ 100 = 10 Squares.

Gable

To calculate square footage of a gable roof: (A + B) x C =

Waste Factor: 10%

Hip

Square footage: (A + B) x C =

Waste Factor: 15%

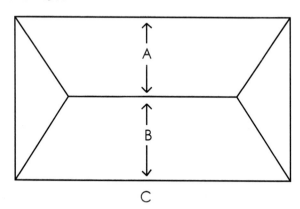

Gambrel

Square footage: (A + B +C + D) x F = SF

Waste factor: 10%

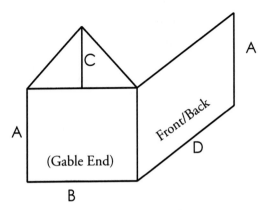

Siding

Siding is measured in square feet or squares, depending on the contractor.

Gable ends:

$$[(A \times B) + (B \div 2) \times C] \times 2 = Y$$

Front and Back:

$$(D \times A) \, 2 = Z$$

Total for two gable ends and front and back: $(Y + Z) \, 2$

Other basic measurements

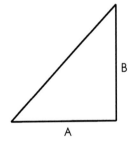

Triangle

$$(A \div 2) \times B = area$$

Trapezoid

$$[(A + B) \div 2] \times C = area$$

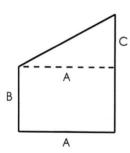

Sloped ceilings

For rooms with vaulted or sloped ceilings, to find the area of the sloping walls, combine the formulas for a rectangle and a triangle:

$$(B \times A) + (C \div 2) \times A = area$$

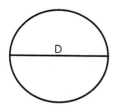

Circle

$$(D \times D) \times .7854 = area$$

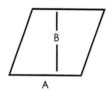

Parallelogram

$$A \times B = area$$

www.QuarterSawnBooks.com

Order Form

$15.95 per copy $_____

Tax: Iowa residents add 6% tax ($0.96 per copy) $_____

Shipping - $4/single copy, $2/each additional copy $_____

TOTAL: $_____

Ship to:

Name:_____

Address:_____

City, State, ZIP:_____

Select Payment Type:

☐ Check or Money Order (make checks out to Quarter Sawn Books)

☐ Credit Card (cards will not be charged until orders are shipped)

Credit card information:

Type of card: ☐ VISA   ☐ MASTERCARD   ☐ AMEX

Name on card:_____

Card number:_____

Expiration Date:_____ (mm/yyyy)   CCV:_____

(The CCV on Visa and Mastercard is a three-digit number that can be found on the back side of the card; on AmEx it is four-digits and is on the front)

Signature:_____

FAX completed form to: 888-344-8795
OR
Mail this form to:

Quarter Sawn Books
P.O. Box 635
North Liberty, IA 52317

For internet orders go to: www.ClaimGameBook.com

Books may be returned for any reason.

www.QuarterSawnBooks.com

Order Form

$15.95 per copy $_____

Tax: Iowa residents add 6% tax ($0.96 per copy) $_____

Shipping - $4/single copy, $2/each additional copy $_____

TOTAL: $_____

Ship to:

Name:_____

Address:_____

City, State, ZIP:_____

<u>Select Payment Type:</u>

☐ Check or Money Order (make checks out to Quarter Sawn Books)

☐ Credit Card (cards will not be charged until orders are shipped)

Credit card information:

Type of card: ☐ VISA   ☐ MASTERCARD   ☐ AMEX

Name on card:_____

Card number:_____

Expiration Date:_____ (mm/yyyy)   CCV:_____

(The CCV on Visa and Mastercard is a three-digit number that can be found on the back side of the card; on AmEx it is four-digits and is on the front)

Signature:_____

FAX completed form to: 888-344-8795
OR
Mail this form to:

Quarter Sawn Books
P.O. Box 635
North Liberty, IA 52317

For internet orders go to: www.ClaimGameBook.com

Books may be returned for any reason.

www.QuarterSawnBooks.com

Order Form

$15.95 per copy $_____

Tax: Iowa residents add 6% tax ($0.96 per copy) $_____

Shipping - $4/single copy, $2/each additional copy $_____

TOTAL: $_____

Ship to:

Name:_____

Address:_____

City, State, ZIP:_____

<u>Select Payment Type:</u>

☐ Check or Money Order (make checks out to Quarter Sawn Books)

☐ Credit Card (cards will not be charged until orders are shipped)

Credit card information:

Type of card: ☐ VISA ☐ MASTERCARD ☐ AMEX

Name on card:_____

Card number:_____

Expiration Date:_____ (mm/yyyy) CCV:_____

(The CCV on Visa and Mastercard is a three-digit number that can be found on the back side of the card; on AmEx it is four-digits and is on the front)

Signature:_____

FAX completed form to: 888-344-8795
OR
Mail this form to:

Quarter Sawn Books
P.O. Box 635
North Liberty, IA 52317

For internet orders go to: www.ClaimGameBook.com

Books may be returned for any reason.

CPSIA information can be obtained at www.ICGtesting.com
Printed in the USA
LVOW051017150313

324467LV00006B/56/P